INSPIRE

EXCITING WAYS OF TEACHING CREATIVE WRITING

EDITED BY EMMA BRANKIN, FRANCIS GILBERT
AND CARINYA SHARPLES

Copyright © Gold Publishing

British Library Cataloguing-in-Publications Data

A catalogue record for this book is available from the British Library.

1st Edition

ISBN: 978-1-913694-04-3

Acknowledgments

Thanks to everyone who assisted with the making of this anthology, including all relevant people at NAWE, the staff at the Department of Educational Studies at Goldsmiths, and the students on the MA in Creative Writing and Education. A special mention should go to the editors Emma Brankin and Carinya Sharples who worked so hard on this book in so many ways; they have our most sincere thanks.

Dr. Francis Gilbert, November 2020.

DEDICATION

To all creative writing educators devoted to pursuing lives well led.

In memory of Francis Gilbert's colleague and friend David Parry, who was a marvellously creative English and Drama teacher, as well as a good friend.

In memory of Suzanne Cleminshaw, the marvellous author of *The Great Ideas* and a good friend of Francis's too!

Contents

INTRODUCTION

FRANCIS GILBERT

Welcome to this inspiring anthology!

Here you will find a series of essays, creative responses and meditations on the teaching of creative writing – and much else besides. The aim is to inspire the reader to write imaginatively, and to learn more about creative writing and how to teach it.

The editors of this anthology (myself, Emma Brankin and Carinya Sharples) are practising creative writers and teachers of this familiar but possibly contentious subject. Creative writing is seen as a contentious subject for lots of different reasons: in academia because it's viewed as lacking rigour, in schools because it might facilitate unsavoury views and images, in society as a whole because it's perceived as a soft subject. Between us we have a great deal of experience of trying to impart our enthusiasm for reading and writing poetry, fiction, drama and creative non-fiction in diverse settings.

We first discussed devising such an anthology in order to showcase some of the great work that the postgraduate students on the MA in Creative Writing and Education at Goldsmiths have done as part of this course during the 2019-2020 session. Some of their work is here.

Lexi Allen offers a concise, original piece based on more detailed research here. She writes of overcoming many barriers – both physical and psychological – to leave excerpts of her creative writing in a number of public settings – trains, libraries, bars and some virtual spaces too. Her work is inspirational because it illustrates how a writer can find a public voice and new resources of confidence in very surprising ways and places.

Matilda Rostant shares her important findings for her research, focusing on the sometimes secret writing of fantasy fiction. She shows how there is an unjustified snobbery about genre fiction in many educational settings, and uses 'auto-ethnography' – a research-informed version of autobiography –

to unearth some important findings about the connections with genre fiction and one's own life.

Tanya Royer demonstrates how creative writers can research their unconscious using a series of mindful strategies such as meditation and free writing. Her findings are startling and moving, and reveal how creative writers can guide themselves to pen original pieces and find out about their own unconscious desires if they follow a strict research methodology.

In his piece, James Ward admits to being intimidated by what he perceived to be his lack of subject knowledge in the field of creative writing. And so, setting out in a similar way to Tanya, he devised a regime of writing and reading exercises, which built up his confidence and unlocked his creativity. Anyone who has similar issues should read his article.

Both James and Tanya (and many other writers here) show the power of what Peter Elbow, the acknowledged champion of this often-criticised way of writing, calls 'free writing'. Elbow wrote in the 1980s (the edition I quote from is a later edition):

> The most effective way I know to improve your writing is to do freewriting exercises regularly. At least three times a week. They are sometimes called 'automatic writing', 'babbling', or 'jabbering' exercises. The idea is to write for 10 minutes (later on, perhaps fifteen-twenty). Don't stop for anything. Go quickly without rushing. Never stop to look back, to cross something out, to wonder how to spell something, to wonder what word or thought to use, or to think about what you're doing. If you can't think of a word or a spelling, just a squiggle or else write 'I can't think of it'. Just put something down. The easiest thing to do is put down whatever is in your mind. (1998: 3)

Free writing plays an important role as a pedagogical strategy in a number of pieces, but most particularly in James and Tanya's.

Moving into the modern age, Emma Brankin explores how social media can be used to nurture students' creative writing. The article is bursting with fascinating and very workable ideas, including the brilliant idea of the 'auto-complete' poem, which is a sort of modern day update of Elbow's free writing concept.

Teacher and writer Sara Carroll shows how teenage girls could be guided to be more critical and feminist in their perspectives. She uses free writing as one of many strategies to encourage her female pupils to think about the ways in which girls are conditioned in oppressive ways by a patriarchal society.

Juwairiah Mussa shows how free writing and poetry can be used as a form of healing during extremely stressful times. Her pieces about living through lockdown are not only powerful examples of creative writing in themselves but also great models to share with creative writing students. Her reflections on the process of writing the pieces are pedagogical in that they guide the reader into thinking about the ways in which free writing can be healing and also help develop a greater awareness of the social, psychological and economic factors that shape who we are.

Carinya Sharples shares with Juwairiah a similar quest to find new ways of expression in her search to find a 'third space' where mixed-race writers can feel free to express themselves and explore their identities. Using various strategies such as 'heritage objects' 'rivers of reading' and the devising of mixed-race characters – all explained in her article – she reveals how creative writing can liberate and enlighten, and also challenge and disturb.

Jake Smith draws upon a rich tradition of experimental writing in order to devise a series of learning activities and lessons that create astounding and thought-provoking writing. He uses experimental reading material as prompts to generate creative writing and offers his own free writing as a possible model to inspire his students.

So to sum up about the pieces by postgraduates on our MA, we could say that there are some common threads: there is a zest to experiment and to use both well-worn and unusual literary forms, from genre fiction to the most esoteric devices; there's a deep commitment to giving both research and learning activities a serious theoretical underpinning; and, above all, there's a profound commitment to nurturing playfulness around creative writing.

And that might have been it for the anthology in its original conception, but Emma and Carinya decided that we would invite other creative writing educators to join the party, by advertising for submissions through the wonderful National Association for Writers in Education's (NAWE) newsletter. This brought a terrific response and as a result we are delighted to offer some amazing pieces from a very diverse range of writers and educators.

Gaar Adams has developed some of the ideas that I first heard in the conference paper he delivered at the NAWE 2019 conference in York. His commitment to making creative writing accessible to everyone shines through in his piece; in doing so, he offers a searing critique of the common 'workshop' format used in many creative writing classes. Drawing upon Eric Bennett's research (2014), he argues that the focus upon personal, autobiographical writing has meant that many creative writers have shied away from important social issues and have, as a result, been sidelined as a political force in our society. This is a point that Aisha Johnson implicitly picks upon in her piece which explores the history of coffee, the coffee house and creativity; we all need to consider the ways in which the most everyday of habits such as drinking coffee, chatting with acquaintances and writing have been shaped globalisation and colonial history.

Camilla Chester provides a wonderful and very useful account of how to mount successful school trips if you are writer, and importantly talks about how to forge strong links with schools. Janet Dean and Angela France examine the ways in which writers can use their own histories, lives and archives in order to inspire their own and other people to write in diverse genres. I love the generosity of spirit in these articles, with the writers showing the real secrets behind successful writing using documents.

Tjawangwa Dema illustrates how 'pedagogies of play' can be developed in poetry classes in order to generate a real enthusiasm not only for poetry writing but also editing poems. My own piece on using the well-worn trope of the Haunted

House to stimulate teenagers to write has a similar frisky if more ghostly spirit.

Kirsty Gunn and Gail Low, writing in tandem, make a very important point about teaching creative writing in education when they write:

> It's starting to feel as though creative essaying—setting exercises like this, working critically alongside the students' own imaginative work—has more capacity for intellectual and imaginative development than the traditional creative-writing workshop.

It's almost as if the idea of writing something creative is inhibiting in some educational settings. Is this about lack of confidence? Neil Nixon, who also teaches in higher education, argues that building students' confidence – getting them to believe they all have talent – is important.

While Geoffrey Heptonstall reveals how Shakespeare and various drama techniques can inspire meaningful creative responses, Stephen Wade shows how that most Shakespearean of forms – the sonnet – (and other poetic forms/devices) can be taught in the unlikely setting of prison or pupil referral units (where children are placed after being excluded from school).

Tamar Hodes focuses upon the ways in which literary techniques such as writing convincing settings, creating ambiguity and using revelations can be taught. One way she does this is by offering her own writing as a model. This is something that Gabriel Troiano does too, using his own powerful extract to get his readers considering how they could explore the concept of forbidden love. Both Tamar and Gabriel reveal that techniques can imparted to students if they are taught in a committed, passionate and reciprocal fashion: teachers should share their writing, too, as possible models for critique and discussion.

Helen Moore has written a really practical and refreshing article about we can use wild spaces and nature to nurture reciprocity between human beings and other living beings. It's both a spiritual and 'nitty-gritty' exploration of what now is

10

termed 'ecoliteracy'; using ecological awareness to infuse pedagogy and learning.

Mark Kirkbride, Patrick Toland and Matthew Tett all provide some invaluable advice about teaching creative writing in the sometimes challenging settings of various schools. They each show how certain attitudes of mind on the part of the teacher and a great set of teaching strategies can stir young people's creativity.

Let's not forget, though, that that this anthology is bulging with that vital ingredient: original creative writing. While Lily Lamont offers the only 'standalone' creative piece, many articles here contain the author's own creative writing; creativity and criticality sit side by side.

So, it just remains for me to say, enjoy and educate yourselves! Do get in touch if you have any points to make and comments to offer.

Francis Gilbert, Head of the MA in Creative Writing and Education, November 2020, Goldsmiths. F.gilbert@gold.ac.uk

REFERENCES

Bennett, E. (2014) "How Iowa Flattened Literature: With CIA help, writers were enlisted to battle both Communism and egg headed abstraction. The damage to writing lingers", *The Chronicle of Higher Education.*

Peter Elbow (1998) *Writing without Teachers*, Oxford University Press. Oxford.

PROLOGUE
Emma Brankin and Carinya Sharples

For the past year we have been working towards our MA in Creative Writing and Education at Goldsmiths. It has been an eye-opening experience where we have developed as educators and writers, honing our understanding of how we can best unlock creative potential in ourselves and others. Having both worked in journalism, we now teach in schools and support community writing groups, and can vouch first hand for how beneficial the course has been to our pedagogy.

From discussing poetry with Raymond Antrobus to supporting students at the First Story writing festival to designing and leading workshops for volunteers from refugee charities (and much, much more), we feel excited to be championing the arts in education, having seen the value it adds to the school experience, for example, when young people can express themselves.

When our tutor Francis Gilbert proposed this book, we imagined it to be a collection of our coursemates' varied and interesting work, but through a callout in NAWE we were able to expand the horizons of the book – and ourselves – with submissions from a wide range of practitioners. These contributors are teaching and writing in universities, schools, community workshops and beyond. We're incredibly grateful for the generosity, insights and patience they have all given to make this happen, and for the opportunity to be part of such a fantastic project.

Very early on in the creation of this book, the world changed dramatically. During this uncertain time, Francis moved his sessions online and demonstrated how productive and engaging writer-educators could still be to students via a computer screen. Now, more than ever, it is important that we are responding to the outside world inside the creative-writing classroom.

This collection of essays aims to be practical but, above all, inspiring. We hope you find it useful in your learning, teaching or writing.

Now it is time to speak

Now it is time to speak,
it's the hardest time to speak.

Stories bubbling unheard, unseen,
so many we could burst.

To speak after so long
feels golden, and so

though they may say I'm this
and they may say I'm that,

and they say I can't write this,
and they say I can't write that

I will write.

For I can hold these words
back no longer.

Carinya Sharples

BEYOND "HARPOONS AND DINGHIES"
BRINGING DIVERSE STORIES AND SOCIAL ENGAGEMENT TO OUR CREATIVE WRITING CLASSROOMS

GAAR ADAMS

Writing is an act of creation. As educators, our hope is to teach students to harness the raw potential inherent in this creation—that whether they build a story based on a real event, adapt one from another work, or devise something entirely from their own imagination, they are unbounded in their own budding artistic practice. But we cannot inspire our students to truly believe in the expansive potential of writing when the stories we bring into the classroom don't carry that same ethos of illimitability.

Critical reading is a crucial part of many creative writing teachers' syllabi: we bring in material—usually lauded writing—and dissect it with our students, perhaps for its colourful characters, masterful structure, vivid language, or some alchemy of its creative parts. But too frequently the stories we offer our students look and sound the same. In doing this, we fail to reveal to our students both the widest possible breadth of others' writing as well as the wildest possibilities of depth in their own work.

For nearly a decade, I led creative writing workshops at a number of secondary schools in the United Arab Emirates where either English or Arabic were the language of instruction. The experience of teaching across languages and in a foreign country may seem too idiosyncratic to apply to classrooms in the UK, but I taught most frequently at institutions that used a British curriculum and it was here where the message I received from my students' work was the loudest: we are doing our students a disservice when we refuse to venture far from classic reading lists or undertake the difficult conversations required to critically examine contemporary work that is socially and politically engaged. Indeed, my students came most alive when I eschewed stale notions of canonical texts and delved into work that rejected a tradition of telling inward-facing stories.

Addressing the first point—veering off the safe, well-trodden path of classic, canonical texts and into more diverse, contemporary work—is systematically difficult for one major reason: the traditional publishing industry is still woefully homogenous. In a recent study by multinational publishing organization Scholastic as recently as 2013 only ten percent of children's and YA books published in America featured a person of colour. (Wisc.edu., 2019) The UK fared no better in an even more recent study by the Centre for Literacy in Primary Education, which found that only one percent of children's books published in the UK in 2017 had a minority protagonist and only four percent included minority background characters. (CLPE.org.uk. 2020) But this doesn't end with children's and YA publishing: a 2017 survey by the Royal Society of Literature found that despite 81 percent of UK respondents saying they liked literature because it "promotes empathy", only seven percent of the 400 writers they cited were from black, Asian or minority ethnic backgrounds. (Kean, 2020)

As educators, simply acknowledging this disparity in publishing and attempting to rectify it with a more diverse reading list is not enough: we must address this second point—examining more politically and socially engaged work and leading our classrooms into more challenging and complex discussions. Even though I witnessed my students at their most inspired when I did so, I found that the very foundation of creative writing education was trying to push me into a "safer" direction.

In 2015, writer and academic Eric Bennett published Workshops of Empire, a deeply researched historical account of the founding of the venerated University of Iowa Creative Writing Program. In the book, he lays out convincing evidence that creative writing as a discipline in post-war America was handsomely funded by the Central Intelligence Agency. While it may sound like a story ripped straight out of a pulpy novel, Bennett explores how – at a critical moment in its growth –

Iowa's program was underwritten by the Congress for Cultural Freedom, an anti-communist advocacy group funded by the CIA. The group developed out of concerted Cold War attempts to counter the popularity of Marxism and build a generation of writers in the US that "fortified democratic values" while disregarding writers with a propensity towards penning work about social justice.

The crux of Bennett's argument is that Iowa's program — as well as the proliferation of creative writing MFA programs that came in its wake (an astounding 50 of those that appeared before 1970 were founded by Iowa graduates) — encourages writing that is "preoccupied by family and self" and avoids politics in favour of literature that prioritizes illuminating small moments in life, like suburban angst or inward anxieties. In other words: the foundation of some of the most celebrated writing programs in the world were built on a system that encourages work that values personal experience over the idea that our identities are shaped by the community, political systems and larger, historical forces around us.

Bennett lays out the ramifications of such a legacy — creative writing programs undermining true artistic freedom and driving away writers from exploring political ideas — quite starkly:

> The thing to lament is not only that we have a bunch of novels about harpoons and dinghies (or suburbs or bad marriages or road trips or offices in New York.) The thing to lament is also the dead end of isolation that comes from describing the dead end of isolation—and from using vibrant literary communities to foster this phenomenon. In our workshops, we simply accept it as true that larger structures of common interest have been destroyed ... and what's left to do is be faithful to the needs of the sentence. ... [But] texts worth reading—worth reading now, and worth reading 200 years from now—coordinate the personal with the national or international." (Bennett, 2015)

As an educator, it feels crucial that I confront the institutional problem of a white, male educator like myself being sheltered by a canon of white, male writers who fixate on inward-facing stories of "harpoons and dinghies". But I must also push beyond this and recognize the larger systemic problem of how I could easily perpetuate this cycle with another generation of creative writing students. As a creative writing educator in the UAE, it was my responsibility to break this chain and inspire my students by demonstrating that there are other kinds of writers as well as other kinds of writing.

In 2016, I taught an eight-week creative writing workshop programme for a group of Year 11 students at a British-curriculum school in the UAE. The student makeup of these institutions was astonishingly diverse on account of the large numbers of migrant workers living in the Gulf. To give some context: a 2005 survey by the Population Division of the United Nations included all six Gulf countries in the top ten of countries worldwide with the highest percentage of international migrants. In Qatar, for example, migrants made up an astounding 90 percent of the in-country population. (Assets.publishing.service.gov.uk. 2017) The majority of people living in the Arabian Peninsula are thus navigating a country — as well as a culture and a language — that is not their own. My students hailed from each corner of the Middle East but also from across South and Southeast Asia—with a large number from India, Pakistan and Bangladesh—in addition to students from countries across Africa, Europe and South America (including Nigeria, Estonia and Chile).

Such diversity often produces the phenomena known as "third-culture kids", a term coined by American sociologists John and Ruth Useem in the mid-20th century that describes people raised in a culture other than their parents' or that of the country named on their passport (where they are legally considered native) for a significant part of their early development years. In the UAE, the third-culture kid phenomenon is further complicated by the fact that citizenship is impossible for anyone who is not born of an Emirati mother or father: that is to say, even if they spend their entire life living in-country, it is still not – legally speaking – "theirs". With very few exceptions, all residents must exit the country after 30 days if they no longer have a work visa, even if it has been their home for their entire life. Although the occurrence of third-culture kids may seem like a phenomenon exclusive to countries of transience like those in the Gulf, a 2017 Department of Education survey6 recommended that questions of ethnicity and language must be more deliberately considered in UK classrooms as well, with nearly one in five primary school students having a language other than English spoken in their home. I would argue that a more diverse reading list is equally important to both demographics: for those who are more readily exposed to languages other than English, it is a question of representation; and for those who are not, it is an equally critical issue of lack of exposure.

After consulting the regular English curriculum of the school I was working in—which mostly examined classic British literature—it was clear that the students needed greater access to other kinds of writing, so I devised a reading list that was contemporary, focused on the Global South, and politically and socially engaged. The first book I brought into the class was Deepak Unnikrishnan's *Temporary People*, a collection of short stories centred on migration in the Gulf. In our initial meeting, we dissected a story about a woman who travels around Abu Dhabi gluing back together migrant workers who have fallen off construction sites. Most of the students were not familiar with magical realism and expressed delight at reading a story with this kind of breadth that was also set in a place they rarely saw addressed in their own reading. This was step one: composing a better reading list so that their marker for successful writing was not entirely composed of dead white men.

I then needed to push our students to examine what worked in Unnikrishnan's writing and bring this to their own writing. After our classroom discussion of the work, I let them loose on a prompt: write a story of migration across generations that uses economic or political factors as the impetus for a character's migration. The aim of this prompt was to provide my students with an initial scaffolding to begin to conceptualize their stories within wider socioeconomic frameworks and global systems. As they tentatively embarked on this exercise and others like it, students began to consider how thinking about these greater considerations behind a character's actions might strengthen their writing.

The work from my class of 10 teenage students included some remarkable stories. One self-described third-culture kid began a short story about famine in Abbasid-era Arabia (the third Islamic caliphate after the life of the prophet Muhammed) forcing an expedition to undiscovered Scandinavia. He was motivated by the recent discovery of an Arabic-inscribed ring found in a 10th century Viking grave, and was curious to investigate why someone would be economically motivated to leave at such a culturally important moment in the development of Islamic society, just after the founding of the religion.

This exercise did not only resonate with third-culture kids: one Emirati teen girl in the class began a screenplay about a Qatari woman forced to leave her country because her children couldn't get citizenship, on account of her husband being non-Qatari (a real law still affecting thousands of half-Qatari children without a paternal claim to citizenship). As the weeks progressed, I watched her screenplay – initially centred on one woman's plight – develop into a story about a subversive, female-led hacking group targeting the Qatari political apparatus. Another student wrote about internal displacement in Iraq, in which people are forced to leave home and yet usually do not have the economic or political ability to leave the country – a phenomenon that, despite 40 million people around the world living in this kind of suspended reality, according to recent United Nations statistics, still does not have a universal legal definition under the 1951 Refugee Convention. Two other students collaborated on a story about the history of ruthless pineapple plantation owners in Indonesia. It was a remarkably fertile batch of work from a single prompt. Most importantly, although these stories explored the greater forces around the characters, they did not have to be without moments of emotional resonance, for as Bennett says about the best writers, "they embed the emotional instant in the instant's full context and long history."

I know many of my own creative writing teachers might have started that first class with a prompt of describing how migration feels; pushing a global phenomenon with deep social and political roots into a smaller, inward-facing story. While these kinds of stories can be successful, to me as an educator it feels critical to begin with a wider lens and encourage our students to tie their artistry into a greater social framework, particularly because I have been told by too many students across too many countries that my class was the first time that they realized their own writing could "do this".

We should always be in the business of inspiring our students to believe that their writing can be and accomplish anything. By bringing into our classrooms a wider array of writing, as well as writing that that truly digs deep into the world around us, we are ensuring that the act of writing—the act of creation—is indeed as rich, varied and vibrant as possible.

With this aim in mind, I recommend a four-point plan of action to both diversify your reading list and encourage your classrooms to become spaces in which writing and conversations that push beyond the confines of harpoons and dinghies are explored:

1. Explore the holes and missing links in your students' exposure to literature. If possible, look at their other syllabi and consider what is missing. Also, talk to them early on about works that have piqued their interest as readers or writers. In a recent class where students wanted to read more memoirs, I brought in books from underrepresented areas that delve into meaty topics, such as Suketu Mehta's exploration of migration and inequality in *Maximum City: Bombay Lost and Found*.

2. Establish your classroom as a place to talk about more than just craft particularities. Build a rapport with your students so that they feel comfortable talking about larger issues such as race, sexuality, economics, etc. I find it helps to lay the groundwork for this by taking 10 minutes at the start of each class to discuss topics tangential to writing. In a recent class, we began by talking about how the students civically engaged each

week and they offered up surprising and entertaining stories about volunteering, voter registration drives etc. (which later led to writing about civic engagement). This has the added benefit of establishing a more communicative classroom for workshopping.

3. Construct a robust, cross-genre syllabus that has room to be malleable. Although it may seem daunting to hand out a formidable reading list across many different genres, consider how a wider array of texts can potentially grab the attention of a wider swath of students. My biggest personal challenge is my reticence to deviate from my own syllabus, but being willing to swap out a particular work might enrich your classroom. Recently, for example, I was looking forward to bringing in work from a particular poet, but when it became clear that many of my students were writing about LGBTQ+ issues, I bumped up Sergio Loo's They Keep Killing Us from a recommended text on the syllabus to a required work we discussed in that week's class.

4. Appraise your own reading habits and strive to get out of any ruts. Consider what you've read over the past year. Has it veered toward a particular genre? Have you mostly been reading work from writers of a certain nationality? It was helpful while teaching in the Middle East that I had studied Arabic literature and read widely South Asian literature in translation, but when I catch myself veering too sharply into a particular genre or region, I do my best to counterbalance that by seeking out new writers and unfamiliar publishers.

REFERENCES

Assets.publishing.service.gov.uk. 2017. Schools, Pupils And Their Characteristics: January 2017. [online] Available at: https://assets.publishing.service.gov.uk/government/uploads/system/uploads/attachment_data/file/650547/SFR28_2017_Main_Text.pdf [Accessed 22 June 2020].

Bennett, E., 2015. Workshops Of Empire. Iowa City: University of Iowa Press.

CLPE.org.uk. 2020. [online] Available at: https://clpe.org.uk/sites/default/files/CLPE%20Reflecting%20Realities%20Report%20July%202018.pdf [Accessed 21 June 2020].

Kean, D., 2020. Books | The Guardian. [online] the Guardian. Available at: https://www.theguardian.com/books/2017/mar/01/literature-report-shows-british-readers-stuck-in-very-white-past [Accessed 22 June 2020].

Tyner, M., 2020. CCBC 2017 Multicultural Statistics. [online] Ccblogc.blogspot.com. Available at: http://ccblogc.blogspot.com/2018/02/ccbc-2017-multicultural-statistics.html [Accessed 21 June 2020].

Un.org. 2007. [online] Available at: https://www.un.org/en/development/desa/population/migration/events/docs/IttMig_170407.pdf [Accessed 22 June 2020].

Wisc.edu. (2019). Children's Books by and About People of Colour. [online] Available at: http://ccbc.education.wisc.edu/books/pcstats.asp

TAKING UP SPACE

CAN PLAYFUL ACTS OF DISRUPTION REDUCE ANXIETY ABOUT
SHARING CREATIVE WRITING?

LEXI ALLEN

The following creative writing research was conducted with the aim of exploring ways of alleviating my anxiety when it comes to creative writing. Through playful exploration, which primarily involved placing my prose in unexpected and unorthodox spaces, I was interested to see if this would make me more confident sharing my work with others. Even though this research was personal, I would hope that classroom practitioners could employ some of my practices to help school children who also struggle with confidence and/or anxiety when called upon to share their work.

BACKGROUND AND CONTEXTUALISATION

This autoethnography examines my anxiety concerning the sharing of my creative writing. I have often found an absurdist and surrealist approach to life to be an effective method of diffusing my general anxiety; thus, I tried to embrace that approach. This project was partially inspired by the creative practices of Dada. In my experience, a form of disruption and embracing our discomfort has often been crucial in tackling anxieties.

A major shortcoming of my research is the fact that I was the only participant in the study, and that, short of panic/anxiety attacks or medical/scientific equipment, it is difficult to really measure my anxiety. Still, this project should offer insight into the ways that sharing creative writing can ultimately become easier and less terrifying.

The research methodology that I have chosen to apply to my research question, 'Would placing my prose in "unexpected" places alleviate my anxiety in sharing my creative writing?' is autoethnography, specifically a narrative/evocative autoethnography.

STUDY DESIGN

I designed the project with two types of settings in mind: virtual and non-virtual/physical ('non-virtual' signifying spaces that I could physically inhabit, such as the London Underground, or a bar in Camden). My supervisor and I agreed that placing my work in three to four spaces in each category was a realistic number of spaces given the scope of the project. I strove for a diverse selection of physical spaces and what I considered to be their virtual equivalents--spaces which would inevitably invite a different readership and a different contextualization of the text. The spaces I chose are as follows:

Physical
- A university library
- London public transport: various stations and trains throughout the network
- Three social spaces in London: BrewDog (Camden); Goat Tavern (Mayfair); The Dev (Camden)

Virtual
- The New College of Florida web-forum and message-board
- The 'Missed Connections' section of Craigslist (London and New York); Google Reviews for various establishments and institutions; and the comments section of The New York Times
- The 'About Me' section of a dating app (Bumble)

I decided to place prose from previously written short stories in a selection of spaces. I specifically chose to work with previously written (not spontaneous) drafts of short stories. I decided that a draft of a story/piece is more raw and vulnerable than is a polished and heavily edited version. It is more anxiety inducing (for me) to share a piece of writing which, I feel-- rather, am certain--is not nearly as good as it could be.

In selecting the stories to share, I merely chose the stories with which I had most recently been working. Because of my deeply personal attachment to these stories--I spent a significant amount of time working with each of them and feel a significant amount of pride in each of them--it would be that much more difficult to share unpolished drafts of these stories.

I chose bookmark-size cutouts--about a paragraph in length--of these stories to use in the physical/non-virtual spaces. For the sake of consistency, I tried to replicate a similar length in designated virtual spaces; however, at certain moments I deviated from this. I made a concerted effort to remove my name from the text whenever and wherever possible. I did not want to attract attention to the issue of the author (me).

The journal that I kept throughout the project was a collection of voice notes, hastily scribbled journal entries (written on napkins, leaflets, and in a designated composition book) and photographs. I structured a list of questions to ask myself before and after I had placed my prose in an unexpected space.

RELEVANT LITERATURE

This autoethnographic study was informed by a diverse array of literature. I relied on the philosophy of Dada, the 20th century art movement, as a cultural reference point and compass.

Dada erupted as a response to the devastation caused by World War I (Rubin, 1968). Dada artists produced creative work that was subversive and disruptive, and challenged the literary/artistic canon. Dada artists, such as Marcel Duchamp and Tristan Tzara, used various forms of media and creative practice, including creative writing, as forms of social protest, challenging and revolting against conventional logic and order (Rubin, 1968). Essentially, Dada was a response to acute emotional pain that seems to insistently defy and refuse rational thought.

Duchamp wrote textual fragments, which he specifically phrased in order to defy literary conventions (Sanouillet and Peterson, 1973). I realised that Duchamp's creative compulsion to resist any artistic conventions allowed him to challenge and reconfigure his own conceptions surrounding his creative practice. This encouraged me to approach my work with a similar attitude, as I was also trying to challenge and reconfigure my relationship with my creative practice. I also consulted Julia Kristeva's theory of intertextuality for a framework to this autoethnography. Kristeva posits that intertextuality is a sort of textual collage from which no text can escape. Our textual work does not stand alone: it is not an island; it is nothing entirely original. Rather, it is the products of the texts that we have consumed throughout our life (Allen, 2011).

ANALYSIS OF THE DATA

In the beginning stages of my research, I focused on the quality of my prose--would they be received as 'good' or 'bad'? As belonging in the literary canon? Were they 'good' enough to categorize me as a writer, as an author? Initially, I conflated these two terms.

Before I placed pieces of my prose--bookmark-size cutouts of my prose--in about 20 books (chosen at semi-random) throughout the Goldsmiths library, I focused primarily on the quality of my work--was it written well? I was convinced that the reader would also, somehow contextualize it within the literary canon. These 'bookmarks' were, essentially, so fragmented--and authorless. Had I stumbled upon one at random with no contextualization, I certainly would not have thought to read it in such a context. Intertextuality calls for us to reference the textual pieces with which we come into contact through other pieces with which we are familiar (Allen, 2011). Virtually any piece of writing that belongs to the literary canon and with which I come into contact, in some sense, appears in book format, or essay format--not in the form of a scrap of paper without any seeming cohesive narrative structure. Thus, it would certainly make more sense to contextualize this bookmark within the framework of a grocery list fallen on the ground, or a receipt, or something placed within a book to keep its place--a literal bookmark. Initially, though, I was so preoccupied with my own compulsion for some kind of artistic/creative talent that my perception was distorted.

My journal entries certainly reflect this. Before placing my prose throughout the Goldsmiths library, I remain focused on the interpretation of my prose (by readers) as 'good'. And, although I am clearly concerned about what the potential reader thinks, at no point do I explicitly mention the reader. Clearly, I am not conceiving of the reader as an actual person. I am obviously preoccupied with and by the intertextual quality of the work; what is its position in this literary dialogue? How does it position itself in this dialogue? I rarely received any kind of response to my work in physical spaces; it happened only on one occasion. In Canary Wharf, a businessman chased me down to hand me one of the torn fragments of paper that I'd left on a train. This confirmed to me that my scattered pieces of prose were interpreted as almost accidental, imperceptible textual pieces of the landscape--did they blend in? That moment, almost innocuous, was transformative for me, as it confirmed to me that my prose had been interpreted in the way that I'd intended for them to be interpreted, but it was also disappointing; I felt unseen. Perhaps, then, my anxiety was transformed and replaced by the desire to be seen. I had, somehow, outgrown this desire for my prose to simply blend in.

Following the placement of these bookmark-size fragments throughout the Goldsmiths library, my journal entry is significantly more joyous, even celebratory and liberated. Whereas my 'before' entry was freckled with question marks, the first sentence of my entry following the placement of my 'bookmarks' throughout the library ends with an exclamation point! Foucault theorizes that 'writing unfolds like a game (jeu)' (1995, p. 225) and that the purpose of writing is not to celebrate the act of writing so much as it is to create a work 'into which the writing subject constantly disappears' (1995, p. 225). Perhaps my preoccupation with writing then does not necessarily allow for a liberation from writing itself, and it was only through literally disappearing from the writing that I could find a sense of joy, or peace, or liberation from the constraints into and onto which I placed myself. Furthermore, Foucault examines what fundamentally constitutes a work (of writing), or work of an author (1969/1995, 226). He then goes onto state that an author is crucial to the rendering of a text as literary--an authorless text is merely a text. 'Literary anonymity was of interest only as a puzzle to be solved as, in our day, literary works are totally dominated by the sovereignty of the author.' (Foucault, 1995, 237). Because of my preoccupation with the notion of an author/a literary work, disappearing from the work--an authorless text (as mine was, when I removed my name from the text) lacking a cohesive narrative and/or rational context--allows me to liberate myself from the possibility for my work to be judged as a literary work, by an 'author'. Rather, I am accepting a sort of nonexistence and am thus freed from the expectation of being 'good' or 'bad', a nonexistence which Foucault examines deeply in his essay (1995). Through a sense of invisibility, I am liberated.

Directly following this (in many ways, transgressive and subversive) act, I write 'At first, I picked books at random trying to covertly hide bookmarks in aisles/books where people weren't [around]. Then I began to think about it more -- how would these words look against the backdrop of the text?' An intertextual interpretation of creative writing, of my work, allowed me to reconsider my prose. Rather than judging myself as an author--who was I? What was I (as an author)?--I could understand the text within a never-ending dialogue. I literally disappeared from my text, essentially (ritualistically) disowning it--physically and metaphorically--and placing it within a dialogue.

As my research progressed, my journal entries reveal a greater preoccupation with the interpretation by the reader, and the playfully disruptive way that text may be read. Following entries reveal my obvious disconnect from my prose-- rarely do I mention the actual content of my work, and rarely do I speak about it as integrated into the literary canon--rather, placing the work in spaces has become a sort of game. In later entries--specifically in the London Underground--I write about how I feel it has become an almost 'compulsion to place my work on the train--if I'm on a train then I must leave a bookmark behind'. This ties back to the notion of the death of the author/what is an author? Additionally, my concern transforms--I become more concerned with aspects hardly relating to writing, but how covertly I can slip my work into a space, or how creative and unexpected a space it may be. I am obviously concerned with a very different type of reader-response. My greatest concern became how easily it could slip/camouflage itself into its environment, particularly by the time I was writing in virtual spaces. I was so preoccupied with others not detecting the creative writing that I forgot to worry about whether or not they thought that my own writing was 'good'--they shouldn't be able to detect it as such. I wanted it to disappear into itself.

Intertextuality suggests that a text is inherently interwoven and imbued with cultural references and citations, and the inescapably intertextual quality of a text offers the reader a certain kind of power (Allen, 2011). Thus, in placing my work in various spaces, I was hyper-aware of the intertextual quality of the work, and my reading of it dramatically transformed; rather than comparing or adjusting my work to that which I think that it should be (literary canon; literary work; author; writers reading and judging my work) I began to perceive the text in a more universal, 'average-man' sense. The text is not merely in dialogue with other literary works, but with other fragments and components of one's life; one's environment.

What does seem strange to me--and what I don't quite understand--is that physical spaces are also littered with spam, so why was I not preoccupied with this? Perhaps it was the fact that my actions felt more disruptive or more cathartic; the internet often feels lazy and not necessarily real or authentic. Perhaps writing these posts from behind a computer screen doesn't feel disruptive enough.

IMPLICATIONS / FINDINGS

This project could easily translate into exercises that might help schoolchildren--as well as adolescents and adults--experiencing issues with any element of the study of English. Maybe they have learning disabilities with which to contend, or are an ESL/ESOL student, or simply struggle with a strong sense of perfectionism (like myself). This project could offer them a sense of relief and unburdening, and could help them to re-evaluate writing and what it means to engage in the practice of writing--whether that is creative or academic writing. It could be reworked and restructured as a sort of scavenger hunt, emphasizing other facets of intertextuality. Ultimately, this project could provide a very necessary and effective form of catharsis for schoolchildren feeling anxious, self-conscious, or insecure about their classroom abilities. I think that this project could also have profound implications for individuals struggling with mental health issues, if slightly reworked or reconfigured. It could emphasize a sense of liberation with regard to placing one's feelings or thoughts outside of oneself, or making them public and visible. Although this would certainly require a slightly different approach to the practice/exercise--perhaps through choosing slightly different spaces, for instance--I think that it could work beautifully for such individuals, particularly those who have difficulty with sharing their struggles.

CONCLUSION

In conducting this autoethnography, I evolved as a writer and an author (and learned that these titles/categories are entirely separate), as well as a human being. My relationship to my prose--and the anxiety which has largely hindered me from sharing my prose with others and identifying myself as a writer--changed dramatically during the course of my research.

Initially, I believed that it was anonymously distributing and sharing my prose with the general public that would force me to overcome my anxiety. I believed that this would function in much the same way that any kind of immersive therapy might help to alleviate a phobia or fear. However, although my anxiety did diminish, it was for a much more complex and unexpected reason.

I re-learned what it means to be a writer and to engage in the practice of creative writing; to explore and allow for a more playful and experimental approach when engaging in the practice of creative writing. Although my anxiety has been mitigated, it has not been mitigated for the reasons I previously believed that it would be mitigated; rather, other 'muscles' (ways of thought) and forms of emotional intelligence and/or understanding were strengthened. I learned to experience and perceive my creative writing outside of the literary canon, and the parameters which encouraged me to restrict myself. Literally seeing and reading my work outside of this context was liberating, as it encouraged me to visualize my prose outside of these metaphorical (and literal) lines. Furthermore, I have come to conceptualize my work as belonging to--and inevitably informed by--this literary discourse, this dialogue. To feel as though my words and thoughts are not entirely my own but are part of a textual, literary collage relieves me of the burden of feeling as though I must be brilliant, or witty, or particularly extraordinary. I sometimes got distracted from writing. Given the nature of the experiment (riding the underground or sitting in a bar with friends), it was not always possible to maintain the level of consistency that I would have liked to. This is a significant shortcoming of this autoethnography.

Ultimately, placing my prose in 'unexpected' (unorthodox/unusual/recontextualized) spaces was a strangely disruptive, surrealistic, and, ultimately, thrilling experience, and I intend to continue saturating these spaces with my prose, and this practice and process deserves much greater attention.

REFERENCES

Allen, A. (2019-2020). Unpublished journal.

Allen, G. (2011). Intertextuality (2nd ed., New critical idiom). Routledge.

Cohen, L., Manion, L., & Morrison, K. (2017). Research methods in education. Retrieved from https://ebookcentral.proquest.com

Duchamp, M., Sanouillet, M., & Peterson, E. (1989). The writings of Marcel Duchamp (A Da Capo paperback). New York, N.Y.: Da Capo Press.

Foucault, M. (1995). What is an author?. In S. Burke (Ed.), Authorship: from Plato to the postmodern: a reader (pp. 233-46). Edinburgh, UK: Edinburgh University Press Ltd.

Muncey, T. (2014). What Is Autoethnography? Making Sense of Individual Experience. In Creating Autoethnographies (pp. 26–53). London: SAGE Publications Ltd.

Rubin, W. S. (1968). Dada, Surrealism, and their heritage. Greenwich, Connecticut: The Museum of Modern Art.

SOCIAL STORIES:

SOCIAL MEDIA-CENTRIC CREATIVE WRITING EXERCISES

EMMA BRANKIN

Reality is nuanced and messy, full of pros and cons. Living
in a networked world is complicated. (Boyd, 2014, p.16)

My initial aim in devising the 'Social Stories' writing exercises
was to use teenagers' familiarity and curiosity with the online
world to improve pupil engagement with creative writing, whilst
encouraging them to experiment with multiple storytelling
modes. In attempting to develop content that was varied and
relevant, opportunities emerged within the exercises to engage
critically with social issues such as identity. Therefore, a further
aim of 'Social Stories' became allowing pupils the space to be
curious-critical of the ever-evolving opportunities and problems
created by social media, and to draw their own conclusions of
these online platforms.

INTRODUCTION

A 2019 study by Common Sense Media found that 84 percent of
teenagers now own a phone and spend at least seven hours
online a day. I have taught in schools where pupils' phones have
been confiscated to stop them accessing online content, such as
social media, that would 'drain' their energy and time. However,
social media has become entwined with identity (Eichorn, 2019)
and teenagers are aware of and curious about this. In Nancy Jo
Sales' study, many teenage interviewees discussed, in their own
words, their 'unhealthy obsession' with their portrayal online
(2016). As one 14-year-old put it:

> We're growing up, finding out who we are and what we
> want to be. We're becoming comfortable or
> uncomfortable with our own bodies ... it plays a role in
> how we feel about ourselves (p.106)

I was struck by the level of awareness articulated by the teens
in the study as to their own malleability when it comes to social

media matters. They seemed able to be obsessed and critical of digital influences in their lives. Valkenburg and Piotrowski suggest that nobody has conclusively proved either 'a dystopian paradigm, in which all media are problematic for youth, nor a utopian paradigm, in which youth universally benefit from media' (2016, p.9).

I believe pupils benefit from being 'allowed' to be expressive and inquisitive on their own terms. In fact, I would argue that the imperfect nature of social media makes it well suited for probing, so students can draw their own conclusions rather than feel they must conform to a universal view. If educators dismiss teenagers' interests (such as social media) as 'junk culture' (p.151), there is a risk of disengagement and devaluing of young people. In harnessing social media for creative-writing lessons, there is an opportunity for teenagers to become more critical and reflective on matters of identity. As Eichhorn (2019) writes, their engagement with social media is already an empowered act as they, not adults, constantly choose how they wish to frame themselves. By giving them the space to reflect, they can become more aware of their agency and the consequences (good and bad) of decisions made online. I wanted pupils to bring into each exercise their vast knowledge and experience of social media, and how it has shaped how they view themselves. Through the act of creative writing, they could similarly inhabit identities, modulate versions of themselves and dictate the route of the lesson.

Social media is a blend of multiple storytelling modes. Within one scroll on Instagram, videos, audio commentaries, static images and text present themselves as a package to derive meaning and connections from. Like Albers and Sanders (2010), I am 'enthralled at the intensity with which young people immerse themselves in arts, multimodality, and 21st century literacies' and see this as 'redefining the world of literacy and our most basic understanding of what it means to be literate' (p.6). Developing this, I believe that any 'preferred' final form for creative writing on the internet has yet to be discovered. In my exercises, I have proposed concepts that combine written, verbal, spatial, visual and audio modes into a final digitised package. It is likely that our social media-savvy students will suggest hybrids that are more innovative and effective. Whether it is sharing or producing digital images, music, video games or apps, 'multimodal text production has become a central part of everyday life' (Albers and Sanders, 2010, p.12). They argue the benefit of moving past a fixed form of writing is that 'no one particular mode (written language, visual, gestural, music, digital and so on) carries the entire message' (p.10). In embracing the concept of 'entangled literacy', I wanted to build on social media's symbiotic relationship to present opportunities for multi-faceted self-expression.

EXERCISES IN PRACTICE

In embracing 'learning that is more powerfully participatory' (Cope and Kalantzis, p.161), it is important that the educator facilitating these exercises is flexible and reactive to the pupils' contributions. It is highly probable that their interest in, opinions and knowledge of social media will lead lessons down interesting, original, unplanned routes.

There are further challenges that should be considered before these exercises are implemented in a learning environment. Firstly, with the internet constantly evolving, and teenagers' technological interests shifting, exercises should be amended accordingly to take into account new apps and trends. The surge in popularity of the TikTok app during Covid-19 lockdown – with Sensor Tower reporting that 118 million people worldwide downloaded the app in March alone, and 60 per cent of users are teens (Chan, 2020) – is a key example of this. Opening up a dialogue about TikTok and expressing my own lack of knowledge of the app empowered the pupils to share their insights. I initially thought its video-based content (featuring primarily dance challenges and lip syncs) would be hard to connect to creative writing. But, after spending some time navigating the app myself, I found that its multi-modal content often focuses on auditory and visual modes being used to compliment or contrast with one another. This seemed to me to lend itself to writing exercises exploring subtext. Likewise, TikTok's song-lyric videos could lead to poetry exercises, and its videos of comical skits used for a scriptwriting exercise.

The use of phones in lessons also demands careful consideration. I believe it would be detrimental to the atmosphere of acceptance and equality if teachers start issuing sanctions to pupils distracted by their phones, undermining the intended aim to treat their interest in social media as an asset. Working with the school's leadership team about their phone policy is crucial here. Of course, phones will be necessary at times but I have purposefully designed the exercises to include limited phone-in-hand involvement until the end. If the educator focuses on atmosphere building then the pupils, excited by the opportunity to be creative, should largely want to use phones for the task rather than for personal use. Coming up with a contract beforehand to establish what is acceptable phone etiquette in the lesson will help.

Where the exercises refer to uploading work, it is important to stress that this should not be to the students' or teacher's own personal social media platforms. My suggestion is that the teacher creates a specific social media channel on the apps used in these exercises. The teacher would be in charge of the account and the password, and pupils would email the work they create to a school email account ahead of the teacher making the final upload.

All of this, of course, operates under the assumption that pupils will have their own phones and/or a working knowledge of social media. Whilst many schools now set homework online and encourage extensive digital communication between teachers and pupils, some children, for financial or other reasons, may not have their own phone. Teachers should be careful to avoid using assumptive language that would make these pupils feel self-conscious. Many studies have found that digital savviness in the workplace is no longer optional (Bittle, 2020), so these less in-the-know pupils will have an opportunity to learn from their peers about a world that, like it or not, will dominate many facets of their adult life.

Writing creatively following a curious-critical exploration of social media could result in pupils making the decision to engage with social media less. In one case, I had a pupil delete their Instagram app after spending time crafting a piece about their addiction to checking for likes. On the other side, you may find pupils wish to engage more with social media, potentially to share their writing on an account. These decisions should come organically from the pupil, and teachers should not impose their own views onto pupils.

CONCLUSION

Below is an excerpt from a pupil's poem that came out of the Auto Complete Poem exercise – an example that I feel illustrates the positive, creative experiences that can result from this approach:

> Nudes are going on
> ...Sexts their only way
> Trending – I'm on top of the world
> Pose for you
> Fake
> I know nothing
> Abuse of the woman

This poem sparked a fascinating and important conversation with the pupils about how they felt women and girls in particular are subjected to behavioural expectations online that boys are not. The writer later developed their poem into a satirical short story about an inanimate mannequin who became a social-media star – the fact she had no personality, opinion or pulse was irrelevant to her followers. I cannot easily conceive of a pre-determined classroom practice that could have resulted in such an outcome. Although time restraints did not allow for this piece to be repurposed into an uploadable package, the possibilities – such as telling the story over an Instagram grid visual (made to resemble the mannequin's 'account') – are there to be explored. I hope that these exercises lead to similarly probing, thoughtful pieces from pupils.

SOCIAL STORIES: THE EXERCISES

These exercises are designed to draw on students' excitement and expertise around social media, to improve their engagement with and quality of creative writing. With so much of social media being about the students communicating a desired image of the self, it became clear that there could be a deeper investigation into how and why this is achieved and the positives and negatives of such thinking. Employing Critical Literacies, Funds Of Identity and Multi-modal Theory, I have shaped as wide a variety of exercises as possible to achieve these goals. The tasks should be set with flexibility and pupils should be allowed to drive the direction of the dialogue between teacher, student and technology. This is why I have proposed multiple extension activities, where possible, rather than dictated a desired route.

ICEBREAKER: STATUS STARTER

Objectives:
- To introduce individuals to the group via a short, reflective piece of writing
- To integrate the topic of social media into the classroom

1. Show a variety of old Facebook status updates from when they were written in the third person.
2. Students lead discussion about what kind of information seems to be shared and why. Teacher can ask open-ended questions if needed.
3. Students write their status in the format of '[Student's name] is ...'. It can be about anything the student wishes. Teacher models some examples.

4. Status can be updated at end of the lesson/start of a new lesson/ when the pupil wishes.

Extension ideas:
5. Write status updates that sum up each month of a year/every year of life/a significant day. Develop into a third-person status poem.
6. Take a character from another project and create status updates that chart their emotional journey.

SYMBOL STORY

Objectives:
- To use both visual and verbal storytelling techniques to create a short video
- To explore symbolism, metaphors and similes

1. Pupils enter a room covered in a variety of images. They have three minutes to choose as many or as few as they wish.
2. Students construct their images in any way they want.
3. Pupils photograph their creation. This is Photo 1.
4. Pupils look at a classmate's work and share their responses. (What catches their eye? Is there any story they see emerging?) Invariably pupils will infer meaning/symbolism in the images, even if not intended. Use this as a springboard to discuss symbolism in texts.
5. From the remaining images on the wall, students choose an image that a) best symbolises their year so far, and b) best symbolises something they wish to achieve by the end of the year. Tell the pupils

they will not have to explain their choices to anyone.

6. Pupils place their two extra images however they wish on top of their current collage, and photograph the work. This is Photo 2.

7. Thinking about the past year, pupils write at least one thing that stands out from each month. It could personal (e.g. March – I got my braces off) or, if they are struggling, more generic (e.g. March – lambs born).

8. Pupils use a metaphor or simile to describe each month (e.g. March/braces can become 'March was a prisoner leaving jail, feeling the sunlight upon his skin once again'). Pupils can use the visuals in front of them for inspiration. If pupils struggle, teacher can model their own responses, pupils can pair up, or teacher can go through images on pupil's collage (e.g. a lion roaring > 'You said in July that you won a fun run and here you have a picture of a roaring lion. When you crossed the finish line, did you hear the roar of the crowd?').

9. Share. (What metaphors/similes were most effective and why?)

10. Continue writing. Pupils can pick one month and develop it, or write about future months.

11. Pupils add writing into their image however they wish (cutting up/ chunking/all together at the bottom)

12. Pupils photograph their creation. This is Photo 3.

13. Pupils look at each other's work and share their reactions to the visual and verbal creations.

14. Using an app such as Instagram Stories, pupils create a short video sequence of their three photographs, adding anything they want (such as

music, more text, emojis) and giving their video a title.

15. Watch videos and reflect on exercise.

AUTO-COMPLETE POEM

Objectives:

- To be playful with language and form
- To explore predictability

1. Using any resource (mind map, poem, short story, song lyrics etc.) pupils underline their favourite 10 words. They do not have to be connected.
2. Turning on auto complete on their phones, they type one of their 10 words into a text message and select the alternatives that auto complete suggests to create the line of a poem. Repeat with another of the 10 words, and so on. Some of it will be nonsense, but pupils should have fun and go with it.
3. Possible discussion on auto-complete and how it operates, what it represents. (Are the sentences created derivative/unoriginal? What does it say about society that we don't want to spend time writing a word out fully? Do they prefer to type with or without it? Comparisons to handwriting etc. Do pupils have things they talk about via text more than anywhere else?)
4. Pupils read their poem and underline any line, phrase or section that stands out, considering the piece's potential.
5. Students screengrab the poem and save the image.
6. Share and discuss.

Extension Ideas:

7. Use their work to create cut-out poetry.
8. Underline a line and use it as stimulus for a short story/character.

9. Write a persuasive argument for or against using auto complete.

10. Erase the last word from a story then let somebody else chose the final word. (How did that feel? Can you understand why they decided to use that word?)

11. Write a short script where one character does not allow another to finish their sentence without interrupting; building the tension, misunderstandings and frustration.

MAKING VS FAKING MEMORIES

Objectives:

- To consider how we can manipulate or distort our memories to cultivate an online existence of choice
- To be playful with the notion of autonomy when storytelling

1. Pupils bring a picture they would be sad to lose. It can be physical or digital. (This in itself should be referenced: why do we often only have digital versions of photos? If a photo only exists in a physical form is it more precious? etc.)

2. Write for three minutes about the photo.

3. Pupils swap pictures after agreeing to be respectful of each other's property.

4. Pupils use new image as stimulus for writing – they should not be influenced by the owner of the photo.

5. Share writing with the owner of the photo/hear writing about their photo. (How do they feel having their photo/memory used in this way? That their story has been manipulated, potentially even erased?) Pupils underline words or phrases they like; score out things they don't. This last step should be encouraged, with teacher ensuring pupils do so respectfully.

6. Pupils add anything additional to the writing if they wish.

7. Discuss the experience. (Did they wrestle back control of the story? Did they accept this new narrative?)
8. Share examples of photos posted online with their narrative changed e.g. the little girl refusing to shake Trump's hand (it was a lookalike Trump), people whose weight-loss photos are stolen, people who are catfished etc. (Why does this happen? Why are people not always in control of their 'story' once they post something online?)
9. The teacher chooses one of the photos at random and makes it visible to the entire class. Using the writing prompts – 'They remembered the feel of…', '…the taste of…', '…the look of…', '…the smell of…', '…the sound of…', 'They wish they could remember…' – everybody writes. Each line can be as long or short as the pupil wishes.

Extension Ideas:
10. Pupils free-write a response to the lesson.
11. The teacher transcribes the final collaborative poem and gives pupils a print out. They can then erase or cut out parts to create whatever poem they want.

SOCIALISING YOUR STORY

NB: This task can only be followed when pupils have completed a previous exercise.
Objectives:
- To engage with social media as a sharing platform for creative writing
- To explore society's desire for approval/validation

1. Pupils select a piece of their writing and divide it into a beginning, a middle and an end. (Could have a conversation here about plotting, setup, complication, climax, resolution etc.)

2. Underline one line from each section that stands out to them.
3. Create a visual for each section – it can be a photo, a drawing or a video.
4. Add each chosen line of text to its related visual.
5. Upload to 'safe' social media platform (such as a school account the teacher is in control of), accompanied by the whole text or just a teaser – students can decide.
6. Discussing expectations can be useful. (What happens if the story gets three likes, or 30 likes? It doesn't change the story, so why should it change our opinion of it? Should, as some argue, likes be removed?) Pupil may wish to disable comments/not post/remove the post – this should be respected.
7. If not uploaded, use the work as a stimulus for writing/swap with other pupils and ask them to use what they see as an inspiration for new stories.

REFERENCES

Albers, P., Sanders, 2010., Literacies, The Arts and Multi-modalities,. London: Natl Council of Teachers of English

Bittle, S. and Technologies, B., 2020. No Longer Optional: Employer Demand For Digital Skills | UK. [online] Burning Glass Technologies. Available at: https://www.burning-glass.com/research-project/uk-demand-digital-skills/ [Accessed 25 May 2020].

boyd, d. 2014. It's Complicated - The Social Lives Of Networked Teens. New Haven: YALE University Press, p.16.

Common Sense. 2019. The Common Sense Census: Media Use By Teens and Tweens. [Online.] Available from: https://www.commonsensemedia.org/sites/default/files/upl oads/research/census_researchreport.pdf [Accessed 25.5.20]

Chan, J. 2020. Top Social Media Apps Worldwide For September 2019 By Downloads. [online] Sensor Tower Blog. Available at: https://sensortower.com/blog/top-social-media-apps-worldwide-september-2019 [Accessed 25 May 2020].

Craft, A. 2010. Teaching for Possibility Thinking: What is it and how do we do it? Learning Matters, 15(1), pp19-23

Craft, A. 2013. Childhood, possibility thinking and wise, humanising educational futures. International Journal of Educational Research, 61 pp. 126–134.

Eichhorn, K., 2019. The End Of Forgetting. Cambridge, Massachusetts: Harvard University Press.

Esteban-Guitart, M. and Moll, L. 2014. Funds of Identity: A new concept based on the Funds of Knowledge approach. Culture & Psychology, 20(1), pp.31-48.

Sales, N. 2016. American Girls: Social Media And The Secret Lives Of Teenagers. New York: Knopf Publishing Group

Frechette, J. 2006 'Cyber-censorship or cyber-literacy? Envisioning cyber-learning through media education', p149-71 in D. Buckingham and R. Willett (eds), Digital Generations: Children, Young People and New Media. Mahwah, NJ: Lawrence Erlbaum

Jewitt, C. and Kress, G. 2008. Multimodal Literacy. New York: Peter Lang.

Kress, G., van Leewan, T. 2001. Multimodal Discourse: The Modes and Media of Contemporary Communication. London: Bloomsbury Academic

Myers, J. 2020. Instagram Poetry: How Social Media Is Revitalizing An Ancient Art Form. [online] Available at: https://www.statepress.com/article/2019/09/spmagazine-instagram-poetry-and-how-social-media-is-revitalizing-an-ancient-art-form [Accessed 25 May 2020].

Newburn, T. 1996. 'Back to the future? Youth crime, youth justice and the rediscovery of 'authoritarian populism', in J. Pilcher and S. Wagg (Eds) Thatcher's Children? Politics, Childhood and Society in the 1980s and 1990s. London: Falmer.

Kalantzis, M., Cope, B., Chan, E. and Dalley-Trim, L., 2016. Literacies. Cambridge: Cambridge University Press.

Usrof, H., 2017. Social Media and Productivity: The Case of Education Sector in Assir Province. International Journal of Human Resource Studies, 7(3), p.243.

YOU DON'T HAVE TO LIKE ME:

A SCHEME OF WORK FOR TEACHING FEMINISM TO KEY STAGE 3 THROUGH CREATIVE WRITING

SARA CARROLL

My initial idea to devise a scheme of work on feminist themes was born out of the disengagement I encountered when feminism was mentioned in a Key Stage Three English lesson – six out of 20 students steadfastly refused to say they were feminists. I teach in an all-girls school with a relatively privileged student body and a geographically distant, but involved, parental community. Through presentations in assembly and the existence of a range of societies proactively addressing diversity and LGBTQ+ concerns, the older students are clearly exploring the important issues of the day, but there is less space for younger students to do the same. In this #MeToo era, when the Everyday Sexism Twitter account still receives many entries daily, I believe that the sooner young women start to engage with questions of gender equality and explore their own agency in the world, the better. Tackling the subject through a dialogic and creative approach in the classroom has the potential to provide a safe space for individuals to grapple with ideas they find difficult. In this article I will set out the thinking behind the lessons and exercises, then provide a brief outline of each lesson.

There is no doubt that to approach feminism in this way is to put politics front and centre of the secondary classroom. Wendy Hesford suggests that feminist teaching requires a rejection of classroom hierarchy, and should reward students for working collectively (Hesford, 1990). She also suggests that one of the main tenets of feminist pedagogy is based on engaging with personal experiences. Democracy and working in a community of practice are both important elements in the creative writing classroom, which suggests there are good pedagogical reasons for combining feminism and creative writing. I was also interested in following the thinking of educational philosopher Paulo Freire's proposal that literacy is part of the process of getting readers and writers to become self-critical about the 'historically constructed nature of experience' (Freire & Macedo, 1987, p.5). One aim in teaching a creative writing scheme of work might be to encourage students to 'read the world' and their place in it, while beginning to equip them with the means of questioning the status quo beyond their privileged bubble.

As a secondary English teacher I am also interested in the effect creative writing can have on the learner in the context of public exams. I have seen for myself the greater sense of engagement that a creative approach develops in so-called low-ability sets dealing with 'literary' texts, yet writing is still rarely mentioned pedagogically as a tool for a student's own learning (Czerniewska, 1992). Students cannot begin to start writing without engaging in metacognition: in order to make language choices, the writer must reflect intensely on the subject they choose to write about and the context in which it will be read (Cremin & Myhill, 2012). Creative writing is essentially a reflective practice and that reflection has the potential to lead to greater self-knowledge, better questioning, increased empathy, and therefore, surely, more effective learners (Bolton, 2009). I like the idea of encouraging creative writing as a skill through a broader, social context; an understanding of which will affect a young person's perception of their place in the world. I wanted the overall title (You Don't Have to Like Me) to set the tone of our discussions: being good or liked is still a lurking expectation for young women (George, 2007) and I wanted the students to challenge that.

I roughly divided the scheme into five one-hour lessons, with an implicit sixth hour for putting together a performance or pamphlet of the creative work. Having an end product seems a good way to generate a sense of seriousness and purpose, and should encourage students to step out of their comfort zones to get a taste of the community support a performance can give (Alvarez, 2014).

DISCUSSION

The lessons each have a directional heading, usually framed in a question through which I aim to establish a dialogic approach that feeds into the writing process. All lessons begin with paired or group discussions, which allows students to interrogate big ideas verbally, whilst drawing on their own 'funds of knowledge' (Gonzalez, 2005). Discussion also helps create a community of practice, where the class works as a group on a common theme. This then leads to the shared experience of writing about it (Wenger, 1999). I am particularly interested in the received idea that as long as the community creates a safe, dialogic environment for sharing ideas and opinions, the process of writing becomes key to a student's sense of self. This felt vital for exploring gender identity with a young age group (Grainger, Gooch & Lambrith, 2005).

Creating a community of practice in an all-female classroom does have its challenges. Adolescent students, in any environment, are constantly in the throes of constructing identity through their own complex communities in the school at large (Paechter, 2002). Those who teach girls will be only too aware of the hierarchy among the students themselves, and it felt necessary to confront this potential difficulty in order to create a safe space in which all pupils could engage in the precious activities of thinking, talking and writing creatively. This was the reason for encouraging students to draw up rules for the community in lesson two; bringing to light the importance of the personal engagement I am asking of them, and encouraging a sense of collective responsibility.

WRITING

I devised the creative tasks with a balance between mutually supportive collaborative work and reflective individual thinking. Many of the exercises begin with free writing that arises from discussion or stimulus material. In my experience, free writing itself can be a bemusing technique for young people, who find it hard to just keep going, and yet once they feel comfortable it can be a useful way of mining for creative ideas (Gilbert, 2017).

It is important to me that the students have a discrete exercise book or journal that is their own private space in which to experiment and express ideas in whatever way seems important to them, giving them full autonomy over their own engagement (Grainger, Gooch & Lambrith, 2005). After any period of free writing, I will ask students to re-read what they have written and underline ideas that interest them or words and phrases they like, thus increasing the sense of ownership over their initial written thoughts and individual words.

After space for thought, discussion and free expression, each lesson contains at least one opportunity to form a more finished product: a poem, script or short story. These pieces will inevitably be first drafts but I am often delighted by the speed at which younger students can produce a very personal piece of writing, dropping inhibitions and drawing on shared ideas quickly. I was keen to include spoken word poetry based on compelling evidence that giving students a voice through creating and performing their own spoken word work develops a confident validation of identity (Dymoke, 2017). I also used this as a place to address the occasionally troubled relationships between adolescent girls head on. Rosalyn George writes about the 'betrayal' that happens when girls bully within their own friendship groups, and yet she reveals that a personal response from the bullied, simply saying what they feel, has the potential to directly counteract the bullying (George, 2007). In the exercise in lesson two, by giving students lines originally written by others I hoped to remove some of the jeopardy of putting one's own opinions out in public – while at the same time increasing a sense of empathy through hearing what has been said to others and the effect this has had. Writing and performing spoken word poetry would certainly be a new experience for my Key Stage 3 students and including YouTube clips of poetry slams by young people can give them confidence that this is a literary space they are allowed to occupy. Whilst not explicitly mentioned in the scheme, I would encourage volunteers to read their work after every writing opportunity.

TEACHER AS WRITER

I have long found it useful to present myself as a participant in the creative writing lesson. I will always do the exercise I set the students, always tell them that I am writing too, but have never once been asked to read my piece! My reason for doing this is to help me empathise with the struggling writer, as well as assess the usefulness of the task. There is also a healthy sense of bonding when the teacher can be seen as a fellow grappler and creator (Smith & Wrigley, 2012). The scheme explicitly includes moments for the teacher to model journaling or writing, where I would hold up my own writing journal, with its diagrams and messy drafts, to show that they don't have to be slaves to presentation (something which can also be a gender issue). The thinking of bell hooks and her theory of 'engaged pedagogy' and 'self actualisation' (hooks, 1994, p.15) gave me confidence with this. Too much revelation from the teacher is uncomfortable but as I am a woman, with a woman's experience, exploring feminism with students in my care, perhaps hooks' ideal combination of 'spiritual' and intellectual engagement from the teacher is another way in which students can find confidence in their own voice.

THE SCHEME

Lesson One: What influence does gender have on me?
Aim: to get students thinking about their gendered place in society and start the habit of creative writing.

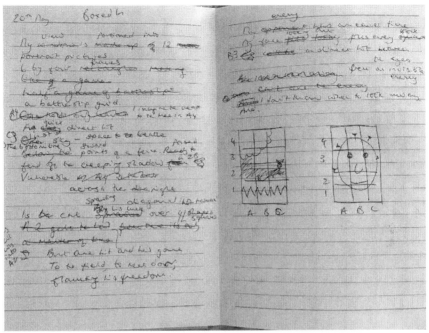

FIGURE 1 AN EXAMPLE OF A TEACHER'S JOURNAL

- (Individual) Make a list of the good and bad things about being female.
- (Small groups) Discuss a series of open questions on being female (e.g. How does being female affect the way I behave? When is being female hard? Does gender really matter any more? What does the title of the scheme mean?)
- (Whole class) Feedback as groups, and explore role models.
- Watch and listen to Taylor Swift's song The Man as the stimulus for a discussion. (What is she referring to? Can you relate to her ideas?)
- (Small groups) Put together a poster with the title 'Being Female in 2020', collaging all the thoughts, ideas and opinions of the group.

- What is a writing journal and how can I use one? (Teacher to introduce and share own.) See Figure 1.
- (Individual) Write freely for five minutes, using one of the phrases from the collage poster as the starting point. When time is up, underline phrases and words you like.
- Plenary: Write a newspaper headline for your experience in this lesson; use it as the title of your first journal entry.

Lesson Two: What do you look like?
Aim: Encourage students to reflect on the responsibility of writing in a community and to start responding creatively to feelings and perceptions.

- Class discussion: '...everything in life is writable about if you have the outgoing guts to do it, and the imagination to improvise' – Sylvia Plath. (Pictures of Plath help the process of identifying a woman writer e.g. Contrasting images of Sylvia Plath on covers of Letters 1940-1956 (UK/US)
- (Whole class) Read and discuss Plath's poem 'The Applicant' (What is the poem about? How does it link with the starter quotation?)
- (Individual) How do you feel about being a writer? Answer open questions in your journal. (e.g. How do you write? What is difficult about it? Why might creative writing be a positive thing? What rules should we have for writing together?)
- (Whole class) Based on thoughts in response to these questions, can we put together a set of rules for the writing classroom?
- (Pairs) Create a spoken word poem based on the line 'Everything in life is writable' (created by Joelle Taylor):

- Write on a strip of paper something hurtful once said to you.
- Teacher to collect strips and redistribute one to each pair.
- Use that one statement as the starting point to write four lines each.
- Put the four lines together with the statement to make a nine-line poem.
- Students to work out a performance for the class.
- (Individual) Free write on a time you felt good about the way you looked.
- (Whole class) What ideas is Lamont Lilly exploring in his poem 'All Natural'?
- Write your own 10-line poem using Lilly's poem and your free writing as a stimulus.
- Volunteers to share work. (Teacher could also share work.)
- Plenary: Use a post-it note to write down what struck you most in today's lesson. Stick it up as you leave the room.

Lesson Three: What women want
Aim: Students to consider the way women's desires can be marginalised and to spend some time taking ownership of their own language.

- Free writing on dreams for your future self.
- (Small groups) Look at newspaper headlines and discuss the language used. (Headlines provided on the pay gap, sexuality, domestic equality, female friendship. Groups given a page of open questions from the teacher.)
- (Pairs) Put some words on trial: work up a defence and an attack of common words used about women and their connotations (e.g. girl, bossy, mother, shrill, loud).

- (Individual) Take back the dictionary: choose your favourite word(s) for every letter of the alphabet based on meaning, sound or association (Anderson, 2006, p.193).
- Write a piece of prose or poetry describing yourself using those words. (The teacher could prepare a model: a simple acrostic for differentiation.)
- Plenary: write one dream for yourself somewhere in your journal.

Lesson Four: Read my lips
Aim: students to consider that inequality can come in many forms, and that confidence with language can help them assert themselves.
NB: Teachers could use any appropriate images here, for example a group of girls acting unkindly and something like the Punch cartoon of Miss Triggs in a meeting (1988) by Riana Duncan.

- (Whole class) How would you react if you were any of the characters in these situations? (e.g. How much power does each person have? Is that fair? What happens if someone in the group is unhappy?)
- (Small groups) Remind yourself of a well-known fairytale. (Provide short re-tellings of Cinderella, Rapunzel etc.) What is the power dynamic in each story? Prepare a short, improvised performance demonstrating that balance of power.
- (Individual) Using 'Once upon a time' and 'They all lived happily ever after' as the framework, write a version of your chosen fairytale (an 'Equalitale') in which the balance of power is more evenly distributed.
- (Small group) Share stories. What did you like about them?
- Plenary: give your equalitale a relevant title.

Lesson Five: What next? Owning it!
Aim: to ask students to reflect on what they have learnt about being young women and to consider how to move forward.

- Pair work, leading to whole-class discussion, on the circumstances in which you might say, 'You don't have to like me'.
- (Individual) Write a metaphor poem: answer a series of questions from the teacher (What colour of the rainbow are you? What animal? Weather system? Musical instrument? Object in the room?) and use them to form metaphors about yourself e.g. I am green moss, my own camouflage etc. (Teacher could share here.)
- (Whole class) 'Perhaps one day, we will have changed society, enough so women are never asked to submerge a true self' – Gloria Steinem. What does that mean in the context of the work we have done?
- Read and discuss the poem 'I want to be a list of further possibilities' by Chen Chen.
- (Individual) Using this poem as a stimulus, write your own manifesto for the future. Start by brainstorming with words or pictures to mine for ideas, then try out short phrases for the poem. (Teacher could model here.)
- Plenary: look back over all your pieces and consider which you would most like to work up and perform/publish.

CONCLUDING THOUGHTS

I have come to the conclusion that a plan such as this, for teaching feminism through creative writing, could have a wider application. My ideas are based around a promotion of 'self-actualisation' and owning language, and in recent times it has become apparent that young people face a future overshadowed by the fall-out from a pandemic, irreversible environmental disaster, and toxic racial inequality. I can't help but think that any pedagogical approach that equips students with the confidence to ask pertinent questions about their own future, nurture assured self-expression and foster social empathy feels more important now than ever. The holistic nature of a creative writing pedagogy, with its reflective, democratic approach, has the potential to do that: it is a compelling methodology that respects the experience and development of the individual within a supportive community of practice – and, quite frankly, we owe it to our young people to give them that opportunity.

REFERENCES

Anderson, Linda. Creative Writing: A Workbook with Readings. Abingdon: Routledge in Association with the Open U, 2006.

Alvarez, Nadia, and Jack Mearns. "The Benefits of Writing and Performing in the Spoken Word Poetry Community." The Arts in Psychotherapy 41.3 (2014): 263-68. Web.

Bolton, Gillie. "Write to Learn: Reflective Practice Writing." Innovait 2.12 (2009): 752-54. Web.

Chen, Chen, and Jericho. Brown. When I Grow up I Want to Be a List of Further Possibilities. 2017. Print. A. Poulin, Jr. New Poets of America Ser.; No. 39.

Cremin, Teresa, and Debra, Myhill. Writing Voices: Creating Communities of Writers. London: Routledge, 2012. Print.

Czerniewska, Pam. Learning about Writing: The Early Years. Oxford: Basil Blackwell, 1992. Print. Language in Education.

Duncan, Riana, Punch 1988, viewed 27th March 2020, http://www.stockpholio.net/view/image/id/8557079931#.Xs5 7amhKiuU

Dymoke, Sue. "'Poetry Is Not a Special Club': How Has an Introduction to the Secondary Discourse of Spoken Word Made Poetry a Memorable Learning Experience for Young People?" Oxford Review of Education 43.2 (2017): 225-41. Web.

Fisher, Robert, "Dialogic Teaching" in Green, Andrew. Becoming a Reflective English Teacher. Maidenhead: McGraw-Hill Open UP, 2011. Web.

Freire, Paulo, and Donaldo P. Macedo. Literacy Reading the Word & the World. London: Routledge & Kegan Paul, 1987. Web.

George, Rosalyn. Girls in a Goldfish Bowl : Moral Regulation, Ritual and the Use of Power amongst Inner City Girls. Rotterdam: Sense, 2007. Print.

González, Norma., Luis C. Moll, and Cathy. Amanti. Funds of Knowledge: Theorizing Practice in Households, Communities, and Classrooms. New York: Routledge, 2005. Print.

Grainger, Teresa., Kathy. Goouch, and Andrew Lambirth. Creativity and Writing : Developing Voice and Verve in the Classroom. London: Routledge, 2005. Web.

Hesford, Wendy S. "Storytelling and the Dynamics of Feminist Teaching." Feminist Teacher 5.2 (1990): 20-24. Web.

hooks, bell. Teaching to Transgress Education as the Practice of Freedom. New York ; London: Routledge, 1994. Print.

Lilly, Lamont, 2020, all natural, viewed 7th April 2020, https://dissidentvoice.org/2020/02/all-natural/

Paechter, Carrie F. Being Boys, Being Girls Learning Masculinities and Femininities. Maidenhead: Open UP, 2007. Print.

Rainer, Tristine. The New Diary: How to Use a Journal for Self-guidance and Expanded Creativity. New York: Jeremy P. Tarcher/Penguin, 2004. Print.

Wenger, Etienne. Communities of Practice : Learning, Meaning, and Identity. Cambridge: Cambridge UP, 1999. Print. Learning in Doing: Social, Cognitive and Computational Perspectives.

APPENDIX

EXEMPLAR MATERIAL FOR LESSON 3

My Lexicon (teacher's own)

A	altruism/ask	ankle/adamant
B	blanket	boulevard
C	celeriac crinkle	
D	dance	Dunstable
E	eggs	eclectic
F	flask	flutter
G	glass	gargantuan
H	happiness	hacienda
I	idiolect	iron
J	jam	jumbly
K	kettle	krispy kremes
L	lace	lullaby
M	misbehaviour	malevolent
N	nutter	numbskull
O	oxygen	oscillate
P	pink	papyrus
Q	quiet	queue
R	recipe	rootle
S	swing	susurration
T	tea	Totoro
U	umbrella	unity
V	vegetables	Verdigris
W	water	wibble
X	X-ray	Xavier
Y	yellow	yarn
Z	Zebra`	Zed

Lexicon Dreams (teacher's own)
I am tea and eggs and oxygen for breakfast,
a flask of celeriac soup and idiolect jam for lunch.
I like to wrap myself in a happiness blanket,
dance a yellow hacienda down a quiet boulevard

and swing to the recipe of eclectic susurration
laced into a papyrus lullaby.

Name Acrostic (teacher's own)
S I like to hear susurration swing
A wear the ankle-bracelet of altruism
R while rootling through recipes.
A All I ask is that you are adamant

EXEMPLAR MATERIAL FOR LESSON 5

Metaphor Poem (teacher's own)
My Thirteen-year-old Self
I am green moss, my own camouflage.
I am a deer blinking in the silent wood.
I am a flute echoing in an empty hall.
I am sharp cold frost on a blue-sky day.
I am the small shiny drawing pin with an angry point.

SUCCESSFUL SCHOOL VISITS:
THE VIEW OF A CHILDREN'S AUTHOR

CAMILLA CHESTER

Writing for children means school visits. I have experienced highly successful visits, and have had very poor experiences. In this article I hope to offer the view of a Children's Author as to what constitutes a successful visit and offer some practical tips for educators on preparing for an author visit to their school.

WHY BOOK AN AUTHOR VISIT?

Not all schools recognise the benefits of author visits and it's often seen as too expensive and low down on the long list of priorities for busy schools. However, successful author visits are known to significantly boost pupil interest, enthusiasm and motivation towards both reading and writing. The benefits of author engagement on school literacy levels can be extremely long-lasting, but it's important that the visit is properly prepared for by both the school and the visiting author.

HOW DO YOU FIND THE RIGHT AUTHOR?

Obviously, there is no point booking an author who writes for teens to talk to reception – you have to do your research. If you already know the name of the author you're looking for then normally a simple internet search will find them. All authors who visit schools regularly will have a website, which should clearly outline their approach to visiting schools and how you can contact them.

Remember: usually the bigger the name; the more money they charge. Personally, I'm a strong believer in using local authors wherever possible. Children relate well to someone who they know lives close by and you will make good links with a local resource.

If you're unsure, a good place to start is Contact An Author. This is a database of many of the UK's authors and illustrators. It is the one I use, but there are a number of others available. They usually allow you to search for an author based on your need: for example, a KS1 author within a 30-mile radius of your school, who is experienced in small group work.

Alternatively, you can go through an organisation such as The Society of Children's Book Writers and Illustrators, using their Speakers Bureau (SCBWI - British Isles), or through The Society of Authors. The good thing about using an organisation is that the author will be a member and therefore usually DBS checked and experienced.

WHAT SHOULD YOU LOOK FOR?

Before you book the author, read their testimonials. Just because they are good at writing books, or are famous, does not necessarily mean that they will be good at school visits. Most of my visits now come through word of mouth or recommendations. One of the most wonderful things that happened to me was when a teacher who had been part of a previous school visit moved to a new job as Head of Literacy and tracked me down to book an author visit for her new school. If a colleague recommends an author to you, make a note of their name.

WHAT SHOULD YOU EXPECT?

If the author is experienced in visits (sometimes debut authors will offer very low rates or even free visits in order to build up their experience), they should have a clear programme of what they offer and how much they charge. This will be their standard visit.

NB: At the moment, the average day rate for an author visit is £350, as set out by The Society of Authors.

I have a set fee for an afternoon visit. This includes a full KS2 interactive assembly, a Y5/Y6-focused workshop and a book-signing session. Having said that, the author should be flexible to what your specific needs are and be able to adapt their visit accordingly. You should expect the author to be professional and businesslike in their approach to working with you, responding quickly to emails and being clear with what they need from the school in order for the visit to go well.

The visit should be interactive: engaging, enthusing and inspiring the children in their literacy work. It is NOT the author's job to teach the curriculum, but it is their job to make pupils excited about reading and writing.

WHAT IS EXPECTED OF YOU?

For the author, school visits are a major part of their income. Although they love their job, they also expect that they will be paid for it and treated professionally. It is expected that:

- Everyone (staff, pupils, parents/carers) will be aware of who they are and when they are coming.
- Their emails/contacts will be responded to promptly and professionally.
- The school will be prepared and ready for their visit.
- They will be paid promptly.
- They will be given feedback and/or testimonials.
- They will be recommended to other schools.

MY WORST VISIT

I'm not going to name and shame the school, but let me share this story as it will give you a clear idea of what not to do. I'd phoned the school to introduce myself as a local author and was given the name of their English Coordinator, who I then emailed. After several months she emailed back to say she had a date for my visit booked – this was out of the blue, but thankfully I was free.

To confirm the booking I emailed her back, outlining clearly what the visit would entail and what I would need from the school (parking space, ability to play a PowerPoint presentation, table, chair, flip-chart stand etc). I attached a pre-order book letter, which was to go out to all the parents/carers before my visit and the invoice for my fee. I said I was flexible, so if this wasn't what they were after to call me and we could work out new details.

I never heard back, despite three gentle nudges, so I assumed it was a standard visit she was after. On the day of the visit I called the school before I set off to ask how many orders they had received so that I knew how many books to bring. The receptionist had no idea who I was or what I was talking about and the teacher who had organised the visit was teaching. I arrived early, with a good 15 minutes to set up. The receptionist I had talked to was job sharing and the new person had no clue who I was. I was left waiting in reception for 20 minutes with all my equipment for my interactive assembly and my workshop, and a bag of books for the signing.

Eventually, another teacher came and just said, 'We're ready for you.' I assumed I would be led to an empty hall where I could set up for my KS2 assembly, but no, I was taken to a single classroom that was packed with two classes of children (Y5 and Y6) plus staff, all sitting ready for my performance. Help! There wasn't even any room for my bags I'd brought with me and I had to leave them outside the door. It was obvious that my visit had been totally forgotten about, but instead of turning me away, they decided to tell the children it was a 'surprise author visit'.

I winged it, improvising as I went and had fun with the kids, but I was never paid for my visit – despite chasing several times – and I only sold one book (to a mum who was dragged back into school after pick-up time by the Y6 girl who was desperate for a signed copy). The visit left me out of pocket and feeling very depressed about being an unknown author with a nasty dose of Imposter Syndrome thrown into the mix.

A good thing did happen from the free visit, however, as one of the boys was so inspired he bought my book later and then dressed as one of my characters for World Book Day. His mum sent me a picture of him via my website. It was amazing and reminded me that even a bad visit, from my perspective, can be positive one for the children – and showed the power an author visit can have.

MY BEST VISIT

Now let me contrast that scarring experience with an extremely positive one. I had contacted the school in exactly the same way and had an email response saying they would like to book a visit, and could I provide a list of possible dates in or around World Book Day (WBD) week? NB: WBD is the busiest day of the year for authors. If you're looking to book for or around that day you will definitely need to do it several months in advance. I had one point of contact in the school, who answered my emails promptly and professionally. When I arrived at the school I had an allocated parking space and as I was getting out of the car several children shouted my name through the playground fence and started cheering. I felt like a true celebrity – it was wonderful!

Book orders were waiting for me in the school office, where a space had been made for me to sign/personalise the books and I was even given a cup of tea and a biscuit. I was then taken to the hall that was ready with the equipment I needed. A staff member stayed with me, helping me to set up and test everything worked. The children were very excited and engaged throughout the entire visit. It was obvious they had researched me and my books. One class were reading one of my books together. The Q&A sessions were full of insightful questions and in the workshop the children worked very hard to impress me with their writing and the books they were reading.

I had a huge queue of parents/carers with their children for the end-of-day book signing. I actually ran out of books and had to go home to collect more – they patiently waited for me. That visit set me up emotionally and financially for weeks afterwards.

HOW SHOULD SCHOOLS PREPARE?

So, you've found your perfect, local author; you've checked she's professional; you have the date and details confirmed; now it's time to get the children and staff excited about her visit.

- The first thing to do is a BIG ANNOUNCEMENT in assembly. Make it a huge deal: Okay, so she's not JK Rowling but nevertheless she's a real author, writing real books. She's definitely a celebrity and she's coming to your school.

- Next, if you have the budget, order her books into the school: get them in the classrooms, in the library, maybe choose one to read as a class.
- At the same time, as a school, spend some time researching her: look up her website, watch her videos on her YouTube channel, follow her blog, sign up to her newsletter.
- You might want to do a school display. It's amazing, as an author, to come into school to see a display board with all your book covers on it, or pictures of your characters.
- Make sure the pre-order letters go to parents/carers at least a week or two before the visit date.
- You could set related homework, such as find out five facts about the author, which the children can do with their parents/carers, so that they too are excited about the author visit.
- Ensure the reception staff are fully onboard with what's happening and are ready for orders coming in.
- Do a countdown to the date – why not even do an advent-style calendar? The children could make them with a 'WOW!' word behind each door. The possibilities of hyping up the visit are endless!
- Keep the author informed and let her know if there's anything specific you would like her to do.
- Make sure the school is ready physically on the day and that when the author arrives she is looked after. Don't leave her alone with children and stick to what you have agreed prior to the visit.
- Give her feedback afterwards: tell her what worked well, what you thought should change.
- Let the children give her feedback for her website.
- See if you are able to forward any of their creative writing onto her afterwards.

- Stay in touch.

EXERCISES SPECIFIC TO MY BOOK

On my website I have a number of curriculum-linked exercises that relate to my debut, Jarred Dreams, which are aimed at Y6. These are FREE to download and can be found under the Teaching Resources Tab: Y6 Discussion Guide > Comprehension Task > Character Development Task. I also have word searches for all three of my books. Jarred Dreams has been selected in some schools as the Y6 Guided Reading book, so these exercises were devised to help teachers with that. Occasionally a class may be doing the activities when I come to visit and I might be asked to lead one. Not all authors will have this, but it's worth checking what is on offer.

Many authors will want to relate activities to their books to maximise book sales – as I say, this is our livelihood. You can always ask an author to devise something specific to their visit, or as an after task, that relates directly to both their book and the curriculum. For example, here is an exercise that would relate to writing persuasive texts and directly links to my second book, EATS:

Read the opening chapter of EATS. Now pretend you are Lucas and Brian and write the covering letter that will accompany their competition entry. Remember you want to win: how will you persuade the chef judges to watch your entry video before all the other contestants?

In conclusion, successful school author visits are always the ones where both the author and the school are fully prepared. Before the visit, the author and the school need to agree the details and maintain regular correspondence. The school needs to ensure everyone (staff, pupils, parents/carers) are excited about the forthcoming visit, which should be interactive and inspiring. A successful author visit can have long-lasting benefits to pupils' motivation and enthusiasm towards the literacy curriculum and it is therefore important that it doesn't become a wasted opportunity.

FAMILY HISTORY: FACT OR FICTION?

OPPORTUNITIES AND CHALLENGES IN USING FAMILY STORIES
AND FAMILY HISTORY RESEARCH AS A RESOURCE AND
INSPIRATION FOR CREATIVE WRITING

JANET DEAN

This article is based on my postgraduate research (Dean, 2015) and creative practice in using family history as a starting point for fiction and poetry, and my experience of facilitating creative writing workshops, courses and writing retreats using family history resources.

I will consider the sources of family history (formal and informal), offer suggestions about encouraging and enabling access to them, and include a range of approaches to using family history as a stimulus for writing. My own experience is of teaching adults, but where possible I will refer to challenges and opportunities for children and young people.

Of the many resources we can draw on to inspire creative writing in ourselves and others, family history continues to be a rich seam. We can access it in a variety of ways, and in this article I'll consider three main groups of sources:

- Personal memory and family stories (the memories of others)
- Family (private) photographs and documents
- Public records, and social and political events

Throughout the article I will attempt to flag up barriers and challenges, including social, emotional and ethical challenges, which confront us when accessing family history, and consider ways to navigate these.

PERSONAL MEMORY AND FAMILY STORIES

Opportunities

Using memory to recall details – physical characteristics, mannerisms, speech patterns, dress, personal habits and so on – is a useful skill for writers and contributes to their ability to develop a wide range of characters and character types. For a writer, memory is a parallel skill to observation.

Some families are full of stories which writers can use to build on or to adapt to other uses or forms: poetry, drama, as well as fiction and creative non-fiction. Family secrets, or fragments of stories, are especially interesting to writers and can fire up the imagination. If stories aren't shared, some writers might need to encourage family members to tell them or write them down. This can be a positive and enjoyable experience in many families, though not universally, as I discuss below.

I am inclined to the view that all memory, whether personal or shared (and even recorded events) can be 'fiction' in that it is always an imprint of what actually happened. If you or I witness an event and we are asked to relate what happened, it is likely that we will report different details, make varied emphases, and tell stories which are not the same. We know this is the case, and it is for this reason that some of the lines between memory, memoir, creative non-fiction (where facts are reported, but feelings and impressions are added) and fiction are blurred.

In my book The Peacemaker (Dean Knight, 2019), I made a fictional story from the family stories that my mother told me repeatedly as a child about her own mother who had died when she was eighteen. I took this approach for a number of reasons: first, the 'true' story wasn't strong enough to stand alone, nor were the real characters well-known or particularly compelling to merit a non-fiction account; second, when I came to do some research of the records, I found that the stories and the 'facts' didn't coincide, so the 'truth' evaporated; and third, all the real people on whom my characters were based were dead, and I could do them no personal harm by fictionalising their lives.

In a recent online writing course, we asked participants to write about family members they could no longer see, whether temporarily because of 'lockdown' restrictions during the pandemic in 2020 or because the person had died or gone away. One participant wrote about her childhood memory of her aunt:

> Her eyes were, I suppose, small and she never wore make-up to try to accentuate them. I think they were brown but couldn't say whether they were light or dark, hazel or chestnut. I would have remembered had they been a vivid green or a dazzling blue, but nothing about Margie dazzled. My teacher may have asked, "Did her eyes smile, glisten, shine?" I would not have known how to draw unhappy eyes. Her ears were, presumably, also small – they were certainly not big or weirdly shaped or in any way distinctive. They were never adorned. They were simply of purpose. (Van Greuningen-Smith, 2020)

In the full piece, the writer had described her warm feelings about her aunt, though she had not been able to describe her aunt's features, which were not specifically memorable. But, in describing this very ordinariness she captures her character and we still see the impression that she left.

Challenges
Accessing memories of deceased relatives can be a difficult area, and not one that children might find possible or bearable. Adults may also find it painful to draw on memories of loved

ones, even where they are motivated to write about friends and family they have lost, and it is helpful to prepare for this. Another consideration is that families are not the same thing for all of us – some of us may have little family history to make a memory from, due to a range of circumstances. My own experience has included working with adults who were adopted, with little or no knowledge or contact with their birth parents, and with adults who are struggling with a determination to write about abusive family situations.

One approach to dealing with family history as a source for writing is to encourage the creation of distance between the writer and their subject. Sometimes and for some people, the process of writing about family is intended to be cathartic and therapeutic, but unless as a teacher you are trained in these techniques, they could lead to difficulties. With most groups, exercises in taking different points of view can be useful in drawing out description and building skills.

Another way to enable wider participation in drawing on memory is to broaden our definition of family to encompass 'community'. If what we are trying to develop in creative writers is the skill of imagining what the world might be like from another perspective, or to build characters that are different from ourselves, it is possible to use people around us to stand in for family members. Talking to people in our social groups – faith groups, clubs and societies, friendship groups – can be a source of tapping into the history of a wider family.

Here are some writing prompts to help writers think about people who might represent 'history', and consider using different points of view to achieve this:

- Who is the oldest person you know? Is it a relative, a grandparent, great aunt or uncle or a great-grandparent? Is it the person in the corner shop, the person who cuts your hair, or somebody you met at a friend's house? Write about them, starting from external descriptions of their features, way of walking/standing, their hairstyle and clothes, their voice and speech, consider their behaviour – what do they do, what interests them.

- Write about them in a third-person neutral voice, stating the facts of what you know or remember about them. Then write in the first person, from your point of view, adding your feelings about them to the description. Then try writing in their voice letting them tell their story of their life, what they used to do and what they do now.

Here is another way to facilitate writers to think their way into somebody else's perspective:

- Think about somebody who is older than you – at least ten years older if you can, but preferably more. It might be a member of your family, or of a friend's family, it could be your teacher or somebody else you know. Now try to imagine what that person would have been like at the age you are now. How would they have looked, what would they wear, what might they be doing that's different? Would their opinions or likes and dislikes be the same?

FAMILY (PRIVATE) PHOTOGRAPHS AND DOCUMENTS

Opportunities

When we add photographs and documents to family memory we get another layer of opportunity. Older members of our families or our communities might have kept photographs, letters, certificates, health records or other documents which predate digitisation. Asking within the family or close community to find out what tangible resources might be available could be a good starting point.

The second trigger for The Peacemaker was a First World War canvas wallet that my aunt gave me a few years before she died. The wallet contained, amongst other things, a photograph of my grandmother and her first husband (which might have

71

been a wedding photograph from 1914), a commemorative document issued by the government which recorded his death in 1916, his burial place in France, and the names and addresses of his widow and his parents – plus, most movingly, the last letter he wrote from France in August 1916, three weeks before he died. These are all shown in the next pages.

FOR KING AND COUNTRY
TO THE
GLORY OF GOD
AND
IN EVERLASTING MEMORY
OF

HUXLEY, Pte. G. H., 1583. 5th Bn. Yorkshire
Regt. Died of wounds 17th Sept., 1916. Age 22.
Son of Mr. and Mrs. Huxley, of Epping, Essex;
husband of Martha Lillian Lythe (formerly
Huxley), of School Row, Rosedale East, Pickering,
Yorks. IV. B. 3.

WHO GAVE HIS LIFE IN THE GREAT WAR
THAT WE MIGHT LIVE
AND WHOSE NAME IS CARVED IN STONE
AT
St PIERRE -Amiens-
MILITARY CEMETERY - FRANCE

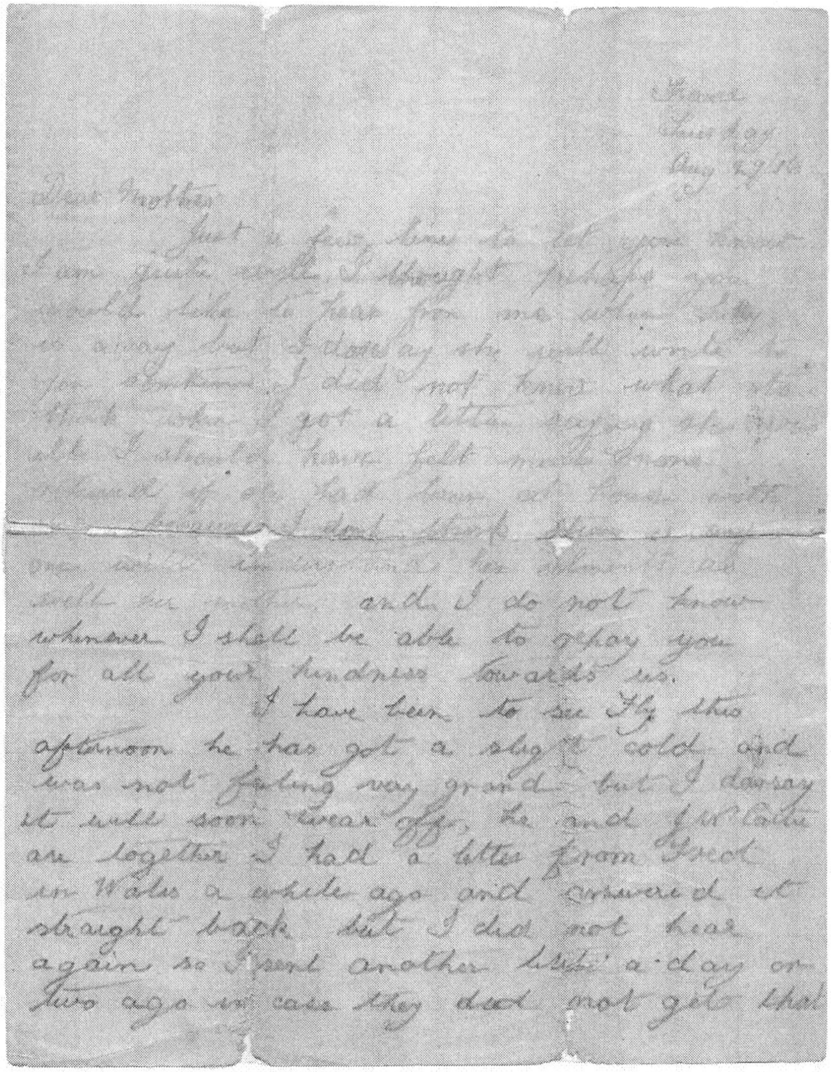

Each resource offered a different opportunity. The photograph contained the facts of a First World War soldier in uniform; and the dark, long-skirted, two-piece suit and wide, flower-trimmed hat considered fashionable by an eighteen-year-old girl at the time. It also contained the opportunity to speculate on matters unknown: how did the couple meet?

What were they like as people? How did they sound? In my novel I use both the facts of the picture and my imaginings of my grandmother and her first husband to invent the story of how they met, and to bring them to life.

In creative writing classes, using the students' own photographs, or anonymous photographs I have supplied, can help to open up the imagination to characters and situations which form the basis of storytelling in either prose or poetry.

The government certificate led me into an area of research I had not anticipated. It gave my grandmother's in-laws' address as 'Epping, Essex', which was a surprise because my mother had told me that this was a Yorkshire family from Scarborough. When I used online family history resources like Ancestry and Find My Past, I could track the family, and in particular my grandmother's mother-in-law, and found a woman with a complicated life who moved from Essex to Leicestershire and then to Yorkshire. None of this information had been retained with any accuracy or detail in my family's oral tradition, but it was discoverable through documents.

The letter, written from the trenches in France, gave another layer of opportunity. I use it almost verbatim in my novel because it portrays the personality of the fictional character I created based on my grandmother's husband – a kind, thoughtful, friendly man – as well as a clear indication of instructions to remain light-hearted in correspondence and not to mention the fighting or locations. Contemporary testimony given in letters is a fascinating and inspirational resource for writers interested in the past. This letter, written in pencil, and gone over to preserve it, also shows how deeply the recipients were affected by its receipt and its contents.

Challenges

Whether families retain photographs, letters and documents will vary, and it is risky to rely on consistent access to such resources in any group or class. But resources can be provided, either copies of publicly available private records and artefacts, or through museum collections and library archives – or if you have them, you can offer your own resources. Students can still make connections, if they wish or have sufficient family knowledge, to their own families through third-party resources, and it can be easier to provide an even starting point in this way, and also to encourage more interrogation of the material if it holds no emotional attachment.

In a recent writing workshop, a participant whose father had recently died, shortly before his 100th birthday, used the process of choosing a commemorative photograph to paint a portrait of his life. We were able to share her emotional experience because she had used description to show her father, just as the photographs did.

> 'I find a photo that I hadn't seen before – him in a light grey suit and tie at a bright café by the sea. His grey-flecked but still dark hair combed into a side parting, dark rimmed spectacles hooked over his ears and a wide grin. Leaning to the camera, enjoying the day. That's the one I choose.' (Tyler, 2020)

Some further ideas for stimulating writing alongside the use of photographs and family documents:

If you don't already know, imagine how your parents met, or your grandparents. Even if you don't know their ages, work out roughly when that was and research what they might have been wearing, how they would look, what they would do for a living, where they worked.

Find a major historical event which happened around the time they met and write about it from their point of view.

PUBLIC RECORDS AND SOCIAL AND POLITICAL EVENTS

Opportunities
Digitisation has revolutionised access to the public record and fuelled interest and enthusiasm for family history research. Paid access to pre-1911 census data, military and parish records, transport lists and newspapers enables those who can afford it to explore millions of records and cross-reference family trees. Libraries and public archives can enable free access to these

records, often with payment for copies of documents. Institutions, particularly universities, but also schools will generally hold licences that enable free access to individuals studying there.

The stories to be found are endless in their variety and great fuel for the imagination. I made particular use of census data and workhouse records to map the fortunes of the branch of my mother's family who lived and worked in the North York Moors for several hundred years. In the archives of the Durham Mining Museum I found the newspaper and coroner's reports into the death of my great grandfather, who was killed by a loose wagon on rails carrying ironstone from the local mine. (Bell, 1892) This story had not been handed down, but a fear of mineworking, always common in my family, was a legacy.

MINES CLASSED UNDER THE COAL MINES REGULATION ACT, 1887.

List of the FATAL ACCIDENTS, and DEATHS arising therefrom within One Year and a Day from the Date of the Accident, in the CLEVELAND IRONSTONE portion of MR. BELL'S DISTRICT, during the Year 1892.

No. of Accident	Date and Hour of the Accident	Number of the Persons killed, &c., No. of Hours before Accident happened to him	Name of the Mine.	Where situate.	Name of the Owner or Company.	Persons killed.	Supposed Age.	Occupation.	Cause of Accident, and Remarks.
6	Dec. 5 11.30 a.m.	6½	Boosbeck East	Rosedale	Carlton Iron Co., Limited.	Frederick Lythe	50	Back Overman.	Run over by a set of tubs on a self-acting incline plane.

The wider public record of newspapers, contemporaneous fiction and non-fiction, theatre and latterly radio, film and internet archives is a fantastic resource against which all our lives have played out. Using these records of our own lifetimes is an interesting way to identify what we have retained in our memories, and what we have discarded.

Challenges
Public records appear more neutral and therefore may generate fewer risks than personal and family records, but all records need to be approached with caution. Such records reflect the social, political and economic context of their times, and comments and classifications which were considered reasonable in the past might offend us today – a typical

example is the word 'bastard' used formally to describe a fatherless child. Terms to describe ethnic origin, racial or religious group, or mental or physical disability, illness or condition might also come across to us now as offensive or crude.

One of the challenges of the public record is its scale, and it is worth considering how to find a thematic or time-related way into records which makes them manageable. Consider how the group or class you are facilitating might react or respond to a thematic approach. For example, I have seen some wonderfully imaginative work done with children in accessing Victorian prison records, but caution is needed not to expose individual children to emotional distress. Similarly, accessing workhouse records that highlight hunger and destitution may seem distanced from most children's lives, or the lives of adults as children, but there are children who may find some accounts of abusive adult behaviour not that different from their own family members'. If you know the students well, you will be able to judge what is right; if not, err on the safe side and pick topics that are less sensitive – political records which deal with social and economic struggles on a less individualised basis might be better sources.

Places where public records are available are family history websites like Ancestry and FindMyPast, which can bring many records together, as well as libraries, archives and museums. Simple searches on the internet will also yield many areas for exploration. Here are some further prompts to guide research, and ideas for imaginative exercises.

Do some research to find out what your ancestors might have done for entertainment – was there television or radio? If so, what programmes would they have watched and listened to? Would they have gone to the cinema or theatre, or listened to music, what would that have been like for them? Write an account from their point of view of a night out or a 'first date'.

Most of us have families who have migrated at some period in history, even if only from one town or city to another in the same country.

Imagine a relative of yours who moved from one place to another for work – what did they do, how did they travel, what obstacles did they overcome? (Be sure to check that this exercise will not be a negative trigger for people in your group.)

Do some research online into passage lists on transatlantic ships from British ports to North America in the 19th Century. Find a family and write about their experience on board. Tell the story of why they were travelling, and what happened when they got to their destination.

REFERENCES

Dean, J. (2015) Lost in Greendale: Creative Opportunities and Ethical Issues In Writing Historical Fiction Based on Family History. MA Dissertation. University of York St. John. York.

Dean Knight, J. (2019). The Peacemaker. Lanham: John Hunt Publishing.

Van Greuningen-Smith, P. (2020). Excerpt from untitled post in a private Facebook Group. Awakening The Writer Within Retreat. Online.

Tyler, M. (2020) Excerpt from untitled post in a private Facebook Group. Awakening The Writer Within Retreat. Online.

Bell, Thomas. (1892) Mines Inspectors Report (C 6986), Durham District (No. 4), Page: 33, Accident Number: 8. Durham Mining Museum. Durham.

LIFTING THE LAYERS:
LONG POEMS INSPIRED BY HISTORY AND PLACE

ANGELA FRANCE

My poetry collection *The hill* (France, 2017) began as an experiment. I had been intrigued by a conversation with Professor Nigel McLoughlin about Paul Muldoon's 2004 poem 'Unapproved Road'. McLoughlin later presented his Text World Theory analysis of the poem at the Great Writing Conference of 2018 (McLoughlin, 2018), in which he showed how the poem could resonate at different levels for readers, depending on their knowledge of a specific place. I, as an English woman with an only superficial understanding of the Irish Troubles, could appreciate the poem for its craft and language; the skill of the subtle, loose, Terza Rima form; the fresh language; and the shifts in time and place. For someone such as McLoughlin, with a comprehensive knowledge of the Troubles and the borderlands, almost every line carries references and allusions opaque to me. Even the title, 'Unapproved Road', carries a different meaning for someone with local knowledge; on first reading I had read it as something like signs I'd seen for 'unadopted' roads, i.e. unadopted by the local council and so not maintained by them. In the context of the borderlands of Ireland, an unapproved road is one that crosses the border but has no checkpoint or official border crossing. Unapproved roads were conduits for smuggling and travel for those who did not want attention; they were often blown up by security services and just as often repaired by local farmers. The title signals, to the knowledgeable reader, a time, setting and political tension.

I wanted to attempt something similar to 'Unapproved Road' and write a poem about a place I knew intimately, which could carry different layers of meaning for different readers. The obvious place for me to write about was Leckhampton Hill, near Cheltenham. I have walked on the hill for over 50 years and grew up with it always at the end of the road, blocking the view like a giant stone curtain. I first learned to love solitude on the hill, scrambling on the rocky paths and playing in the remains of quarry workings every weekend and school holiday from about 10 years old. I grew up knowing some of the history, that there had been trouble over the quarries and there were riots over closed rights of way in 1902. Locally known history can take on the quality of urban legend in its variances and focus on a single incident; I began researching the history, using legal documents and newspapers in the county archives so that I could be certain of the details I wanted to allude to in the poem.

I was aware that a short poem could only be a moment in a season, a single spot in a landscape that varied from woods, to grasslands, to limestone quarries and outcrops. It was not difficult to allude to physical traces of the history in a poem because they were present in the landscape: Iron Age workings, a colony of Roman snails, and the ruins of an engine house and lime kilns from quarrying. The human dramas were not as obvious on the hill itself but were preserved in the county archives. It became apparent during my first visit to the archives that my aim of blending the history with my contemporary experience of the hill would not be achieved in one, or even a few, short poems. I was specifically looking for details of the riots in 1902. A new quarry owner had closed rights of way in 1896 and built a cottage for his foreman on a 'pit' where local people held fairs on holidays. Appeals to the Rural District Council achieved nothing so a group of working men, known as the Leckhampton Stalwarts and led by a clay-digger called Walter Ballinger, marched from Cheltenham town with around 2,000 people and demolished the cottage. The county archive holds six boxes of legal papers relating to the rights of way and the riots, letters, local news reports, and photographs. There was a *List of aged witnesses brought to court* (Anon, 1904), mostly working people, who testified how many generations had known and used the hill before its closure, together with transcribed witness statements from each one on the list. There were newspaper reports, including a verbatim report of the speech from the back of a cart before the protesters set off to march up the hill. There were letters from landowners and solicitors, letters to the Rural District Council, and letters to newspapers. One man wrote frequently to the local paper and became a strong presence throughout the project; William Sparrow, a road-sweeper. Sparrow's letters to the *Echo* were furious, witty, and intelligent. His language was rich and colourful, and contributed to the difficulty I was having in finding a way to enable these voices to be heard while weaving history with a contemporary account of the hill. Co-opting such language as Sparrow saying the press made a great deal of "fustian and flapdoodle" (Sparrow, 1902) into a poem in my own voice, or in a 'found' poem would read as inauthentic at best; Sparrow needed to speak in his own voice.

I visited the archives regularly, sorting through boxes of papers and photographing documents to study at home. The story and the characters were so fascinating that I had to find a way to tell it. I have no interest in versified history but as I spent more time with the documents from the riots I kept getting sucked into the history as if disappearing down a wormhole. I found I could not write poetry while I was in the archive, nor while directly working with the documents, but needed to take time away from the history, sometimes walking on the hill, in order to get a sense of that history as part of the present, one of the many layers that make up the now of the place. I had to also take space away from both the hill and the history at times, before I could write anything worthwhile. The introduction to *The footing* (Lewis, 2013), an anthology of long poems based on "the ideas and practices of walking", suggests that "Landscapes are disturbed and reordered by currents of memory and history." (Lewis, 2013, p.8). For me, it was as if I had to go away in order to allow all the different impressions, layers, and voices to settle within me, and away from the sources, before I could find a way to make poetry of the "disturbed and reordered" (Lewis, 2013, p.8) landscape.

Once I had accepted that *The hill* needed to be book-length and that it could not be rushed I was able to settle into a rhythm of research, taking time away, and writing. Recognising the length of the project also enabled a more expansive view in which the different voices and layers of time could be accommodated, and I could see form as the way the layers could be both differentiated and work together. Creating short, newspaper column-shape pieces spaced throughout enabled me to include the rioters' story, without having to resort to notes, and provide a space for Sparrow:

> Sparrow says men from
> Bath Road hide in the
> garden crouch behind
> brassicas skulk in
> rhubarb
> [...]
> Sparrow writes the
> letters tells the world
> Sparrow says the world
> don't listen says the
> press are fustian and
> flapdoodle no friends
> of the hill
> (France, 2017, p.22)

At this stage I became aware that there was too much focus on the riots, fascinating though they were. If the hill were to be fully invoked on the page, there needed to be recognition of its older layers of history. The flora and fauna have been there through, and before, human habitation and presented an opportunity to perform older voices. Giving creatures a voice in poetry is fraught with difficulty; there is a risk of anthropomorphism or cuteness, either of which can seem inauthentic and alienate the reader. I struggled to find a voice for the creatures of the hill until I discovered 'Anglish', which is English with the Latinate influences removed (The Anglish Moot, n.d.). Anglish is, admittedly, something of a gimmick but I found it feels good in the mouth and connects with something ancient, for me and for the reader.

> Brock says
>
> delve deep

```
                under stone
claw sharpstrike into roots
                        and earth
find allworld below
            for shelterness

my jaws make a hallowing
of sinless worm and slug

I am needful of night-swart
uncleft in my woodside ledemark

leave sun-tide
            to aquern and wort-cropper
                        beingless to me
```

(France, 2017a, p.25)

Using form and white space expanded the possibilities for incorporating material from the county archive while continuing to make poetry. Documents I felt were critical in understanding the emotional and practical relationship local people had with the hill were the list of 'aged witnesses' and the corresponding witness statements (Anon, 1904). I used some of the witness statements, paraphrased for rhythm and sound, as short prose pieces and these, together with Anglish poems, and the column-shaped poems above, created a narrative frame within which the more traditionally lyrical hill poems could develop.

Aged Witness #3: Sparrow Hiscock

I have walked on the hill as long as I've been alive. I was sent to learn the baker-trade from Isaac Crump. I was young and strong, carrying bread to customers over the hill and no wagoner nor squire stopped me on tramway path or stoneway. I followed the common wall track to Cubberley then to Cowley over the hill top by Hartley Bottom. Dale's no right. He's wrong to think he'll ban us from our hill. We've always walked here and we'll be there Easter; with our donkey rides and music, celebrating the people's will. (France, 2017a, p.24)

The hill has been the most absorbing, fascinating, and difficult poetry I have written. It is hard to know where to go next. It became clear that standard poetry reading could not properly represent all the characters and layers, so I developed it into a multi-media performance with recordings of an actor for the rioters' voices and photos from the time. I received Arts Council England funding to tour with the performance (France, 2017b). While I am still touring, it feels as if the hill, Sparrow and Ballinger, Brock and Nadder have not let me go. During the writing of The hill, and since, I have been reading a lot of other poems written about place and have started to question the commonalities I find. What is it about engaging with a place closely that seems to demand a longer form? My own experience with The hill, in not anticipating the length of the work, is not uncommon; I emailed some other makers of long poems to ask about their experience. Paul Henry has said that he usually writes short lyric poems, but says of his poem The glass aisle (Henry, 2018a), set on the Monmouthshire-Brecon canal, "each day, from the outset, I was writing fragments of verse that would eventually lead me towards the long poem" (Henry, 2018b). Penelope Shuttle said of Heath (Shuttle and Greening, 2016), a book-length collaboration with John Greening about Hounslow Heath, "it was initially an experiment to write a few poems for a possible magazine feature, then as a pamphlet, and then we realised it was such a rich subject that we were on our way to writing a full collection." (Shuttle, 2018). It is as if fully engaging with a place, through thought, imagination, and research, creates a pressure that leads to the work having its own momentum until it reaches the length it needs to be.

Poets have written about place for a long time; the Romantics, in their quest for the sublime and the numinous wrote a number of long-form poems of place. Wordsworth's *Lines composed a few miles above Tintern Abbey* (Wordsworth, 1798) and Shelley's *Mont Blanc: lines written in the Vale of Chamouni* (Shelley, 1816) are two fairly typical examples. There are distinct differences between the work of the Romantics and contemporary poems of place. For the Romantics, the poems were about looking *at* the landscape in search of the sublime and recording the effect on the poet while contemporary writers are more likely to be *in* the landscape, whether urban or rural, and engaged with it.

There is very little specific detail in either poem; the descriptions are quite general and from a distance. While Wordsworth notes human activity, it is seen as part of the pictorial effect and a trigger for romantic speculation with no recognition of the real human lives:

> Of vagrant dwellers in the houseless woods,
> Or of some Hermit's cave, where by his fire
> The Hermit sits alone. (Wordsworth, 1798)

As a poetry reader, I am no longer satisfied with the panoramic view offered by the Romantics; I want to visualise the setting, to engage with the place invoked on the page and it is only specific detail that can enable that experience. All of the long poems of place I have read offer rich detail, regardless of the vantage point or size of place. For example, "shining like tin, the hen-fish swishing her tail / making a little vortex, lifting the gravel" (Oswald, 2002, p.9); "in the roots of fir trees / in the brick-earth where brambles coil / from under roadside flints" (Shuttle and Greening, 2016, p.109).

Reading other long poems of place has led me to question why so many of the works have layers of history. Many of the poems also employ other voices, both historical and contemporary, in the layers that make up the whole. Alice Oswald's books *Dart* (2002) and *A sleepwalk on the Severn* (2009) both employ braided voices, of living and dead characters. In both cases, the weaving of voices shows a symbiosis between river and human that intensifies and illuminates Oswald's descriptions of place. The title poem of Paul Henry's *The glass aisle* uses the device of a telephone engineer up a telegraph pole "caged in a tree" (Henry, 2018a) to pick up lost voices. Henry has said the poem began as a ghost poem but the discovery of a census of workhouse inmates, from an old workhouse on the opposite bank, "chillingly validated a supernatural experience and they became crucial to the poem" (Henry, 2018b). The workhouse inmates provide a litany throughout the poem, sometimes just the bare details from the census:

> John Rosel, Tinker, Carmarthen
> George Butcher, Weaver, Frome (Paul, 2018a, p.33)

Other times, the inmates' voices offer fragments of their stories, like bubbles rising to the surface of the canal:

> When my boy cried in chapel
> they sent me to the Master's room... (Paul, 2018a, p.30)

The effect of these voices, for me, was indeed chilling. Their being italicised suggested a constant whisper in the background, like the sounds of the water of the canal or the creaking of the canal when frozen (the glass aisle of the title).

At 183 pages, John Greening and Penelope Shuttle's collaborative call-and-response sequence about Hounslow Heath is a much longer work than the others I have read. They both use a range of voices, alive and dead, some of which are friends and family as well as historical, imaginary, and legendary figures. Hounslow Heath has changed from a broad expanse of edgelands, frequented by footpads, highwaymen, and travellers to 'a smallish nature reserve, squeezed between high-rise flats and the Post Office depot' (Greening, 2018), constantly crossed by flights from Heathrow. The call and response form, the time-shifts carried by the different voices and the precise and sensory detail create an impression of the older expanse of heath as a revenant, flickering in and out of vision around and over the small piece of land the poets walk in the present.

Returning to the questions that arise for me in reading long poems of place, it seems to me that a short poem can only be a slice of view, a moment in time, as if seen through a coin-operated seaside telescope. For a place to be fully invoked on the page, as readers we need to experience breadth and time, more than the equivalent of one foot on the path. This is not to say I don't appreciate shorter poems set in a specific place.

Patrick Kavanagh's *Shancoduff* (1938), for instance, is fresh and engaging, with gorgeous language:

> My hills hoard the bright shillings of March
> While the sun searches in every pocket.
> They are my Alps and I have climbed the Matterhorn
> With a sheaf of hay for three perishing calves. (Kavanagh, 1938)

However much I enjoy poems like Kavanagh's for their craft, music, and language, the place is a setting, rather than the place as an experience on the page. As I read more poems of place that bring human history into the poets' engagement with the language, I become less satisfied with a romantic, panoramic, view of the land. While it may not be true of larger countries, there is not a single acre of England that has not been under human management at some time. To write about any part of this country without acknowledging the effect of humanity on the land is inauthentic at best, and dishonest at worst. I discovered when writing *The hill*, under the compulsion of the vitality and honesty of the voices that emerged from the archive, that engaging with the human history becomes a sort of social ecology alongside the natural ecology; a way of showing how the past shapes the present both physically and culturally so that the place is performed on the page.

WORKING WITH HISTORICAL DOCUMENTS
Please note: most archives prefer that documents less than 100 years old are not disseminated, in case of living relatives.

For adult writers:
- Visit a place you know well, either physically or in imagination.
- Make notes about what you see. Use precise details, not generalities; use all the senses; try looking close-up, middle distance and long distance.
- Look up the history of your chosen place. Most County Archives are searchable online, also try local newspapers,

some keep their own archives, some are kept by libraries. You may not need to see the actual documents; sometimes the title of a document or a newspaper headline is enough to spark imagination.

- Look back at your own notes in the light of the historical documents. What has changed? What might characters from history see? What traces of the past can you see in the present?
- Finally, don't let the facts get in the way of a good poem or story. There is little point in just re-telling, let your imagination go where it will.

For young writers:
- All places have at least one famous person in their history (look at the region, if the place you live in is too small).
- Research the person: what did they do, what family did they have, where did they live (look for a blue plaque), what inventions were there in their lifetime?
- Look online for archived newspapers mentioning them or search for documents at the local County Archives.
- Let imaginations run:
  - What would that person think of the world now?
  - What would it have been like to be in that person's family? If they were out fighting wars or climbing mountains, what would their children feel?
  - Write them a letter about what has changed since they were alive, what questions would you like to ask them?

REFERENCES

Anon, 1904. *List of aged witnesses brought to court.* [testimonials] Gloucestershire County Archive. Boxes 1-6 DA21/141. Gloucester: Gloucestershire Heritage Hub.
Ayers, A., 2013. The strait. In: B. Lewis, ed. 2013. *The footing.* Sheffield: Longbarrow Press. p. 36.

France, A., 2017a. *The hill*. Rugby: Nine Arches Press. pp.22–25.
France, A. 2017b. The hill. Film of live performance
http://angelafrance.co.uk/thehill.html
Greening, J., 2018. *Re: Heath*. [email] (Personal communication, 26 August 2018).
Henry, P., 2018a. *The glass aisle*. Bridgend: Seren. pp.30-33.
Henry, P., 2018b. *Angela France questions and answers*. [email] (Personal communication, 14 August 2018).
Kavanagh, P., 1938. Shancoduff. In: *Ploughman and other poems*. London: Macmillan. Available at:
https://www.tcd.ie/English/patrickkavanagh/shancoduff.html
Lewis, B. ed., 2013. *The footing*. Sheffield: Longbarrow Press.
McLoughlin, N., 2018. Slipping unnoticed across the border: hidden narrative and the liminal in Paul Muldoon's Unapproved Road. *The 2018 Great Writing Conference*. Imperial College, London, 23rd June, 2018.
Muldoon, P., 2004. Unapproved road. In: *Moy sand and gravel*. London: Faber & Faber.
Oswald, A., 2002. *Dart*. London: Faber and Faber.
Oswald, A., 2009. *A sleepwalk on the Severn*. London: Faber and Faber.
Shelley, P.B., 1816. *Mont Blanc: lines written in the Vale of Chamouni.* [online] Available at: <
https://www.poetryfoundation.org/poems/45130/mont-blanc-lines-written-in-the-vale-of-chamouni [Accessed: 21 June 2020].
Shuttle, P. and Greening, J., 2016. *Heath.* Rugby: Nine Arches Press.
Shuttle, P., 2018. *Re: Heath*. [email] (Personal communication, 25 August 2018).
Sparrow, W., 1902. *Letter to the Gloucestershire Echo*. [letter] Gloucestershire County Archive. Boxes 1-6 DA21/141. Gloucester: Gloucestershire Heritage Hub.
The Anglish Moot, n.d. *History of Anglish*. [online] Available at:
https://anglish.fandom.com/wiki/History_of_Anglish
[Accessed 21 June 2020].

Wordsworth, W., 1798. *Lines composed a few miles above Tintern Abbey.* [online] Available at: https://www.poetryfoundation.org/poems/45527/lines-composed-a-few-miles-above-tintern-abbey-on-revisiting-the-banks-of-the-wye-during-a-tour-july-13-1798 [Accessed 21 June 2020].

HOW TO READ A POETRY CLASS:
TEACHING POETRY IN THE 21ST CENTURY

TJAWANGWA DEMA

'Inviting compassion into the bloodstream of an institution's agenda or scholar's purpose is more than productive, more than civilizing, more than ethical, more than humane; it's humanizing." Toni Morrison (2020)

Alongside Morrison's infusion of empathy, I would like to bring Edward Said's politics of writing and interpretation to bear on spaces of creative writing (CW) instruction by asking: Who teaches? For whom is the teaching being done? And in what circumstances? This provocation is as much a note to self as to other early career instructors who engage with the CW classroom. While institutional contexts matter it is not particularly necessary here for the use of the word 'classroom' to distinguish between spaces of instruction in and out of campuses, online, at festivals, detention centers or wherever else instruction is taking place. This thought piece invites ways to think together by gesturing towards approaches by poets, creative thinkers and critics invested in mapping what can be read as potential ways forward for teaching poetry in the 21st century.

I am a poet and perhaps lack a critic's detachment but I am invested in the practice and teaching of poetry. Here I give particular attention to the CW classroom as a transformative space that courts possibility, and integrates and interrogates those who would dismiss inclusiveness or claim ignorance of (implicit) bias.

Poets do not produce work in a vacuum and by thinking of students as literary citizens (regardless of their country citizenship) we complicate their role to one of engagement, responsibility and consequence in the classroom. Perhaps the CW classroom, in particular, insists on learners who are cognizant of the responsibilities of engaging modes of self-expression as those modes by definition involve storytelling and world-building, which in turn can shape perception. Thus, I hope to offer some questions for the CW instructor to consider as they design, structure and teach a class that aims to shape and produce citizen learners who will become makers out in the world.

It was W B Yeats who famously said 'We make out of the quarrel with others, rhetoric, but of the quarrel with ourselves, poetry' (Yeats 1918, p. 29). How can we as instructors – who have our own limitations to contend with – make sure we do not circumscribe the student experience and that alongside the rhetoric of technique and theory we are equally served by productive quarrel. I'm suggesting that a space that intentionally embraces enquiry allows room for shame-free 'not-knowing' *and* learning. A polyphonic space that welcomes specialized cultural knowledges without making them pre-requisite, minimizes grandstanding at the gates of some old republic by those who would insist on shibboleths before entry. In turn, the republic is endlessly renewed, re-inventing itself and encouraging meaningful and plural restlessness. This second coming is not without complication. The centre may not be able to hold but it invests a lot of energy in doing so. The university can be a genealogically conservative system that only strategically courts innovation, therefore tensions may arise between older departments/faculties and the need for renewed and restless ways of working. How then do we as teachers ensure, as Andrew Motion (2016) puts it, that poetry 'seem[s] an endlessly ingenious thing, but also as natural to the species as breathing.' In all the dozen countries where I have run workshops, I found that asking questions was a good place to start – not just for the students but for myself.

I am suggesting that, as part of its student-teacher-institution-world contract, good literary citizenship solicits concurrent engagement with rights, responsibilities, rewards and risk. Some of the ways this rubric of R's can read is: rights (structural and pedagogical support), responsibilities (rigour, respect), rewards (community, development) and risk (failure, not belonging). This proposed contract considers the gaze of all parties who seek to serve and/or learn in the context of reasonable autonomy. I posit that in the study, reading and writing of poetry there is articulated a social contract that, in alliance with craft-building, requires one to see, hear and respectfully commune with others in order to read as attentive and empathetic on the page. These are practices of the kind of literary citizenship I am suggesting here. I use the idea of space as a framework for my own teaching; all CW instructors aim to facilitate ways for learners to engage the white space of the page, I complicate this by intentionally thinking about the physical space of the classroom, the head space of those who occupy the classroom and their ability to take up space in the literary and non-literary world beyond the classroom.

BIAS

In quarrelling with myself about teaching and therefore text, context and the many gates through which we enter the prickly garden of language and imagination, I turn to Kwame Dawes' (2020, lines 9-12) poem Yard Boy:

> That when Kamau, who told me to call him "Kamau" when I called him in reverence, "Professor Brathwaite", and then, "Prof B", which is where we settled, me being well-trained in the rituals of eldership, for what do we call our teachers, those who teach us?

Thus, Dawes not only maps out who taught him and how, he wields an invitation for the reader to consider the relationship between pupil and educator. A re-reading of the poem invites the idea that it matters who teaches as much as it matters what is taught, because in many ways the two are entangled. One could look to the experiences of black, indigenous and people of colour (BIPoC) students in American MFA programmes as a way to explore these entanglements. We know, too, from a recent in-depth study looking at 'diversity' in UK trade fiction publishing that BAME writers are perceived as 'represent[ing] a riskier investment for publishers' (Saha and van Lente 2020, p.

14). Teachers, however, cannot afford to view any students as lost causes, as educational risks.

In his book *Dear Upright African*, Donald Molosi (2019, p. 38) suggests we, 'Point out to [African students] the irony that the same colonial powers that forced us to trivialize [African forms of] performance, art, history, and literature are now using the powers of [the same forms] to control the world. Teach the African child to be led by passion and ability toward a profession'. When we encounter a student who respects writing but is struggling, especially with the false binary of BIPoC/BAME identity *versus* craft, how can the choices instructors make around poetics, race and class in the classroom help the students' sense of belonging (not assimilation) as concerns writing and thinking about writing? How do we work with them to name and value their knowledges, influences and process? I think this begins with a vision of the classroom as a place where we carry the burden, hopefully alongside parents, of teaching students how to make homes for themselves within language. To be clear, those homes will be as wide ranging as their individual makers, and on this spectrum, some may be concerned with identity and preservation, others not, but even a project preoccupied with preservation requires rigorous imagination, perhaps even demands it.

While we metaphorically await institutional responses to why in 2018, only 2.7 percent of teachers in state funded schools in England identified as black or 'mixed' black (*by ethnicity* 2020), how are you as an instructor – whatever your ethnicity – stepping into this systemic chasm? Whatever your choice of contested shorthand (BAME/BIPoC etc.), people not racialised as white are often refused the right to be their full and free self in the world. They in turn may push against useful elements of their training such as 'theory' or 'craft' because it is falsely positioned as the preserve of 'real poetry' and/or whiteness. In what ways does your classroom – whether conversationally, critically, citationally or creatively – actively resist replicating systems of oppression?

Diversifying reading lists is by no means the full extent of decolonial work, but surely the size of gatekeeping around the canon(s) is an indication of value. In her book, *The Faraway Nearby*, Rebecca Solnit (2013, p. 3) offers us this:

> What's your story? It's all in the telling. Stories are compasses and architecture; we navigate by them, we build our sanctuaries and our prisons out of them, and to be without a story is to be lost in the vastness of a world that spreads in all directions, like arctic tundra or sea ice.

Solnit sets up a delightfully useful framework for the value of stories. If part of the project of the humanities is to humanize the scholar, as Morrison suggests, then perhaps what diversifying texts offers us isn't just an equitable representation of the world but a forced encounter with a relational-self for the student who is problematically all-present, absent or misrepresented in the text. I posit that the classroom remains a community with pre-existing habits of perception and, if unchecked, it will reproduce bias and problematic systems, in particular anti-black views, in micro and macro ways.

A further consideration is that overburdened communities (based on class, economics, ethnicity, etc.) cannot access or afford (more) debt and since CW arguably rarely financially pays back the investment in fees, this narrows who can afford to study it formally. Who is able to pay for a writer's retreat or take the year(s) required to study a course that does not pretend to link directly to employment? In this regard, study either becomes a non-option or necessitates auto-didactic learning. Does your institute or workshop offer scholarships? If not, what do you think are the implications of this choice?

Speaking of exclusion, in terms of course content not everyone is ready to welcome all poetry, especially spoken word, into the classroom. Yet structuring CW courses requires more than diversifying student and reading lists. In his paper 'Spoken word is dead: long live poetry?', Pete Bearder (2020) raises the question of the prioritization of 'Page-centric poetic dogmas [that] have dominated [British] educational institutions'. I agree with Bearder when he suggests that

'Another consequence of this neglect is that pockets of experimentation and expertise get ignored or forgotten'. Though hardly a utopia, slam and spoken word poetry communities for many, such as Javon Johnson (2017), 'have created more open and accepting creative writing spaces and programs. They have fostered environments in which participants search for something beyond.' Spoken word communities may often be under resourced and undervalued but we lose much if we imagine that makes them unsophisticated or underdeveloped. A program that dis-engages spoken word or performance poetry in the classroom negates a worldview and *its practices*. This exclusion is not simply a matter of preference or policy, it is a political act.

As interlocutors in the classroom, instructors need to be prepared to invite and catalyse discussions and conversations with a variety of student personalities. This must be done without overburdening some students with the task of constantly explaining 'culture' and 'context' to their peers. How do you support and bring together varied interests, yours and student goals, pre-empt and integrate challenges, or interrupt missteps and bias meaningfully and safely?

POETRY IS A DOING WORD

We are told often enough that the word poetry comes from the Greek word 'poesis' and is a verb meaning to make; as my 10-year-old nephew would say – it is a 'doing' word. I extend this requirement for action to the monumental task of teaching poetry, to move beyond the imparting and giving of knowledge to helping students to contribute new knowledges. I do not presume to prescribe ways for other instructors to work, nor are my suggestions substitutes for formal pedagogical training. Instead I ask, in what ways can our approach to teaching poetry be pragmatic? I am talking about how we teach the mechanics of poetry, rigour, as well as craft, while acknowledging that what is also happening in those moments is a larger project of teaching poets to be readers and creative re/producers who are alive in the world. Following Simon Armitage's (2014 p. 92) poetic suggestion to 'Think, two things on their own and both at once' allows me to believe in poetry's capacity to house both the productively didactic and the delightful. After all, instructors dialogically use poems to show how to deploy and disrupt, build and dismantle language and lest we forget, Ngugi wa Thiongo reminds us that 'language is a carrier of a people's culture' (Eyoh 1985 p. 157).

Not all writers choose or are able to teach but some of those who *can*, teach. As many parents may have learnt during the Covid-19 pandemic's stay-at-home period, teaching is an impressively laborious undertaking. Some of the most pertinent questions for instructors at the moment are not regarding which poems to share with students, but rather what a classroom that supports students equitably and does not objectify or trivialize any worldviews might look like. In thinking about and practicing teaching, faculty will invariably factor in how over-extended they are by academic citizenship and how this affects their own writing time. Burnout is real and there is much to consider about teaching in general, including pay and pension contention, workloads, administrative opposition to curricular innovation, job precarity, under/mis-funded schools, league tables, unsupportive management, and the power imbalance created by treating students as customers not co-respondents in the development and assessment of their learning.

It would be inappropriate and impractical to prescribe that any and all instructors take on more work, and radical work at that, without considering their contentions around autonomy and service. However, not everything about the classroom is dystopian or reducible; it can be a place of joy and discovery. Sara Black (2020) writes that, 'Teaching is not closed, cold transmission. It is an emergent event, where students do the unpredictable, where learning occurs as a relational effect between student and instructor, and sometimes student and student.' She goes on to explain that as an instructor, she creates and watches over her 'space', noticing who is struggling even if they don't verbalise it, diagnosing misunderstandings, reading and addressing moods, revising seating arrangements, factoring in safety and comfort, as well as allowing for and managing silence. A space that is always emergent, accessible and working to be safe insists on irreducibility as a way of being read. This complexity allows the possibility for all students to be in the same room *as themselves*, and counters the violence of performing allyship or ticking diversity boxes while ghettoising select students into a metaphorically adjacent room.

Paulo Freire writes that 'Knowledge emerges only through invention and re-invention, through the restless, impatient, continuing, hopeful inquiry human beings pursue in the world, with the world, and with each other.' When we get teaching right, learning is a language, not (just) a series of certification hurdles. The implication is that students are able to become lifelong learners and years later are 'still clearing the ground/ [their teacher(s)] started to cultivate in the way a poem grows' (Dawes 2020, lines 62-63). Much like writing, teaching CW is a project of failure and hope. As Matt Beighton (2020 p. 17) points out 'Perhaps the most important thing to remember at the outset is that we will inevitably fail. Our input will never engender a lifelong passion for creativity in *every* [italics my own] child whose path we cross.'

While learning style debates are beyond the scope of this provocation, the hope is that once instructors have begun to work towards building a culture that supports literary citizenship for all, despite any systemic or curricular opposition, they are then able to demand rigour while remaining responsive. Writing is labour; lack of craft cannot be excused by content, no matter how urgent or necessary. Craft demands that the poem be able to stand outside the body, identity and intention of its author, and the student must be prepared for the world outside of their various echo-chambers. I do not care to prescribe what students write about but I do care how they write. I am interested in the reflections, influences and interrogations that inform their processes of imagining and editing, of inventing and re-inventing voice. Whatever else, the student and instructor want to avoid a failure of imagination within and around the work.

PEDAGOGIES OF PLAY

When Lauren K. Alleyne asks Matthew Shenoda 'What are some things that you find sustain the poetry outside of poetry?' Shenoda (2020) replies:

> You have to live a life; you can't simply engage in the world of creative writing. That's an incredibly limiting world. You have to explore the world ... whatever your passions and interests are outside of writing I think have to be engaged.

I am curious about employing a version of 'play' in the adult classroom as a way to reconstitute approaches to learning. In speaking about David Whitebread's early childhood development theory, Patrick Butler (2016) says, 'Carefully organised play helps develop qualities such as attention span, perseverance, concentration and problem solving'. I am struck by how those qualities are amongst the tools I prize most in my bag of writerly tricks. Based on a comparative case study of four adult playful classrooms, David J Tanis (2012) observes 'play and playfulness were most frequently manifested in the classroom through risk taking, storytelling, and physical activities. Students themselves have identified cognitive gains in terms of engagement, retention, and understanding. More significantly, students indicated that play and playfulness created a unique learning environment that felt safe and encouraged risk taking.'

Some of this pedagogical play will invariably happen outside the classroom and I want to suggest that an instructor who engages with their local literary community is not only modelling engagement but may gain a sense of what related skills are missing/under-resourced within the classroom and community. Community engagement can thus be both joyful and a kind of creative research, where the knowledge gained can help shape workshops, panels, lesson plans or institutional policies.

Mandy Coe and Jean Sprackland (2005 p. 62) write that, "From our feedback it is clear that some of the best projects schools have experienced with writers have taken place not *in* schools but *out* of them." However, the authors highlight that out-of-school teaching requires logistical planning, timing, resources, limited student numbers, and staff. If this is not an option, how can you work within the assigned classroom space? My sense is that bringing a carefully chosen writer into the classroom is one way of teaching in-out of school. It offers an opportunity to incorporate work and playfulness through live literature, open discussions as well as engaging exercises that build confidence and prize abstraction and imagination.

RE-VISION
There are many ways to set about cultivating a historically, contextually and compassionately realised approach to teaching. As a poet I am drawn to the idea of 'reading' as a highly accessible tool. Edward Hirsch (2007) begins his essay 'How to read a poem' with the words, 'Reading poetry well is part attitude and part technique. Curiosity is a useful attitude, especially when it's free of preconceived ideas about what poetry is or should be. Effective technique directs your curiosity into asking questions, drawing you into a conversation with the poem.' I want to close by asking us to substitute the words 'poetry' and 'poem' above with 'a CW classroom'. If the goal is to support the growth, preparation and 'humanizing' of our creative scholars this will depend on instructors' writing and lived experience, training, and school environments but also on their empathetic reader-response of the class as a dynamic work-in-progress.

Enthusiasm, knowledge, experience and caring probably aren't enough in the face of systemic opposition to innovation in teaching. Moreover, there is a 'cost of caring' as Morrison puts it. The question is whether the possibility of an inclusive canon – arising from an engaged classroom that is willing and able to bear the cost of creating, interpreting and shaping the world – is compensation enough for your troubles? Naivety aside, if we can remember for whom we teach perhaps what is a risky educational investment in humanity can be read as an ethically and creatively rewarding journey. We can be purposefully ambitious too; demanding our contractual rights from institutions and students while keeping our responsibilities to the same by simultaneously considering this labour to be both an institutional transaction as well as a collaborative project of hope.

REFERENCES

Armitage, S 2014, 'Homecoming', *Paper Aeroplane selected poems 1989-2014*, Faber and Faber, London, p. 92.

Bearder, P 2020, 'Spoken word is dead: long live poetry?', applesandsnakes.org, blog post, viewed 28 May 2020, https://applesandsnakes.org/2020/05/26/spoken-word-is-dead-long-live-poetry/

Beighton, M 2020, 'The Teaching of Writing', Writing in Education, issue 80 Spring 2020, pp. 17-19.

Black, S 2020, 'The problem with Stephen Grootes' views about online learning', *Daily Maverick*, 11 May, viewed 1 June 2020, https://www.dailymaverick.co.za/opinionista/2020-05-11-the-problem-with-stephen-grootes-views-about-online-learning/#gsc.tab=0

Butler, P 2016, "No grammar schools, lots of play, the secrets of Europe's top education system', 20 September, viewed 29 June 2020, https://www.theguardian.com/education/2016/sep/20/grammar-schools-play-europe-top-education-system-finland-daycare

By ethnicity 2020, viewed 14 July 2020, https://www.ethnicity-facts-figures.service.gov.uk/workforce-and-business/workforce-diversity/school-teacher-workforce/latest#by-ethnicity

Coe, M. & Sprackland, J 2005, *Our thoughts are bees: Writers Working with Schools*, Wordplay Press, Southport.

Dawes, K 2020, 'Yard Boy', viewed 20 June 2020, https://www.unl.edu/english/kwame-dawes/yard-boy

Eyoh, H. H 1985, 'Language as Carrier of People's Culture: An Interview with Ngugi wa Thiongo', Ufahamu: A Journal of African Studies, 14(3), pp. 156–157, viewed 28 June 2020, https://escholarship.org/uc/item/32j2p716

Freire, P. 2005, *Pedagogy of the Oppressed,* 30th anniversary edn., Continuum, New York & London.

Hirsch, E 2007, 'How to Read a Poem', Poets.org., blog post, 27 November, viewed 1 July 2020, https://poets.org/text/how-read-poem-0

Johnson, J 2017, *Killing Poetry: Blackness and the Making of Slam and Spoken Word Communities*, Rutgers University Press, New Brunswick, Camden.

Saha, A & van Lente, S 2020, *Re:thinking 'Diversity' in Publishing,* Spread the Word, viewed 10 July 2020, https://www.spreadtheword.org.uk/wp-content/uploads/2020/06/Rethinking_diversity_in-publishing_WEB.pdf

Shenoda, M 2020, 'Reclaiming our Humanity: An interview with Matthew Shenoda', *The Fight & the Fiddle*, Winter/Spring 2020, viewed 1 July 2020, https://fightandfiddle.com/2020/04/13/reclaiming-our-humanity-an-interview-with-matthew-shenoda/

Solnit, R 2013, *The Faraway Nearby*, Granta Publications, London.

Tanis, D. J 2012, 'Exploring Play/Playfulness and Learning in the Adult and Higher Education Classroom', PhD thesis, The Pennsylvania State University, viewed 2 July 2020, https://etda.libraries.psu.edu/files/final_submissions/8092

Molosi, D 2019, *Dear Upright African: a call to action for taking history into our own hands,* The Mantle, New York.

Morrison, T 2020, 'The Price of Wealth, the Cost of Care', The Source of Self-Regard, Vintage International, New York.

Motion, A 2016, The Guardian, 9 April, viewed 30 June 2020, https://www.theguardian.com/books/2016/apr/09/my-hero-my-english-teacher-by-andrew-motion
Yeats, W. B 1918, *Per Amica Silentia Lunae*, Macmillian Company, New York, viewed 25 June 2020, https://www.gutenberg.org/files/33338/33338-h/33338-h.htm

BIBLIOGRAPHY

DuBois, W.E.B 1999, 'From A Negro Student at Harvard at the End of the Nineteenth Century', *The Souls of Black Folk*, in H. L Gates Jr and T. H Oliver (eds.), W. W. Norton & Company, New York.
Kwakye, C and Ogunbiyi, O 2019, *Taking up Space: the black girl's manifesto for change*, Merky Books.
Larson, S 2015, 'Degrees of Diversity: Talking Race and the MFA', Poets&Writers, blog post, 19 August, viewed 25 July 2020, https://www.pw.org/content/degrees_of_diversity
Said, E 2000, 'Opponents, Audiences, Constituencies, and Community', *Reflections on Exile and Other Essays*, Harvard University Press, Cambridge, pp. 118–147.

THE HAUNTED HOUSE:

TEACHING CREATIVE WRITING THROUGH COLLABORATIVE LEARNING TO 9-13 YEAR OLDS

FRANCIS GILBERT

Many teachers of creative writing find teaching the 9-13-year-old age group tricky for a few reasons. These children are usually in a time of radical transition: getting ready to move into a new school, or starting in a new one. They are still, in my experience as a teacher and parent, children who want to be grown up but aren't ready for the fully adult material you can teach 14-16 year olds, and yet don't want 'baby' stuff. This makes teaching them difficult. What exactly should you teach? How should you teach it?

Having had decades at the chalk face and a few years as a teacher-educator, I feel I might have discovered an answer. I've found that using the well-worn trope of the haunted house works a treat – it's never failed me yet. Why is this? Well, the reasons are quite complex, but in brief, I've always found that children of this age are not only very familiar with the ghost-story genre but also extremely keen to share their stories with each other.

KEY THEORY

The following series of learning activities draw upon my enthusiasm to help students discuss, imagine and write both collaboratively and individually.

At the heart of this approach is the idea that children create their own 'simulation' of a haunted house: they pretend together that certain characters – a bully, a coward and vain, selfish, jealous people – explore a creepy domain, full of spooky sounds, smells, tastes, textures and sights. Each of the characters are taught a lesson.

This unit of work is underpinned by some serious learning theories. Perhaps most significantly, it is informed by the idea that learning is 'is building knowledge as part of doing things with others' (Watkins 2011, p. 11; Gilbert 2017), or what educational theorists call 'social constructivism'. The focus is upon children learning how to write through collaborative discussion: talking about shaping plans, maps, ideas, descriptions, characterisations and narratives in groups, and coming to a consensus about what might be the most effective way of constructing an imaginative world. Watkins writes:

> As people are engaged together, they are also empowered – both to contribute and to influence. This view helps us see that the settings and situations which provide the most potential for learning are those in which participants are engaged in real action that has consequences not only for them but for their community as a whole. (2011, p. 12)

The students are also drawing upon their own funds of knowledge (González et al. 2005). Carlos G. Vélez-Ibáñez and James B. Greenberg (1992) describe this concept as:

> those historically accumulated strategies (skills, abilities, ideas, practices) or bodies of knowledge that are essential to a household's functioning and well-being (p. 91-92)

In my experience, ghost and horror narratives play a significant role in all children's lives; these are frequently the stories that children tell each other at home, in the playground, on holiday; these are the types of films, TV shows, computer games etc that they find thrilling. I've always learnt a great deal about my students by simply asking them to recount ghost stories they've heard, read about or watched: every child has a different story to tell.

The skill that is required by the teacher in this project is to steer children away from clichés or to get them to make the clichés – the picture with eyes that move, the ticking of the clock, the creak of the door etc – live afresh. The collaborative nature of this project makes it easier for the teacher to intervene when things are going wrong. The teacher can take part in group discussions and plans, and get children to use an unfamiliar object, picture, poem, literary extract/story etc as inspiration to write something that is original and imaginative.

The haunted house simulation is multi-modal in that it uses many different modes – drama, embodied learning, group work, pictures, photographs, drawings, objects, movie clips – to inspire the construction of the haunted house. Kress (2005) explains the multi-modal method in this way:

> A multimodal approach is one where attention is given to all the culturally shaped resources that are available for making meaning: image, for instance, gesture, or the layout – whether of the wall-display, or the furniture of classrooms and of course writing and speech as talk. Mode is the name we give to these culturally shaped resources for making meaning. Multi refers to the fact that modes never occur by themselves, but always with others in ensembles. Multimodality characterized therefore by the presence and use of a multiplicity of modes. (p. 2)

The different modes are used to build a sense of context: the children piece together a picture of a haunted house in fine granular detail, drawing upon their funds of knowledge to make it uniquely spooky. The unit makes great use of audio and sensory detail. I've found the most successful part of this story is when pupils shut their eyes or are blindfolded and the other group members take them on a 'sensory journey' where they experience smells, tastes, sound effects, words that describe the room, and textures that they feel in their hands in the form of objects (things like slime work well). Many of my pupils have told me that they've found this an absolutely thrilling experience. Obviously, it requires a high level of good behaviour, but I've noticed that even so-called 'badly behaved' classes will behave well for this project because they are intrinsically motivated to do it.

Built into this unit is the notion of re-drafting. I have found it is particularly successful in this regard because it does not require children to individually make a piece of writing 'better', something many children (and grown-ups) find extremely difficult, but asks them to take an existing narrative – a certain character encountering a haunted room – and improve it by getting everyone to work out how this character might be taught a lesson. The teacher can intervene at this point because they can say that this is what writers do: they try to make much of their writing 'character-based' and ensure that the action is shaped by their character's unique personality. When I've taught this unit, I've drawn upon Dickens' *A Christmas Carol* to illustrate this: the haunting of Scrooge is inextricably linked to his mean, miserly character. The students can learn about some important concepts outlined by Aristotle in his *Poetics* (Tierno, 2002) such 'hubris': the bullying, vain and selfish people often find that their pride is significantly deflated in the haunted house, and all of the characters, except for the coward, experience some kind of 'nemesis' or retribution. The coward often exhibits 'hamartia', namely he/she has the 'tragic flaw' of their cowardice; and all of the characters undergo moments of 'peripeteia' or reversals of fortune, with many of them experiencing 'anagnorisis' or moments of realisation where they perceive their flaws and resolve to change them.

Since many of the students are working in groups at a reasonably leisurely pace and often re-drafting work, there is plenty of opportunity for the teacher to intervene if they see a 'good teaching opportunity'. In this sense, the pedagogy developed by the Grammar for Writing project is useful; the teacher can say, at suitable moments, whether words need to be changed and improved, or sentences and paragraphs re-structured. Furthermore, the teacher can encourage students to do this in groups using the guidelines set out on the excellent Grammar for Writing website (University of Exeter, 2020).

Another pedagogical approach could be to write alongside the students, where appropriate. So, for example, the teacher could join groups for certain writing tasks and/or discussions, or write their own haunted house description and share their thoughts and feelings about their progress as they do so. Research shows that teachers better understand what the real issues are regarding writing when they write alongside their pupils (Cremin 2006, 2017: Wrigley & Smith 2012: National Writing Project, 2020).

The project also involves students taking notes, summarising and using visuals to capture their thoughts. Marzano et al.

(2001) have shown that explicit teaching of these strategies can really improve levels of achievement in all subjects. This unit has enough flexibility in it for teachers to do just this in an organic way. They could use pupils' note-taking, visual organisers and pictures as examples and models, or share some of their own.

THE RESEARCH & CREATIVE WRITING EXERCISES IN ACTION
First, the teacher of this unit needs to explain the what, why and how of the simulation. In brief you might say:

- What? Students are going to sit in groups of five and map out, draw, discuss, plan and write descriptions/stories about an allocated area of a haunted house.
- Why? This is a simulation: you are going to plan for a 'make-believe' recreation of a haunted house. You're doing it to develop your powers of imagination, your descriptive writing skills and to enjoy working and writing together.
- How? You'll be working first as individuals and then in groups, and writing both collaboratively and individually, as well as making your own group haunted house podcast.

INTRODUCTION FOR STUDENTS: USING VISUALS
The first activity is individual, with the teacher giving students some visual stimuli, video clips and literary extracts to get their imaginations racing. I used the following pictures, but you can use whatever you feel works for you.

Figure 1 Walking in the misty sunset to the haunted house

Figure 2 The dining room, first floor

Figure 3 A bedroom

Working with photographs or pictures is usually very popular with children. With each of the pictures, the teacher asks them to discuss and write notes on the five senses in these situations. With Figure 1, I asked the students to work in pairs and 'hot-seat' this person (my son) walking through the mist towards the haunted house in a strange sunset. Hot-seating consists of one participant being in role – pretending to be the person walking to the house – and the other participant asking questions, which get the person in the hot-seat to consider what the walker in the mist might hear, see, touch, taste, smell etc and also talk about why he is heading towards the house.

With Figure 2, the person in the hot-seat considers what happened when they were invited to eat a scone and drink tea at this table (you could even provide some real food here). Key questions to ask the person in role would be: who has invited you to eat at this table? What do you talk about? Why have you come to this house? What do you want?

With Figure 3, using hot-seating and/or paired discussion, they think and discuss why they are going to sleep in this bed, and what they think, feel and sense.

However, you don't need to use photographs or hot-seating, because what you want to do at this stage is give the students a 'taster' for haunted house scenarios. Trailers or video clips of haunted house films always engage students. For example, the trailer for *The Woman in Black* (2012) is always a winner, even if the students have seen it before. You can pause the trailer at the part where Daniel Radcliffe opens the door to the haunted house, and then get everyone to jot down the sounds, smells, textures, sights and tastes of that particular moment. You could then discuss the ways in which the trailer follows the conventions of the ghost story, but also offers some surprises. This can then lead onto a discussion about how the genre works: it has very well-known conventions but the successful stories always add their own special 'take' on the tropes. For example, *The Woman in Black* uses the rocking chair in creepily unexpected ways.

You could use some ghost stories or poems to whet their appetites. Longfellow's poem, 'Haunted Houses', is old fashioned but effective in this regard, while Michael Donaghy's 'Haunts' is very short, poignant and creepy too. These poems can be read and enjoyed, with pupils underlining what they find engaging, and then discussing in pairs or groups why they find them creepy – or not as the case may be. The point is that you have a discussion about the topic, using the poems as a springboard for the conversation.

The overall point of this part of the lesson is just to give students an introduction to the topic, a taster so that they are ready to move on to the next part...

STEP 1: CREATING A SCENARIO

Once they've been given this introduction, the students are now ready to work more fully in their groups, devising their own haunted houses. They can use some of the ideas they gained from the whole-class exercises discussed above, or they can make up an entirely different haunted house.

The teacher then needs to divide up the class into different coloured groups of five: blue, yellow, green and red. Each group is allocated an area of the haunted house and its surroundings. These are the ones I used:

1. Blue: ground floor, dining room and cellars
2. Yellow: first floor, library, master bedroom
3. Green: second floor, children's bedrooms, attic
4. Red: gardens, grounds, surrounding area

First, as a group, they will need to discuss what this section of the house contains in terms of furniture, food, decorations, walls, windows, musical instruments etc, and also who actually used to live here. They will need to determine why the house is haunted in this section of the house. Everyone should draw their own impressions and map of the house, labelling and annotating it as appropriate. Give them 10-20 minutes to do this. Don't let them linger too long, but equally if they are working productively, do allow them more time. Then ask for a report back, and gauge as best you can how well each group is doing. If you think they need a bit more input; in a gentle way, invite some constructive criticism and suggest some fresh ideas.

STEP 2: SENSUAL WRITING AND PLANNING

Next, each person in the group has a sense to exclusively work upon. They need to list, draw and then write a few sentences about their sense and their allocated section of the haunted house. This is how I divvy it up:

- Person 1: Sounds (the wind, clocks ticking, the scraping of fingernails at the window)
- Person 2: Smells (damp mist, mystical incense)
- Person 3: Sights (get the students to consider the lighting, candles, shadows, small objects)
- Person 4: Tastes (what do certain ghosts taste like if they enter your mouth?)
- Person 5: Textures (the tread of the floor underfoot, the slimy walls, the smooth wallpaper)

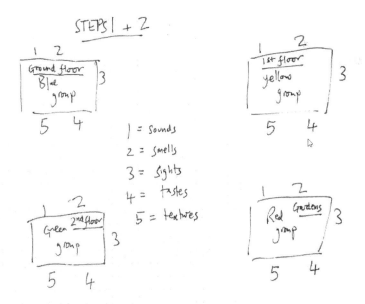

Figure 4 My rough teacher's plan of steps 1 and 2. You can draw your own.

Figure 4 shows that everyone on the tables has been given a number from 1-5, and each group has a colour. Each numbered person has a sense to consider and make notes upon, thinking about the sense in relation to the haunted house.

STEP 3: CHARACTERIZATION

Now each group is asked to jointly plan out and then individually write about different people who enter the house. These are the characters I use because they chime with many of the concerns of this age group:

- Person 1: A bully
- Person 2: A coward
- Person 3: A jealous person
- Person 4: A vain person
- Person 5: A selfish person

The students need to draw a big outline of this person, writing inside the body of the outline what this person thinks and feels about him/herself, and then outside them what other people – parents, friends, teachers etc – think/feel about them. They consider these questions: what does this character want? Why have they entered the house? What will they learn from being haunted? Here, or previously if appropriate, the teacher can explain the two major scenarios for ghost stories:

- Ghosts who get their revenge (the driving force behind *The Woman in Black*)
- Ghosts who teach the living a lesson and are often benign (the thematic heart of *A Christmas Carol*)

The groups should report back to the whole class after this phase of planning has happened. When I've worked on this project in two-hour lessons, the lesson will have finished by

116

now, so you might want to set the completion of this for homework.

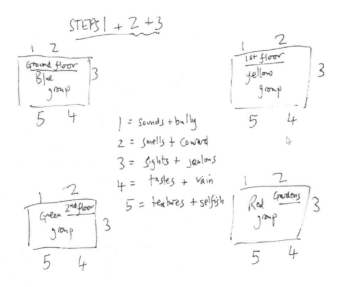

STEPS 1 + 2 + 3

1 = sounds + bully
2 = smells + coward
3 = sights + jealous
4 = tastes + vain
5 = textures + selfish

Figure 5 Teacher's rough plan of steps 1, 2, 3

STEP 4: THE QUEST

The next step is to give the groups some preparation time for the next major activity. The idea is that after 20 minutes' preparation, certain characters will sit down with another group, and that group will take them on a sensory journey that enables them to experience that group's part of the house: giving them possibly something to eat (obviously something edible), creating a soundscape, possibly a smell scape, getting them to feel objects and textures. The characters should ideally be blindfolded or shut their eyes when they sit down to go on their quests. The characters should also then share their unique stories, explaining why and how they are bullies, cowards, jealous, selfish and vain etc.

Most groups will have one person visiting them, but one group will have two people visiting them using the group size I've suggested (see Figure 6). This usually isn't a problem and can be very helpful if you have noticed that there is a group which is struggling: send two characters to see them so that they gain some more ideas.

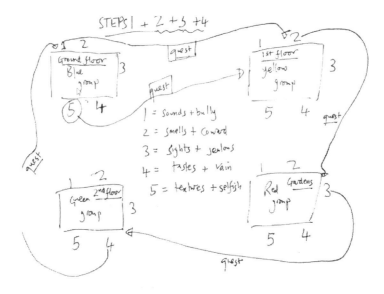

Figure 6 Step 4: The quest, sending an envoy to another table

Figure 6 shows what happens when an envoy, one person from each group, is sent to another table to experience that group's haunted house. The envoys go on a quest around the room, absorbing the different simulations, and then report back to their original group.

STEP 5: REFINING THE NARRATIVE, DEVELOPING CHARACTER AND STRUCTURE

Once the groups have shared their sensory journeys and the characters' life stories, you now talk about how writers can improve their narratives by considering characterisation deeply. To do this, you ask everyone on their table to refine their sensory journey to really teach the relevant person a lesson. They will need to talk in some depth about this: what might happen to the selfish person? How might the ghosts teach him/her lesson? What might the jealous person encounter, why might ghosts want to get their revenge on him/her?

Then re-run the sensory journey again, but with the envoys responding in role. So, for example, they could respond like Scrooge at the end of *A Christmas Carol*, where he implores the ghosts to believe that he will reform his ways. You might want to read a section of this dialogue or write your own script based on one of the characters to model this for your students. It's actually quite challenging to do, and takes some thought.

Now refine the journey and record the encounter in the form of a radio play, and/or write the radio script. This step is conceptually the most difficult of them all; deploy it flexibly. If you think that the people on the quest, the envoys, need to travel around a few groups so that the groups get more versed in enacting out their sensory journeys etc, then do this before embarking upon this step.

STEP 6: ENCOURAGING MORE CREATIVE EDITING, RE-DRAFTING, WRITING AND READING

Having produced a collaborative script and/or radio play, the world is your oyster! The class could now write a class novel about the haunted house, with each group writing a chapter about their allocated room. Or you could encourage individual work, with everyone writing about their allocated character and their unique journey in the haunted house.

You could jigsaw (Capel et al, 2016, p. 204) the groups by giving everyone in each group a number between 1 and 5, and then getting all 1s to sit together, all 2s to sit together etc, and then asking them to draw/map out and label/describe a complete haunted house. This is a great way of mixing groups up, and getting everyone in the class learning from each other. Other tasks might include making a documentary about the haunted house, holding a 'reality TV show' in it, or devoting an edition of a newspaper or magazine to it.

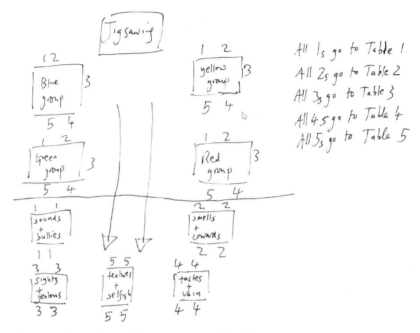

Figure 7 Jigsawing: All 1s go to a table, all 2s etc

In the above Figure 7, the top part of the diagram illustrates the class before the jigsaw happens: everyone is sitting in a group with a different number from 1-5. The teacher then tells all 1s to go to one particular table in the room, all 2s to another table etc. The bottom half of the diagram illustrates what happens when the jigsawing has happened: all 1s are sitting together, all 2s are sitting together etc. The point is that the students who have been given the same thing to think about are sitting together, sharing their ideas.

ADAPTING THESE IDEAS FOR OTHER CLASSES, TOPICS AND MODES

The principles for this project could be applied to any 'world-building' unit of work. So, for example, students could be allocated different parts of a village, town, city, country, planet or universe to imagine, take notes upon, discuss and write about. Similarly, they could be provided with photographs, video clips, poems and literary extracts to motivate and stimulate them into coming up with their own ideas. The principles of collaborative learning would all apply: students would work in groups, envoy around others, and jigsaw to share ideas.

The project could also be carried out online, using discussion forums on a platform like Moodle, which gives teachers the ability to put students into groups and allocate them different tasks, which they then share with the whole class later on.

FINDINGS

I have run this simulation with many different classes and in many different ways during my three decades of teaching pupils and teachers. My chief findings are this:

Pupils and teachers are very motivated by this idea. They love creating haunted houses and rooms together. They particularly like getting someone from their class who is not in their group to experience the room they've created.

You generate a positive feedback loop with this activity. Children love sharing ideas about spooky things, and this sharing creates a positive feedback loop. I've found that many children who are not engaged with school have a great deal of knowledge about this area.

Clarity is very important. One of the difficulties with writing this article is that I've realised this project sounds quite complicated when really it isn't. In reality, it's quite simple, but the whole thing must be done in clear steps. So, first get everyone into groups, second give them part of the haunted house to consider, and third allocate each person a sense to discuss and write about. Then go from there.

Flexibility is important. Don't plough on with the above steps if they are not working with your class. Go back to the basic idea, which is to get the groups describing and 'building' a haunted house in their imaginations and in 'real life'. If you have come up with a better idea of how to do it, do it!

Have a clear, final product in mind and model it. I modelled the audio recordings of the simulations in real time with my students: 'Welcome to the dining room of the haunted house, shut your eyes now, and smell the strange smell of gravy from the silver dish, and listen to the ghostly laughter of the guests sitting around the table...'

Get your head around jigsawing and envoys. If this article has not explained this sufficiently to you, then read other sources and have a go at it. These grouping activities work very well because they mix and match pupils, and everyone works with different people, which is very important with group work.

Teacher passion and intervention is crucial. You will find eventually that everyone gets on with the work without you having to do a thing except observe, but to begin with you'll have to work very hard to get the whole project off the ground. That means you'll need to keep walking around the groups checking to see they've got the right ideas. If pupils come up with an idea that is not something you've instructed them to do but is a good idea, then let them go for it. Don't inhibit good ideas. Equally, if the pupils are clearly not on the right track, make sure you are strict about enforcing what they should do. You'll need to be passionate about the project too; show your pupils how thrilled you are by the whole concept of the haunted house.

WHAT NEXT?

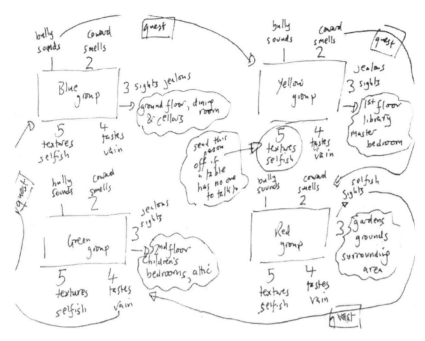

Figure 8 Summing up the strategies of the project

I hope I've shown that the combination of collaborative learning and a topic that really engages students is a winner for creative writing teachers. Once you've understood its principles and basic strategies, it is a 'high-impact, low effort' teaching tool that requires relatively little preparation and can be tweaked endlessly to suit the needs of any given class. If the teacher notices that the collaborative learning is not working, they can always ask students to write individually on their set topic. Furthermore, it can also be adapted so that it works online; in these days when so much is shifting into the digital sphere, this is an interesting option.

The next steps for you would be to:
- Have a go yourself!
- Find some interesting poems, passages, stories etc that really chime with you about this topic.

- Consider how you might do this online. Using technologies like Zoom/Microsoft Teams/The Big Blue Button, you are able to put people into groups, and you could get students doing this simulation online.
- Learn more about social constructivism: read Watkins' work (listed below) as a starting point. When you deeply understand how collaborative learning works, you'll be much more confident about doing it.

REFERENCES

Capel, S., Leask, M.,Younie, S. (2016). *Learning to Teach in the Secondary School: A companion to school experience* (7th ed.). Routledge Ltd - M.U.A.

Cremin, T. (2006). Creativity, uncertainty and discomfort: Teachers as writers. Cambridge Journal of Education, 36(3), 415-433.

Cremin, T., & Oliver, L. (2017). Teachers as writers: A systematic review. Research Papers in Education, 32(3), 269-295.

Donaghy, M. (2000) 'Haunts' poem in *Conjured*, Picador, London, URL accessed 18th March 2020: https://poetryarchive.org/poem/haunts/

Gilbert, F. (2017) The Creative Writing Teacher's Toolkit, Writing in Education, NAWE, York. https://www.nawe.co.uk/DB/wie-editions/articles/the-creative-writing-teachers-toolkit.html

González, N., Moll, L., & Amanti, C. (2005). Funds of knowledge: Theorizing practice in households, communities, and classrooms. New York: Routledge.

Kress, G. (2005). English in urban classrooms a multimodal perspective on teaching and learning. London: RoutledgeFalmer.

Longfellow, H. (1807-1882) 'Haunted Houses', poem, URL accessed 18th March 2020: https://poets.org/poem/haunted-houses

Marzano, R. Pickering, D., Pollock, J. (2001) *Classroom Instruction Strategies that Work: Research-Based Strategies for*

Increasing Student Achievement. Association for Supervision and Curriculum Devleopment, Virginia USA.

The National Writing Project (2020) website, URL accessed 18th March 2020: https://www.nationalwritingproject.uk/

Tierno, M. (2002). Aristotle's poetics for screenwriters : Storytelling secrets from the greatest mind in Western civilization (1st ed.). New York: Hyperion.

Vélez-Ibáñez, C. G., & Greenberg, J. B. (1992). Formation and transformation of funds of knowledge among U.S.–Mexican households. Anthropology & Education Quarterly, 23(4), 313–335.

University of Exeter (2020), Grammar for Writing Pedagogy, Centre for Research in Writing, URL accessed, 18th March 2020: http://socialsciences.exeter.ac.uk/education/research/centres/writing/grammar-teacher-resources/thegrammarforwritingpedagogy/

Watkins, C. (2011) Learning: A Sense Maker's Guide, Association of Teachers and Lecturers. London. https://www.chriswatkins.net/publications/

Smith, J., & Wrigley, S. (2012). What has writing ever done for us? The power of teachers' writing groups. English in Education, 46(1), 70-84.

CREATIVE ESSAYING:
CREATIVE ESSAYING AS CREATIVE-WRITING PEDAGOGY

KIRSTY GUNN & GAIL LOW

It's the first class of a year-two module: 'Creative Writing: Prose Poetics and Practice'. Given the tension between this set of words, I outline what paths this module might take. This is not only a writing module, I say, but also a creative reading module. The students' ears prick up. What's that? Reading? On a creative-writing programme? Yes, reading is fundamental; the course is underpinned by a belief that slow, attentive explorations of texts create better awareness for writing practice. We read to write and to reflect on craft, I say. I continue doggedly, making a distinction between reading as a hermeneutical activity—meaning-making—and reading as poetics, an understanding of textual and rhetorical effects. Then, for this is a module about creative writing, you put this into practice, I say, by having a go.

I am not teaching these classes alone. Two of us stand down here in the front, delivering our 'Creative Lectures', as we have titled them, in order to disrupt expectations that lectures are where someone simply tells students stuff. Ideally what's in mind here should work really well: designing and teaching these sessions together, with one noting reactions while the other talks. The teacher-student—the teller and the told—paradigm is broken up into a discussion between two that spills out into a dialogue with many. Thus, shared conversation is embedded into the two or three hours after an introduction, some informal back and forth. And it softens a lecture's delivery, this kind of approach. Team teaching may not be deemed economical within our current academic management system, but it generates a spontaneity so necessary for the imaginative health and writing. Differences in perspectives and enthusiasms are not hidden but laid out for all to see. There is not just one voice sounded.

To grab their attention in this first week, I give them a short story that I think will appeal to even the most demanding student. 'Dog' by Mark Slouka (2012) is a richly affective and surprising short story in the realist American mode yet also shot through with something other worldly, familiarly strange. I ask them to take a line each to read and then pass the reading baton around the room so we get to hear all their voices. To 'come inside' the narrative as I think of it. The reading goes well and the class settle into the cadences of Slouka's lines. Some are clearly moved by the sadness and loneliness that is at the story's heart; others are nodding, exchanging 'that was quite good wasn't it?' glances at each other. Now I invite them, in small groups, to discuss the story and to note some initial responses and thoughts. First thought best thought, I say. Just react to the text. Write. Don't worry about being right or wrong. After that, I ask each of them in turn to read out one of their ideas. The class starts to loosen up. They are now less members of an audience and more participants. Everyone, even the most shy, contributes and I can see their confidence growing in speaking out like this. It's exactly the boost needed for the next part of the afternoon's exercise: to turn reading into writing.

Given the emotional intensity of 'Dog', I say, and the way that story conveyed such affect, I now want you to make a short story of your own. Here is a character, I tell them: A woman who is very sociable, loves parties, who suddenly finds herself alone in a park or on a walk somewhere. Here is a situation, I add: She meets another person and something awful happens. It can be as little as a bee sting or as massive as an electrical storm. Now, I finish: That's all you need. You add all the details—whatever you want them to be, and as much or as little as you want—the season, the landscape, the woman's clothes, whether or not she knows the other person she meets here. Let your pen hit the paper and just... write. Scribble down everything you can think of. I'll call time in ten minutes and give you another five or so to polish up what you've done.

There's a second of silence—a sort of shock—then off they go, and once time is up, I ask each to read aloud their opening sentences and to each I give a short burst of encouragement and feedback. Again, confidence is what I am building here. Each student has now composed the draft beginnings of a short story that with further work and drafting could lead into a really good short story. Yes, some are starting to enjoy the process. This mightn't be 'Creative Writing' as they see it but still... this could be interesting. Some stay afterwards to ask questions: How can they make the most of the course? Should they use their workbooks to write stories? What else has Mark Slouka written? Others emerge from the mid-to-back rows of the lecture hall and form disconsolate clusters. Finally, this group comes down to speak as one: Will we have to do this kind of thing every week? We thought this course was going to let us be able to do our own writing... And I think: How is what you've just done here not your own writing? At what point has reading and thinking about literature become something you, a student enrolled on an English and Creative Writing programme, have not wanted to do? These thoughts continue and start to nag. What's happening in our departments to so distance expectations from the core reality of the texts and good – even great – literature we have passed down to us to learn from? What's going on?

After a couple of weeks of paired close reading and writing discussions and exercises, I announce the first assessment. I quote from Harold Bloom, 'Literary criticism ... is in the first place literary, which is to say personal and passionate' (2011:4). Also, you are writers and not simply critics. For that first essay, think about what it is in the writing that moves you, pleasurably or displeasurably. Choose from the reading list and write in a way that enables the reader to see you thinking on the page; that makes that reader turn around in surprise and want to engage fully with both you and the text. Have a voiceprint that intrigues or charms, and a reflective thoughtfulness—a mindprint—that draws a reader into an intimate conversation with you. Don't treat the text like an object only to be analysed in a scientific manner. Instead inhabit it; make it come alive. Show your thinking process, not simply your thoughts already fully formed. I have at the back of my mind John D'Agata's marvellous definition of an essay as 'an art form that tracks the evolution of consciousness as it rolls over the folds of a new idea, memory, or emotion', and where 'we're made to feel privy to another human being's thought process' (Steinberg, 2016).

You could start with a puzzle, I say, a problem of reading, and your essay might take your readers on a journey from that point. You don't need to declare straight out what the essay will do. You might not know where exactly you are headed... And it can be exciting not to know. Show your thinking on the page and don't be afraid of affect, putting something of yourself into the work. Read like a writer also: write about the way the text has been put together. Structure, use of adjectives, rhythm, lyricism... The course title has 'poetics' in it, I remind them.

There is a bewildered buzz around the room. No one much liked what I've just been saying. The mantra 'Just Write!' in the Creative Lectures has been one thing but what kind of essay shows tentativeness, hesitancy or confusion? What exactly is required? Don't think about a right or wrong way, I respond. In my mind, cultivation of an openness to not being able to get-it-at-once puts us at the start of a learning journey. I say to the students: Don't fear uncertainty, but use it to feel your way along the line, always grappling and reading more as part of the process of exploration – and write about that! Everything I've said seems to go against the grain of much of how they have been trained to think: that a display of mastery and expertise is the only way to write. I counter those responses, observe how 'getting it' sometimes allows us to dismiss the work, to file it away. Mark Doty's poem 'Difference' (2008: 120) highlights the importance of a sensitivity to words and it fronts our module's online pages. Take this to heart, I say:

> What can words do
>
> but link what we know
> to what we don't,
> and so form a shape?

I have a word that I love to use when thinking about putting disparate ideas together, something which seems to work well in essays by Doty and others: 'stitching'. To me it describes perfectly the delicate joining together of pieces of writing, both as a means of working as well as its result. So now, I announce with an earnestness that belies my own anxieties, I want you to forget all about the template school-room essay! And just dive in with your responses to the text. Write a whole lot of mini reactions, if you like, to the texts you are going to investigate, and then think about stitching those various sections together. Let go of scholarly abstracts or summaries, stolid chunks of expository information, and instead think of literary criticism as personal, performative and imaginative.

There is more puzzlement and bewilderment; all this seems counter-intuitive, and the students are not convinced. Some come down to the lectern after the session to argue querulously. If there isn't a tight and linear structure and logic, how is that a proper essay? Tell us exactly what you want. One asks more cannily, how do you grade? Another says, 'Then what kind of essay gets an A?' When I tell these students that writing isn't a production line where quality control is enforced in identikit fashion and, I think but don't say, in some educational consumer culture we've allowed to be established—that those are the wrong questions to ask—some of them are filled with high emotion and real rage.

But why should there be essay templates? In the Humanities, especially? That is where my thinking is headed, more and more. I myself am writing another kind of essay by now: a joint project shared between the two of us who teach writing and 'Creative Essaying' as we call it. Writing and thinking on the page together in a kind of porous 'I': one's thinking opening out into the other's as the essay goes on. I describe what it feels like to write with someone else, to turn over one's words to another and not be fearful of giving up control. I talk about how interesting it is to challenge the conventions – the marking out of territory – that sit behind the unself-conscious use of the first-person pronoun. You might even want to experiment with writing essays like that, I suggest to the students in another session. Write with a friend. The person sitting next to you. That's a sure-fire way to open up thinking and let go of having a conclusion in mind in advance! In one particular session of our shared year-three module, we actively sabotage the use of the singular first person by stitching together the whole class's brief, first-person pieces of non-fiction writing to make one united piece. We also translate their initial first-person exercise into the third person.

I set an object essay exercise to get them thinking. Look in your bag for an object that has some resonance, I say, write down some close descriptions of it: what it looks like, its colour, the weight of it in your hand, whether it is smooth or rough when you run your fingers over it. Think about how it makes you feel, and write about that in a separate paragraph or two. Then write more, setting the object in context. Where might it come from? What does it remind you of? What is it like? As with all the timed exercises in our Creative Lectures, students have a limited period for writing in short bursts. Ten minutes for a description, another five for writing about how the object makes them feel, and so on. But they don't have to 'join up' these fragments yet. I give them another 10 minutes to 'stitch'—that word again, so useful!—the pieces together at the end. Before we leave the hall, I tell them: Now, try following that same process when it comes to writing your essays about the books on your reading list. Let yourself follow the line of your thinking and stitching and see what you end up with. This can be fun!

It's starting to feel as though creative essaying—setting exercises like this, working critically alongside the students' own imaginative work—has more capacity for intellectual and imaginative development than the traditional creative-writing workshop. The following week, I set them a little exercise after our initial reading and discussion of various 'definitions' of the essay by John D'Agata, Robert Atwan, Chris Arthur, Judith Butler, Brenda Miller, Philip Lopate and others. We look at specific excerpts from Arthur's 'Thirteen Ways of Looking at a

Blackbird' (2012: 135—55) and discuss the structure of his essay: segmented, circular, centering around a concrete object (a briefcase) to signal his thinking; how ordinary domestic events, items and so on can yield extraordinary stories if we but pause over them thoughtfully and carefully. I discuss segmentation in essay form (Arthur's has 13 parts), and how his deliberate use of these segments render the essay structure as collage, mosaic, bead-like.

The exercise that follows is titled, provisionally, 'Some ways of looking at an essay'. It comprises about five distinct short segments that might initially begin with or respond to a series of prompts, such as 'An essay is... ' and 'An essay does...'— conveying at a slant, through metaphor, analogy or figurative language, what an essay is. For example, 'An essay is walking in a forest without following a map and stumbling on...'; 'An essay is like climbing up stairs in a dream'; or 'An essay marshals you through a series of doors in a maze.' Then, I say, find me a personal memory of something that might be tangentially related to essay writing, and write about it. In addition, compose a paragraph about a place where you write—it might be a desk in your room, or on your bed—describe that place in some detail and the feelings and experiences that occur when you put pen to paper or type on screen. Finally, find the briefest of striking passages from your reading about writing and, in your own words, react to what they say. Then stitch all your compelling and interesting passages together, edit and redraft with an eye for how it looks, and ear for tone and voice. You may find that the segments need to be differently ordered. You may find that you circle around some things. See what happens when you put them all together and where that writing as writing takes you.

What is the outcome of all this making and thinking and talking? Despite my own excitement for moving creative-writing teaching into this new arena, I have to confess that there has been a mixed response. Some students take to the process with enthusiasm—it's new to them, sure, but they're excited. Excerpts from the best of their work can be seen in our online magazine, DURA (https://dura-dundee.org.uk/category/essay/)

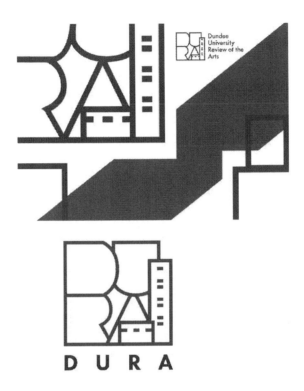

Others take a little longer to come at literary study in this new way. For others again, this kind of writing is never going to suit them. They have projects in mind and they want to get to them, fast: to finish their novel, to write the next one, and the next. What they simply want to get on with is 'my writing'. And, yes, still those questions continue to prowl: Why is it that students of English—even those with a more broad view of the subject—see literary studies as content-delivery machines? As a subject that's only about context, biography, history and all the rest of it? How have we let a discipline that arrived in universities to serve the study of the imagination let imaginative enquiry so fade from view? Yet a content-delivery machine is precisely what we seem to have made of so much of literature teaching, and the creative writing discipline as well, come to that, with its increased focus on 'vocationalibity', as one bureaucrat put it to me recently, talking of 'degree content and outcome'. By way of retort—by way of rebellion!—I won't let essays in my classes simply be about conveying information. I want pleasure. I want affect. And I want these for our young people too.

This aspect of creative writing teaching, this essaying, I have found, is durable, communal and generous. It is kind; it listens. It has an open ear and happily translates. It is supple and enabling and the very opposite of 'my writing', and I think it may be able—despite our new post-lockdown world—to take us far. So bring on the changes, I say... 'The mind I love must have wild places', wrote Katherine Mansfield (1997:163). Okay, I will tell the incoming students, let's see how wild you can be...

REFERENCES:

Arthur, C. (2012) On the Shoreline of Knowledge. Iowa City: University of Iowa Press.

Bloom, H. (2011) The Anatomy of Influence. New Haven: Yale University Press

Steinberg, S. and D'Agata, J (2016). 'John D'Agata Redefines the Essay', Electric Literature, July 14. Available at https://electricliterature.com/john-dagata-redefines-the-essay/#.h9ockv8lc. [Accessed 16.8.2017]

Doty, M. (2008) Fire to Fire: New and Selected Poems. New York: Harper Perennial.

Mansfield, K. and Stott, M. (1997) The Notebooks of Katherine Mansfield Volume 2 (Lincoln: Lincoln University Press).

Purpura, L. (2006) On Looking. Louisville: Sarabande Books.

Slouka, M. (2012) 'Dog', Ploughshares 38(1), 152—160, 209—10.

VENETIAN WHISPERS

GEOFFREY HEPTONSTALL

They spoke of mercy,
making eloquent pleas
that I heard as spoken
in good faith, withdrawing
my knife from the merchant's flesh.
My heart was touched as his was not.
Later I learned of mercy's bound
when none was shown me.
Even my daughter was taken.
I am abandoned again,
my life defiled
in the name of another God.
This has to be the death of things.

Snow was falling out of season,
melting in the waking sun.
The limbs of the beggar were cold.
As a heap of rags he was buried
beneath the waste of the citadel.
The sight of stars in a clear sky
became his dreams to die for.
'I gave you an empire,'
he croaked to the worthies.
Coins were thrown in contempt.
Like a ghost the old man vanished,
but not before warning.

All that I have known is no more
than this, my forfeiture,
which is to some a virtue.
Their justice mocks my name.
Without a name I am unknown.

My head is dashed against the wall.
I am chained with nails
that tear spirit from flesh.
I am the child behind the wire
waiting to be born.

The above poem is inspired by *The Merchant of Venice*. I imagine Shylock speaks, making the plea that in the play he does not. But it is not meant to be an improvement on Shakespeare's text; it is a response to Shakespeare. The approach is an extension of the character; I have attempted to write what Shakespeare implies. I am raising the questions the play arouses: Is Shylock a villain or a wronged man? Was Portia's eloquent plea for mercy no more than a hypocrisy given that no mercy was shown to Shylock? My interpretation is that Shylock was wronged, but Shakespeare invites seemingly infinite responses. The responses we have now are shaped by the history that divides us by many centuries from the Elizabethan poet. As the final lines of the poem indicate, the shadow of a terrible history continues to fall on any consideration of Judaism in the gentile world.

WHAT NEXT? POSSIBLE CREATIVE WRITING ACTIVITIES

Poetry and other forms of creative writing allow us to imagine different sides to a character and explore their inner thoughts. By entering the head of a text's protagonist or minor character, the creative writer can not only see the world through their eyes and better understand their behaviour but also develop their technique in terms of character development. Here are a few classroom exercises to help students explore the character of Shylock further – followed by some more general exercises suitable for understanding any misunderstood or minor character in a book or play:

Shylock-related activities
Poetry cut outs/black out poetry: Print out an extract of one of Shylock's speeches onto sheet of A4 paper and instruct the

students to either 'black out' words and sections using a thick black pen, or cut up the paper and re-arrange words and sentences, to create a new interpretation of the same words.

Imagining Shylock now: Without his wealth, Shylock is destitute – as we see in the second half of the poem. He has gone from a hated Jew to a contemptible beggar. Rich or poor, he is mocked. Having read and discussed the poem, ask the students to do their own version: imagining where Shylock lives, what he sees, what he feels etc, what his hopes are etc.

What does a 'pound of flesh' weigh today? The description of a 'pound of flesh' is a visceral, powerful image of the reality of capitalism: that in order to be rich, someone else must suffer. What is the equivalent of a pound of flesh today? The cost of a new mobile phone, a diamond, cheap clothes...? Instruct students to write a modern-day poem or short story of greed and inequality that explores this image further.

General activities

The hot seat

- Ask for a volunteer (or nominate a student) to take the role of a much-debated character in the text, or a character who doesn't speak much.
- The student takes the 'hot seat' at the front of the classroom and their peers ask them questions, which they respond to in character.
- If another student thinks they have a better or different answer, they can raise their hand to take over the hot seat and offer their 'take'.

The diary entry

- Note down or draw five key points in the character's story: this could be a turning point, a dilemma, an accident, an argument, or another significant event.

- Write a diary entry in the voice of the chosen character, written as if on the night of when the incident or occasion in question happened.
- Ensure students are writing about the emotions of the character too and their wishes, as well as what happened.

The time-machine

- Re-imagine a scene in the book or play as if it were taking place today and discuss how it would be different. Would the language be different? The outcome? The setting?
- Ask students to rewrite or update the scene to a modern-day setting in a location of their choice.
- Alternatively, ask students to create a modern-day character that enters the period scene. What do they do? What do they say? How do the original characters react?

The rivals

- Ask the students to pick two characters from the text who are mortal enemies – or simply who disagree. Alternatively they could look at the two sides of one character.
- Instruct the students to write a two-voice poem in pairs: where one student writes one line and the other student writes the next, offering a different or opposing perspective on what was written.
- The students perform their poem, taking it in turn to read their lines in order to build up a complex character or illustrate the division between two characters.

CATCHING THE LIGHT

TAMAR HODES

Foliage shimmied and shone in the cut-glass light. Harry squinted, shifting his gaze from the beech tree to his pad, as if willing it to fall onto the page for him. He loved this time of year, his favourite for drawing; the world amber, as if coated in syrup. Everything was clearly defined: the maple tree, fiery and vibrant; the silver birch, flirtatious and fluttery; and the giant oak, shedding its ochre leaves and lowering them gently onto the ground. He noticed the way that the outlines of leaves stamped themselves against the sky like transfers, peeled to leave their image embossed.

Beside him on the grass lay his treasured box, the chalks rigidly side by side, an extensive rainbow. Harry selected the sepia and started shading the leaves of the horse chestnut. His aim was not to copy nature but to capture the essence of the day as it appeared to him; the light benign and warm, a slight breeze which periodically shook the tree, as if ruffling the feathers of a bird, so that a few leaves fell, but some clung resolutely on.

The roughness of pastels felt appropriate for autumn, where nothing is static and yet there is a kind of beauty in its movements, as if the landscape were slow-dancing: half-dreaming, half-awake. At this time of year, it seemed to him that nature was caught between life and death and that it was this transition, this changing identity, that was its appeal.

Angling the chalk, he aimed to recreate that fuzziness, that hazy chaos that he found so alluring. Using a red stick, he dotted the rowan, replicating the berries randomly brightening the tree.

These were the times when Harry felt at his happiest: no human sounds, just a wood pigeon rumbling its throaty song and a thrush, pitching its soprano voice above the baritone line. Surrounded by colour and softness, Harry had the chance to slip the scene onto his page, and that gave him satisfaction. People could be disappointing; nature was authentic, unashamed of its own contradictions.

Harry was able to remove everything and everyone from his life, as if he had entered another country in spite of being so close to home, his back turned on his house and on reality and facing towards the trees which offered a new perspective. The complex world fell away. He had often had the sense of being on the outside, removed, never at the centre of activity. And he was becoming more comfortable with that. The figure on the deck looking out to sea; the man on the cliff edge surveying the landscape around him; the traveller turning one last time to look at his homeland before departing. Surely they had the best views.

He remembered years earlier that he had liked a girl called Ginny. They were in primary school together. He thought she was pretty, her red hair twisted into plaits, her cheeks pink and her eyes bright. They often sat together in class and he looked forward to seeing her each day. One morning, arriving before she did, he left a pencil drawing he had made of her in her place. When she came in, slinging her satchel on the floor, she saw the sketch and, rather than being pleased, she was uncomfortable. She stared at it as if in a smudged mirror and did not like what she saw. Harry remembered how he had felt awkward, too, as their friendship instantly crumbled.

He felt more at ease with trees. So many leaves, so many brittle branches, and the challenge was to show the effect of it, the overwhelming result. Sometimes he wondered where it came from, this desire to capture, the need to record what he had seen. But it came naturally to him, as if the chalks were guiding him, not the other way around. He felt as if nature were passing through him on the way to the paper and he was a mere conduit, a channel, and he liked the role of being an intermediary. His thoughts and the sun and the trees and peace, bathed together easily in a kindly light.

Time slipped away. He could not have said how long he sat there, the warmth on his nape, his hands moving fluently, his thoughts suspended somewhere in the sky. If only all days were like this, removed from others yet connected to nature, to a landscape which never let him down, which changed but remained essentially the same.

And that was it. People stayed the same, made the same comments, complained about the same issues. They did not develop. Or sometimes they altered completely and suddenly, without warning.

Nature got it right: constancy but variations within so that your eyes always had somewhere to look, your ears had something to listen out for; there was the roughness of the bark and the smooth leaves and the prickly grass and all of it altering each day. He was thankful for the seasons and the light and dark and for everything in between and he tried to replicate that movement on paper. Colour, texture, hope: he attempted to convey it all. And as he worked he thought about life and his dreams and the sunlight gave strength to it all.

'Harry,' called his mother from the kitchen door. 'It's time for tea. Put your things away and wash your hands, please.'

Harry closed the lid of his pastel box, picked up his pad and walked back into the house. He laid his materials on the kitchen table and his father ruffled his hair as he passed.

'I've finished another one,' said Harry proudly, giving the picture to his mother as if passing an exhibit as evidence in a court case.

'Lovely,' she said, but when Harry was in the downstairs bathroom, he heard her whisper:

'Oh god, another one of those wretched pictures to go on the fridge. I could curse your sister for giving him those pastels.'

'I know,' said his father, snapping the ring off a beer can. 'I wish he'd just go out and kick a ball like a normal twelve year old.'

THE FIRST DAY

Helena looked over at the tiny figure sitting next to her in the car. Betsy barely took up half the seat. Her little face was tight with anxiety.

'You'll be fine,' said Helena, reassuringly. 'Everyone feels nervous on their first day.'

She moved her hand off the steering wheel to touch and comfort Betsy. She squeezed her hand for an instant; then returned it to the wheel. She needed to concentrate. Here in the New Forest, three horses were heaving their suede bodies slowly at the side of the road. One walked nonchalantly in front of the car and seemed in no hurry. Helena braked. She had heard of accidents caused by wandering animals here and she didn't want an unfortunate incident, today of all days. Betsy needed her to be calm.

'Look at the horses. Aren't they lovely?'

Betsy nodded.

They waited a minute and the animal edged slowly away.

They drove on. Betsy was quiet. Helena glanced over. She wanted to stop the car and just hug her, hold her tiny body close to her own and kiss her. But she knew that they both had to be brave and move on.

The horses were behind them now and they were surrounded by green bushes and trees. A few rabbits nibbled the grass on the verge.

'Look, bunny rabbits. You like rabbits.'

No response.

'You know, you're going to be fine. It will feel a bit strange at the start but you'll soon settle. Everyone there is very nice.'

'But what happens if they don't like me?'

'Of course they'll like you.' Helena laughed to show how ridiculous that idea was. 'Everyone is new at the beginning. And then they settle.'

'Will I have any friends?'

Helena felt tears prick her eyes. Would she ever stop feeling protective of her?

'Of course you will. Wherever you go, people like you. You're so friendly.'

'What will we do there?' Betsy's voice was small and slightly squeaky.

'Oh, all sorts of lovely activities. Maybe some painting or drawing. Baking. Singing. All things you enjoy and you're good at.'

Outside, Helena saw the first signs of early blossom sprigging the trees. Maybe they were a good omen. Was that even a bit of blue in the otherwise granite sky?

'Will I have lunch there?'

'Yes. You'll enjoy that. I've told them that you don't have a huge appetite.'

'Will I have to eat all of it?'

'No. Just leave what you don't want. Okay?'

Betsy nodded.

'And then I'll pick you up at three and see how you've got on.'

Helena sighed. She was pleased that there were no other cars on the forest road today. She needed as much calm as she could get. Why was life so hard? Why did she find leaving Betsy so difficult? Would she settle? Would it improve as time went on?

She had to admit that her devotion to Betsy had probably destroyed her relationship with Miles. He had felt excluded from the tight bond that the two of them had, and his inability to break in. He had pleaded with Helena to let Betsy make her own decisions, to stop mollycoddling her.

'She has to look after herself,' he would say. 'Think for herself. She's far too reliant on you.'

'She needs me,' would be Helena's response and then she would storm out. Except that on one occasion Miles did the storming out and he hadn't returned.

A ray of sunlight broke through the trees now. More blossom. The trees were fuller here, as if they were bursting with life and freshness. The foliage was the green of hope and new beginnings.

They left the forest now and entered the outskirts of Lyndhurst. Betsy was playing with the toggles of her coat, twiddling them in her tiny hands.

'I'd like to stay at home with you.'

'I know,' said Helena, 'but I have to go work and you'd be lonely and bored all day on your own.'

Betsy shook her head in disagreement. She could be stubborn although at times she seemed rather defeated.

Helena thought now of Betsy's belongings, pink with prettiness everywhere: white linen hearts, floral bags, trays and boxes full of shiny brooches and tinny trinkets. How they belied this vulnerability.

They drove up to the gate which was open onto the drive.

'Here we are,' said Helena as cheerfully as she could.

The red brick building was solid and smart. There was an attractive garden in the front with picnic benches where lunch could be eaten on sunny days, a neat pattern of gravel paths and trimmed bushes edging them, a buddleia attracting butterflies, bird feeders filled with nuts.

Helena got out of the car and went round to help Betsy undo her seatbelt. She came tentatively out. They walked together, hand in hand, to the front door, Betsy clutching her pretty, floral bag.

There was a sign, letters engraved into a gold plaque: Lyndhurst Care Home for the Elderly. She rang the bell and a petite Chinese lady in a pale blue uniform answered.

'Hello,' she said warmly, 'you must be Betsy.'

Betsy didn't answer. She looked to Helena for reassurance.

'Yes,' said Helena for her, 'my mother has come for her trial day.'

She let go of Betsy's hand and passed it to the lady. 'Come with me, then,' said the woman to Betsy. 'I'll look after you. We'll see you at three,' she said to Helena.

'See you later, Mum,' said Helena, as she left them, and went back to her car. 'Have a lovely day.'

She looked up. The door was firmly closed.

WRITING STORIES WITH TWISTS
IN THEIR TALES

Stories which turn dramatically at the end are enjoyable to read and, in my opinion, even more enjoyable to write. There is a secret thrill in guiding the readers through the narrative, leading them to assumptions that are ultimately dashed or turned upside down. Because the story hangs by a dangerous thread, the writing has to be especially convincing and plausible. There are many great tales that demonstrate this device such as *The Verger* by Somerset Maugham, *The Necklace* by Guy de Maupassant, *The Last Leaf* by O'Henry and *The Awful Fate of Melpomenus Jones* by Stephen Leacock. In this article, I am going to analyse two of my own stories, *The First Day* and *Catching the Light,* which both employ ambiguity and twist endings; then I will help students to devise their own. Although generally I like to write without knowing where I am going (setting out without a map), when it comes to these manipulative tales there is a need for meticulous construction (planning the route before you begin). It is my hope that your pupils' writing will benefit from employing similar preparation techniques.

CONVINCING SETTINGS

Because you are trying to convince readers of a truth that you will then reverse, almost like a magic trick or optical illusion, the description of the setting needs to be detailed and realistic: this is the writer as conman. It helps to name the location, to root the fiction in a real place. In *The First Day* I mention the New Forest and Lyndhurst and have tried to make the description as visual as possible: 'three horses were heaving their suede bodies slowly at the side of the road'; 'A few rabbits nibbled the grass at the verge'; 'A ray of sunlight broke through the trees,' 'The foliage was the green of hope and new beginnings.' I have also tried to convey spring without naming it. It is both literal and symbolic: Helena hopes this will be a fresh start for Betsy.

In *Catching the Light*, the setting is the garden of Harry's house and I have, again, tried to evoke this place clearly in the reader's mind: 'Foliage shimmied and shone in the cut-glass light,'; 'the world amber, as if coated in syrup,' 'the maple tree, fiery and vibrant, the silver birch, flirtatious and fluttery, and the giant oak, shedding its ochre leaves and lowering them gently onto the ground.' Colour is helpful as a persuasive tool and so is sound: 'a wood pigeon rumbling its throaty song and a thrush, pitching its soprano voice above the baritone line.' The season is autumn, conveyed but not named. Again, it is both literal and symbolic: it is glorious but it also hints at an ominous ending.

DELIBERATE AMBIGUITY

You need to have decided what you want the grand revelation to be. In my case, the twist in *The First Day* is that the reader believes Betsy to be a child but she is, in fact, an old woman. In *Catching the Light*, it is the reverse: the reader believes Harry to be an old man but he is actually 12 years old. The names you choose are important: Betsy could be a girl or an old lady; Harry could be a boy or an old man. Once you know what the twist will be about – age, status, identity, innocence or guilt – you need to build on that ambiguity. In *The Verger*, this hinges on literacy; in *The Necklace* on fake jewellery; in *The Last Leaf* on reality or artifice; in *The Awful Fate of Melpomenus Jones, a deus ex machina*. You should include sentences or phrases that could apply to both the fabrication and the truth. As the reader can go back and check, these tricks need to be cleverly written and watertight. Here are some of the ambiguities I included: in *The First Day* the following could all apply to a girl or an old woman: 'the tiny figure'; 'Betsy barely took up half her seat,'; 'her little face, tight with terror'; and her anxiety about going somewhere new, making friends, liking the food, 'Will I have to eat all of it?' Objects also add to the deceit: Betsy likes 'white linen hearts, floral bags; trays and boxes full of shiny brooches and tinny trinkets.'

In *Catching the Light*, the following lines could refer to a boy or old man: 'These were the times when Harry felt at his happiest'; 'He often had the sense of being on the outside, removed'; 'People could be disappointing. Nature was authentic, unashamed of its own contradictions.' The titles of the stories also add to the duplicity. *The First Day* is not actually about starting school but going to live in a care home and *Catching the Light* does not only refer to Harry's attempts to depict nature but also the reader's epiphany on realising that his parents do not appreciate his talents and are dishonest in their reactions to him.

USING OTHER CHARACTERS AS ALLIES IN THE DECEIT

In order to make the case more credible, other characters can support the pretence. In *The First Day*, we learn that Helena's over-protectiveness of Betsy led to the collapse of her relationship with Miles, 'on one occasion Miles did the storming out and he hadn't returned'; and in *Catching the Light* there is a reference to Harry's earlier attempt to try and impress a girl called Ginny by leaving a drawing on her seat at school: 'She stared at it as if in a smudged mirror and did not like what she saw.' By asserting that this incident happened 'years earlier', I am tricking the reader into assuming that this was over 60 years ago instead of, in fact, only two years before. These minor characters support the notion that the characters have a life before and outside the story and make the trick more possible.

THE GRAND REVELATION

This will be near the end of the story – but not quite at the end, or it might feel like the punchline to a joke or the answer to a riddle. In *The First Day*, the reader realises that Betsy is not Helena's daughter but her mother when Helena tells the care worker: 'my mother has come for her trial day.' But the parallel carries on a little longer. Helena says that she will collect Betsy at three, which is also school closing time, and she passes Betsy's hand to the carer as if she is the teacher in a school. The story ends with the line, 'The door was firmly closed', which evokes the feeling of exclusion that a mother might have on leaving her child at school for the first time – or a daughter leaving her mother at a care home. Similarly, in *Catching the Light*, the reader realises the truth when Harry's mother tells him, 'It's time for tea. Put your things away and wash your hands, please,' but the story continues further. The mother pretends to like the new pastel drawing but is actually fed up with all the artwork on the fridge, while the father wishes his son would 'just go out and kick a ball like a normal 12 year old.' After the truth is out, allow the story to exist briefly in the new reality.

GUIDANCE ON WRITING STORIES WITH A TWIST

- Decide what your story's twist will be so that you can build towards it.
- Choose a setting that you can describe convincingly, maybe somewhere you know well.
- Decide on two or three main characters. More minor characters can help to support the central lie.
- Choose a time frame. It is best to place this on one occasion (the real time in each of my stories is about 20 minutes) although, of course, there can be flashbacks and references to the past. Think of the season, time of day, weather, light.
- Start writing your story. Describe the location, then introduce the characters (there might be some dialogue) and start building your piece, including constant ambiguity to direct the reader in one (false) direction.
- Towards the end, but not quite at the end, reveal the truth and anticipate the reader's reaction: shock, surprise, amusement or satisfaction. Describe the new situation a little further.
- If you can, and this is hard to plan for, try to reveal a central truth about life. Jean Cocteau wrote that a writer is 'a liar who always speaks the truth.' If your story does not convey a deeper message, it is simply an exercise, a clever game. In

The First Day (inspired by visits to care homes for my mother, who had dementia) I was exploring the parallels between caring for children and caring for parents and how, over time, children and parents sometimes swap roles. In *Catching the Light*, I was interested in how children who are talented or gifted are not always appreciated by their families, as they are not acting the way that they are expected to at that age.

The First Day was published in *Wiltshire View* in 2014 and in *Salt's Best British Stories* (edited by Nicholas Royle) in 2015.

This article is dedicated to the memory of Hayley Davis, Tamar's cherished school friend who later lectured in Goldsmith's Department of English and Comparative Literature from 1991 to 2005.

COFFEE BEASTLY

AISHA JOHNSON

Long long slender back
Surround fields to move, covered in arms toe to head with a
wink outside of the scarf covering thick black curls
Dark smooth skin
Aviation flitters make up rooms of sweaty hands hung late
Imagine them pressed to the windows, yet another
destination
Sweaty is the beans turning inside of the palms of my hand
rigid lines engraved like a map I've walked to be here
They call this blue collared or white collared
Dress and Sense
The overseer is not a tribe of
This morning
Blood & thick ills running down dirt ridden alleys
Punters? Will there be? The clock of his watch, gather, collect,
gather to select
Glances through eye glass shaded rims to the fastest of
workers
Slow and steady is work and the sun is ablaze
Crops on land and scythe on sheaf
Difficult leaves
Tempting plane research and new love for gas
Culture vultures'
Cigarettes smoulder
Long flight is their press and stress
Welcome ending car buyers, platters, clatter and laden fruit
best picked lychees
In sheer tights, Louboutins clicking
Scent from the hills of their homes
Written is theirs, told is mine.
I seek and sit by my large stone of ground and clay
Mouth to mouth existence

Scent is on me around my fingertips, I imagine sniffing you by
the hotel pool
Strong coffee
The colour of my skin
Staring all black eyes behind lashes curled in curiosity
Seeing the chief accepting back the uncle who paid too much?
Many ladies by his side?
Did he dream of Stockings?
Laughter and a little tear from the sores
Binding bush green flourishing into my thoughts of you
Reminding my body of height not air miles
Buses to higher learning to pots to hunt, to stick fight
My might is strong taste on your lips, the fruit skins are
scattered sweet scents
Remembering us.

COMMENTARY

The first purpose-built coffee houses in England were
established in Oxford during the 1650s, taking inspiration from
Turkey. They earned the nickname 'Penny Universities' as they
attracted educated, well-to-do patrons who came to enjoy the
"mind-stimulating benefits of the beverage" (White 2018).

Coffee became so popular that in 1882 the Coffee Exchange
was established in New York, which later became the Coffee,
Sugar & Cocoa Exchange (United States Federal Trade
Commission 1954). The futures of coffee trading were and still
are predicted by brokers, with city traders negotiating prices
with the companies who import the coffee.

Today, the sustainability and ethics behind coffee is
increasingly important to consumers. Ethical trade companies
such as Fairtrade ensure that the workers get paid a reasonable
price for their hard and ongoing work to supply the Western
world. However some coffee workers and farmers continue to
be underpaid or exploited.

This poem came to me at a time of change and decision-
making. I was living in Newcastle, in the North of England, and it

was bitterly cold. Before starting to write in the morning, I would go to a small cafe close to Whitley Bay train station (which it's important to say with a Geordie drawl). The owner, a cheery Maltese gentleman named James, introduced me to a lot of different types of herbal teas before we got onto coffee (I think he was concerned for his clients' health).

The first was a coffee from Eritrea. It was so strong that I was buzzing for hours. In the corner of the cafe was a barrel, which sparked thoughts of import and the traders behind the coffee. It saddened me that the impact global capitalisation was having on the producers of cheap clothing could also be happening with coffee. The poem grew out of that.

I feel humanity can only go forward if we seek to understand each other beyond a point of interest: to know what lies behind our different cultures and to see that we are all one. I truly believe sitting down and chatting to someone can reveal so much more than hours and hours spent online. Also, that through artistic expression, we can get closer to finding the meaning behind our social actions and be inspired to make changes in our daily actions.

CREATIVE WRITING ACTIVITY FOR A SMALL GROUP

Step one:

Take a pen and paper and write a quick response to each of the questions or prompts below. If you can't answer the question personally, use your imagination:

NB: For children unfamiliar to coffee, you might ask them to interview a parent and/ or guardian.

- Do you remember the first cup of coffee you had? How did it make you feel?
- What effect does coffee have on you?
- What actions/memories do you associate coffee with?
- Look at the coffee in your cupboard, where was it produced?

Next, have a discussion with others in your group. Share your answers to the questions above and/or select one of the points below:

NB: For children, this could take the form of a research project.

- What is social mobility? Do those who cultivate the produce we buy have a right to social mobility? What might this look like for them?
- Would you be happy with that?
- What is ethical trade? Does it mean that we are alleviated of further responsibility?
- Does the feeling of being privileged make you want to travel and see how others live? Have you had an experience of this before? How did you feel? How do you feel now?
- What was the effect of the 'Coffee Beastly' poem on you? Do our personal stories have an impact on others?

Now we're going to write a story about a person working at a particular stage in the globalised commodities trade.

- In pairs, construct a character and decide what their role is, what their situation is, and what future plans they have. Think of someone who produces the beans for the coffee you make – or if you prefer, choose another product that you use regularly in your day-to-day life that is produced overseas.
- Present them to the rest of the group and answer any questions they have – in character, so you get into the role.
- Write a story about the character, individually or in your pairs.
- To finish, share your stories and discuss what you have learned. How does this make you feel? Will this affect your purchasing choices in future? Why do you think in the West we are so reliant on coffee? What could you do to

experience the same benefits of drinking coffee – without the coffee? What has your character taught you?

REFERENCES

United States Federal Trade Commission. Economic Report of the Investigation of Coffee Prices. 30 July, 1954. https://books.google.co.uk/books?id=JQsiitPqyMQC&dq=coffee+1882+exchange&source=gbs_navlinks_s (accessed 6 July, 2020).

White, Matthew. British Library. 21 June, 2018. https://www.bl.uk/restoration-18th-century-literature/articles/newspapers-gossip-and-coffee-house-culture (accessed 6 July, 2020).

WORKSHOP PROMPTS:
PROMOTING ACTIVE LEARNING

MARK KIRKBRIDE

The aim of this article is to demonstrate how the more learning that can be packed into workshop prompts and exercises, the greater the sense of discovery and therefore engagement among participants.

The prompts included here are all open prompts, as opposed to those of the 'Finish this sentence...' style, because I find they allow for greater originality both in idea and execution. Each can be used as a springboard to make something that is entirely the writer's own. Lately I've been fortunate to work with a group of very versatile writers in my role as arts facilitator for OPEN Ealing arts centre in West London and they've kindly donated work to illustrate some of the prompts.

Writing is a craft and, like any craft, we learn as much in the practice of it as we do in the theory. Yet what if the one can come wrapped in the other? Embedding elements of the learning process in the exercises and prompts allows participants to join the communion of writers down through the ages and make the key discoveries themselves.

The theory underpinning this approach is that a lesson learnt for oneself will always have more impact than information acquired second-hand. Rather than being told what works and what doesn't, the writers are trusted to make their own creative decisions, which places the learning firmly in the doing. For the workshop tutor, this means thinking critically about the creative process at the start rather than at the end, and determining not only what works, or doesn't, but why – a process of reflection that I find informs my own writing.

Active learning can be illustrated with a very simple example: characterisation for beginners. For a group new to creating fictional characters, I would get them to list five or six character traits for one individual along with a flaw that could have interesting consequences (e.g. impulsiveness, a short temper, perhaps a bit nosey), plus about the same number of physical characteristics, putting both lists in order of importance. Then I would get them to write a piece introducing this brand-new person to the reader as if they were describing him or her to a friend: mentioning each of their character's qualities, plus their appearance. When satisfied with what they'd written, I would ask them to write a second piece conveying as many of the same characteristics as possible, certainly the major ones, along with at least one physical detail, without describing their character at all. This would inevitably necessitate some class discussion as to how it would even be possible. Once they'd established that this meant through action and dialogue, I would get them to dramatise their character's traits in a scene using another character to bounce off. In order to produce some fireworks, ideally the second character would be the main character's opposite. Mutual lack of comprehension could lead to a misunderstanding, one-upmanship or even a full-blown argument. A prompt to get things going might be: *Two characters meet who haven't met in a long time, with consequences.*

If one asks which of the two approaches conveys more information, characterisation by description or characterisation by dramatisation, description wins. If one asks which is more enjoyable to read and works better for the purposes of fiction, dramatisation wins. It's also generally agreed that even just one bit of physical description, if memorable enough, is preferable to a whole list. The writers have demonstrated – to themselves – what works, what for, and why.

Another example would be dialogue for newer writers. Given that dialogue can only ever be an approximation of real speech, I'd get the class to discuss ways in which the messiness of real speech could be rendered without it becoming unreadable, for example hesitation, trailing off, contractions or swallowed words, incorrect vocabulary, mangled grammar, and non sequiturs. Then I would get them to use these cracks in the surface of dialogue to recreate the realness of speech while hinting at emotional depth beneath it with the prompt: *Two people are arguing about one thing, in the moment, but it soon becomes apparent that they're arguing about something much more deep-seated.* Given that adults very rarely say what they mean, dialogue is effectively the surface of emotions. The very chinks that make it seem real give glimpses of what's bubbling underneath – and this is often far more interesting. The threat or promise of undercurrents eventually surfacing provides tension and keeps one reading. The above prompt allows the class to discover for themselves that a lot of the ways in which one can recreate the realness of speech also provide glimpses of those deeper undercurrents. Once again, the learning is in the doing.

Although the whole point of signing up to a creative writing course is to study what works and the pitfalls to avoid, saving years of trial and error by relying on the experience of those who have learnt the hard way or been similarly taught, allowing new writers to work things out for themselves has huge benefits. If as much of the teaching as possible is contained in the prompts and exercises themselves, those present become active participants in their learning. Key points can always be reinforced in discussion and feedback but it is much better if the writers make the important discoveries for themselves. There will be a buzz about the class with everyone fully present and keen to make further breakthroughs on the back of their own efforts.

To get the creative juices flowing, I sometimes use the parlour game Consequences as an ice-breaker. Each writer adds an element to a single-sentence story, then folds the piece of paper to conceal their contribution and passes it on. Although this exercise has occasionally unravelled (literally), I am frequently amazed at the level of creativity brought to bear on the prompts themselves – with work produced straight off the cuff and under the clock. It is always a privilege hearing or reading these stories for the first time.

Below are some more exercises and writing prompts with learning designed in, which are suitable for writers with a wider range of experience across all creative writing contexts, together with examples courtesy of OPEN Ealing's writers.

Motivation and Character Arc

EXERCISE: *Your main character wants something that's the opposite of what they need. Which one do they get?*

With an outer want and an inner need, this task forces writers to think about motivation, character arc and the emotional journey, almost without even needing to use the terms, because the main character should have realised something or be changed by the end of the story.

Dialogue

These are some more dialogue-related tasks:

EXERCISE: *One half of a phone conversation. Write about someone on the phone trying to go about their business but clearly distracted by whatever the person at the other end is saying.*

This is good for practising the bits of action in between dialogue, with physical reactions to lines we can't see. One approach would be to write out the complete conversation and then cut half.

In her piece 'Driving', Samantha Stotland cleverly dispenses with the need for the physical reactions themselves because they're inferable from the speech:

> 'Hi! No, it's fine. I've finally got my phone set up for hands free in the car. I don't know why I didn't do it sooner, it's so easy. Oh, my love, why are you crying?'...
>
> 'He didn't! What a pig! I'm so sorry. Whoa – stop! ... No, it's fine. Some idiot just stepped on the zebra crossing. I nearly ran them over, but they leapt back.' ...
>
> 'How many women?! Don't you beep at me, I was indicating. Sorry, I am listening. So what did he say?' ...

'The Riviera? That'll be lovely for them this time of year. No, I know that's not the point. Please stop sobbing. Take a deep breath, try and calm down. … No, I'm still here. I didn't know they'd made that into a one-way road. But it is very narrow. There wasn't anywhere to turn around, but thankfully the other driver backed up and let me through. A couple of pedestrians looked a bit confused. Well, of course he'd say that to you…' …

'That's outrageous. He can't possibly expect you to move out and her move in. Wait, this isn't right. Oh, I see, somehow I'm on the ring road.' …

'How much?! That's simply not fair. Yes, yes, I know – you did everything at home. Ooh – I've missed my exit again. I think I've already been around twice.' …

'Sirens? Yes, I can hear them too. And there are flashing blue lights. Oh. They want me to pull over. No, I've no idea…'

EXERCISE: *Write a story with something vital left completely unsaid. It's there beneath almost every line but is never referred to overtly.*

This is an exercise in subtlety and restraint in dialogue. If suitable for the age group (given the subject matter), the obvious example for class discussion would be Ernest Hemingway's 'Hills Like White Elephants' with its third-person objective point of view.

Interior Monologue

EXERCISE: *Write a story in which a character's thoughts are totally at odds with what they say.*

An exercise such as this can take the fear out of writing interior monologue, with plenty of scope for individual interpretation, as in Kirstie Ferrett's story 'Words Unspoken':

There it was! The question I had been expecting all conversation, delivered brightly by my friend Helen and then left to hang in the air like the mic drop moment she believed it to be.

'Of course I'd love to be Nathan's Godmother,' I replied without hesitation.

I was glad she asked via a phone call so she couldn't see my bored, impassive expression …

God knows I was not meant to be a mother in any way, shape or form. My CEO position, designer wardrobe and liking of partying hard did not quite mesh with a squalling child…

I always imagined bets being placed on the moment I would finally crack at my lack of motherhood and weep inconsolably.

'What's so funny?' Helen asked, sharply bringing my attention back to the conversation…

I made my explanation based around feeling excited at the chance of a cuddle and that seemed to placate her …

The call ended and I made a note in my diary of the christening date. Looking at the notepad I had been doodling on I registered the scrawlings of graphite that had kept my right hand busy during the call …

In the darkness the computer monitor took on a mirror-like quality and reflected the pencil marks the right way round to read, 'I want a baby!'

Description

If description is ballast, some is needed to stop a story floating off completely but too much will weigh it down.
EXERCISE: *Write a story with the right amount of description needed – no more, no less – using either of the following two prompts:*
PROMPT 1: *Lost. Either someone is lost or someone has lost something.*

An example would be this piece by Karolina Perez Sima about finding one's way geographically and in language:

Click clack. Was that the sound shoes make in English? Or was it stomp stomp? She wasn't sure. Hers sounded more like toop toop in her head. Attached to her brain like a tapeworm to its host, her first language ripped flesh when she tried to remove it.

'Those things never translate, do they?' she thought, glancing between her phone and her surroundings. The map on her phone was leading her in circles, but she didn't mind. She was starved for the city, sampling the views.

The bricks around her were old. Mould in their cracks was timid yet persistent. The quasi-symmetrical structures alienated her, as if she were in an odd dream, recreating itself. The houses had been designed to look the same but now resembled a distorted mirror image, one wall caving in, finally giving up on its centuries' long history of bear and bull markets pulling and pushing it.

'How sad!' she thought, and kept walking. It was her new real and she had to place herself within it. 'Yes, "stomp, stomp"!' she said to herself like a madwoman, deciding this verb was stronger. She would be too, now that she was here.

The streets were filled with people, faces like compass needles, showing her the world...

PROMPT 2: *Forbidden territory. Your character enters a place when expressly told not to, and the consequences of that play out.*

Atmosphere and Setting

EXERCISE: *Write a story in which the setting is almost a character in its own right.*

PROMPT: *Hints of the past.*

This task helps demonstrate how effective setting is in establishing atmosphere, as amply illustrated by Lydia Stone's 'The Western Belle':

The Western Belle bobbed on her mooring in the gentle autumn breeze. She was the plainest and the littlest of the five pleasure craft that transported tourists up and down the river, and was often overlooked in the height of the season for the other boats with their shiny hulls, well-stocked on-board bars and fancy modern amenities.

But if you happened to be rowing past her at the equinox, and on a full moon, you might hear more than just the lapping of water on the buoys and the creaking of age-old wood.

As the sun set, Albert roped his dinghy to the side of the Western Belle and clambered aboard, running his gnarled fingers lovingly over her worn railings and tapping his feet on the faded blue deck. The moon emerged from behind a cloud, and the whispers began. They grew louder, into shouts, and then the ghostly gunners appeared, running down the deck firing their weapons in all directions. 'Get down! Get down!' they cried. Bombs whizzed past and crashed into the water causing the little boat to rock. Arms reached down and pulled swimmers aboard.

'Get off the beaches, come on! Come on!' they shouted. The engines started with a rumble.

If you were watching from the bank, all you would see would be Albert, his eyes closed, rocking back and forth on the deck. But Albert knew. He'd been there, at Omaha Beach, lived through it on this very vessel.

Brave old girl, he thought. We came through.

And he went below to pour himself a single malt from her poorly-stocked, tiny wooden bar.

Language

EXERCISE: *Write about one thing in terms of another. Use the language of one context in an unrelated context.*

This exercise is useful for turning the attention back on language and especially diction. JG Ballard's 'The Assassination Of John Fitzgerald Kennedy Considered As A Downhill Motor Race' can be used as an example. Ballard's story does exactly what it says in the title but this exercise can yield unexpected and extremely interesting results, as is the case with this excerpt from Laurie O'Garro's 'The Premiere':

By the summer of 2016, Prince Harry's frequent trips to Toronto, where Suits was filmed, were beginning to pique the interest of British newspapers.

'PRINCE TO STAR IN LEGAL DRAMA'

read one headline, while another said,

'ATTRACTIVE ACTRESS GIVES PRINCE ACTING LESSONS'

When the Prince was caught on camera in Los Angeles at a gala evening hosted by Tom Hanks and attended by Hollywood's own royalty, including Meghan Markle, the British public began to feel uneasy. The papers struck a more serious tone, wondering where his foray into the world of acting might be taking him, and whether it was a distraction from his charity work. Was it wise for him to take time out from his organisation of the 2017 Invictus Games to rub shoulders with the likes of Johnny Depp, they asked.

Speculation continued on and off about Harry's long-term plans, and there was talk of a move to the United States.

By late summer 2016, however, media interest shifted to predictions about what a post-Brexit Britain would look like and the forthcoming elections in the US. For now, Harry's private life and ambitions were yesterday's news and he was free to conduct his affairs in private. Or so he thought.

He of all people should have known that the tabloids' appetite for juicy gossip could not be sated by the goings and comings of Cameron and Trump. By the end of that year the lenses of the media were once again trained on him and he felt obliged to announce that he would be replacing Patrick J. Adams, the actor who plays Markle's love interest...

WILD WRITING:
CO-CREATIVE PRACTICES & INSPIRATIONS

HELEN MOORE

In this essay I offer ways to engage in what I call 'wild writing'. My approach stems from my practice as an ecopoet, socially engaged artist and Forest School leader, and my online mentoring work guiding people on co-creative writing journeys into deeper Nature connection. I outline what I mean by wild writing and co-creative practices, and share some key aspects of my methodology, developed through my 'Wild Ways to Writing' programme. I also offer two writing exercises for inspiring students to experience the natural world in ways they may have never previously done, and to write from those experiences as a group and individually.

UNDERSTANDING INSPIRATION & CO-CREATION

The word 'inspire' connects us with the breath and the air we share with all beings – inspiration being the insights, ideas and experiences we 'breathe in', and then, as educators, 'breathe into' others. And if inspiration is a prerequisite for unleashing creativity, this suggests that it, and the creative process it catalyses, are fundamentally collaborative experiences. We may write alone, but our inspiration derives from others, including the work of other writers.

Similarly a tree doesn't grow in a vacuum, but in response to light, soils, water, weather. And it interacts with others through mycorrhizal relationships between fungi and tree roots. Trees are also home to birds, creatures and insects, and may be supported in their reproduction through a range of symbiotic relationships. Co-creation is therefore at the heart of all experience: all beings are infinitely interconnected through the web of life, the ecosystems and communities we inhabit. A key concept for wild writing, co-creation is always more than just humans working together. Ultimately it can involve consciously working with whatever sense we have of the Universe, and/or the Divine.

APPROACHES TO WILD WRITING

Before attempting to inspire others, I suggest you engage with wild writing first. Be inspired, and this will allow you to guide the exercises more skilfully. I invite you to read the following with an eye to initially embarking on an adventure yourself. These approaches can then be adapted to suit the needs of your participants and the particular context in which you plan to work.

The first step towards wild writing is about switching off from our digital, human-made world, and establishing space in our often busy schedules for uninterrupted connection with the natural world. It's also about allowing the wilder aspects of our being to be stimulated and expressed; for us as 'humanimals' to drop into our creaturely bodies, using our five senses and other 'ways of knowing', which allow the rational mind to become less dominant. According to Bill Plotkin, there are five ways of knowing: sensing, feeling, imagining, intuiting and thinking. (Plotkin, 2003). Through them we can open up to the wild voices and natural languages around us, and, as William Wordsworth encouraged, let Nature be our teacher. At the same time we remember that we're Nature too – although we've been conditioned to think and behave otherwise.

In Indigenous cultures, and in many of the world's faith traditions, Nature is sacred, and all plants and creatures are recognised as sentient, ensouled like us. In our modern industrialised world, we generally think quite differently.

However, writers in the Romantic tradition resonated with this world-view – William Blake, for example, believed that 'every thing that lives is Holy'. (Blake, 1793) This English poet and artist living in eighteenth-century London witnessed the Industrial Revolution rapidly transforming the hills, meadows and river-systems of the English capital, and the construction of what he called 'dark, satanic mills', where adults and children often worked in terrible conditions. Blake criticised social injustice, including racism, and valued all life – even the 'little

Fly', to whom he apologises in one of his poems for having thoughtlessly swatted it. (Blake, 1794)

Wild writing begins with ensuring we have our writing tools (low tech only, so paper notebooks and pens/pencils), plus everything that supports our basic needs while we're out (waterproofs, warm layers, a flask of hot tea, a bottle of cold water, sunscreen, sunhat, walking stick, a mat to sit on, essential medications etc). Having taken care of the practicalities, we can drop into an extra-ordinary mode, where our being is freed to be wilder than usual. The intention we bring to our wild writing adventure helps this too. Try to stay open to what life wants to show you today.

In honouring this as a co-creative practice, we may choose to cross a metaphorical and literal threshold (a field gate, the entrance to a park, a footpath to a beach, lake or forest) to enter into sacred time and space for experiencing and expressing Soul – our own and the ensouled world we inhabit. Try to avoid speaking to anyone you encounter – a nod or a smile can suffice. If appropriate, you can also allow yourself to feel drawn to paths, places, and other-than-human beings – see this as an enchanted journey on which you're guided to follow.

WILD WRITING ITSELF

Before beginning any writing, we allow ourselves simply to be. To shed the stresses of our day, we may need to shake the body and slow down – literally slowing our walking pace, with our steps following the rhythm of our breathing. Entering a more meditative state, and allowing our mental chatter to subside, our bodies can soften, and our senses may then receive more information about the world we're moving in: the breeze and textures reaching our skin, the scents wafting into our nostrils, the taste of the air, the sounds in our ears, the colours, shapes and patterns before our eyes. The poet Ezra Pound described artists as 'the antennae of the race', so we too can become an antenna, picking up signals, signs, wild language. We allow associations, intuitions and wild imaginings to arise in response to these stimuli – giving them all house-room. For example, we

166

may look up and notice a cloud in the shape of a creature, and we see that without any judgement, as a child might.

Open to your intuitive guidance as to when to take out your pen and notebook. And when you do, you're simply splurging, not trying to shape a poem or story, just letting the words come, reassuring any judgemental voices inside that you don't need their advice (you can access your inner editor at a later stage). Forget spelling, punctuation, grammar. Open to hearing the quiet inner voice guiding the words, and let them fall onto the page, like beads on a string.

Let your language be wildish, if it feels right. Perhaps the word to describe the texture of the tree bark you're gazing at doesn't quite exist, so invent one. Play around. And if you feel stuck, ask yourself questions, and try to answer them. You could also use the prompts that follow to nudge your consciousness. Keep trusting that the words will come. At this stage it's not about getting it 'right', just about getting it written! When it's time to conclude, you could mark the ending in some way, giving thanks for the experience, and crossing back over the threshold into ordinary life.

In subsequently going about your day, stay open to thoughts, feelings, sensations, associations, memories and dreams. Inspiration arises at any time, and we learn to honour such promptings. Leave your notes a while, and return when you feel ready. Read them with an open mind and heart. Look for the seeds of a poem or story, the kernel of an idea you'd like to develop. Spend time with that, perhaps collaging in lines from your notes. Remain open to where this goes. If you can, come back to it again, polishing it further, asking yourself if your language and imagery communicate the feelings and pictures you have internally. And now you can let your inner editor check the spelling and grammar, and perhaps shape the form of the words on the page. This, and perhaps subsequent edits, will enable you to complete a piece of wild writing.

TWO EXERCISES FOR ENGAGING A GROUP

Even in urban spaces, access to a mature tree is usually possible, so begin by choosing one that your group can readily reach, preferably with a walk so that they can make some of the transitions outlined above. Before you set off, spend time preparing the group for this exercise by eliciting a pool of tree knowledge: different species; their life-cycle and longevity; their role in ecosystems and as oxygenators of the atmosphere; the biodiversity they support. Invite other knowing too: trees sacred in other cultures, trees in mythology, trees used for timber. And the students' own experiences too: favourite trees they've explored or climbed; tree-top walks; tree-houses; Christmas trees. You could also read some tree poems: for example, Robert Frost's 'Tree At My Window', or Charlotte Mew's 'The Trees are Down'. Or you could use my poem, which traces the history of a mahogany rocking chair. (Moore, 2015)

A HISTORY OF THE BRITISH EMPIRE IN A SINGLE OBJECT

> "The first axiom for camp is… do not make yourself uncomfortable for want of things to which you are accustomed" – Complete Indian Housekeeper and Cook, 1890

I own a Victorian rocking-chair that folds –
a piece of 'campaign furniture'
with which the British Empire was built.
Rockers bear me on a curved sled
mental-travelling across continents,
the seat a plugged lip, which speaks
of indigenous peoples, the hidden values of the antique.
Had I at any moment considered
Mahogany as tree
a glittering crown which rose above
gargantuan forest skirts? How it began as minute heliotrope
hooked up to the light?
How in dry seasons Mahoganies
would shed their glossy leaves,

baring pugilistic fruit-fists
that were tanned & leathered –
trade winds pummelling out their seeds
spinning them away
to wait for germinating rains?
Nor had my thoughts flown to the Scarlet Macaw
whose crack beak could winkle seeds
from inside those fibrous pericarps;
nor had I walked with tedium-drilled officers
in backabush British Honduras – men who hunted
for sport; who'd have some old Creole bake a pie
with five hundred Parrot tongues.
In those rainforests,

which the Maya knew as distinctly as kin,
Peccaries wandered, rubbing their scent
against giant buttresses – Mahoganies with girths
wider than the lengths of three prone men.
                              O, Nine Benevolent Spirits!
O, Maya healers, who observed the Moon's phases;
the motion of bitter sap to trunk or roots;
the absence of dew; and who gathered herbs for teas,
poultices, decoctions. Caoba, Copal, Trumpet Tree,
Sapodilla fruits beloved of Tapir, Paca, Agouti….
                              O, brutal British axe!
Like convicts at Tyburn, Mahoganies
were quartered, stacked by the tonne for transportation.
Lying below decks, as if so many wounded slaves
piled one above the other, their timbers shifted, creaked,
sap oozing from their fibres.
Then all along the docks, the esteemed furniture-makers
came tapping their canes –
frock-coated men puffed with Honourable
East India Company business,
fingers chiselling at the blood-orange grain,
society minds prizing the exotic wood's
workability, its resistance to decay.

Soon it would be fed to their workers' lathes & planes –
Hillard & Meal, of Craven Street, Strand,
crafting the secrétaires, the sofa-beds,
the travelling rent tables, washstands & chiffoniers
which flaunted comfort & prestige
for Empire's executors.   O, Bengal, Scinde, Lucknow!
In this metamorphic chair,
from which a Captain's wife might have come to extol
their crinolined infant, I rock the souls of all those generations
consumed by duty –
Governor-Generals functioning from the collar up;
officers' hearts locked in strong-boxes,
tear-ducts dry as husks;
civil servants melting over pink-tinted maps;
men like living stiffs with swordsticks;
men most at home with mess silver & big-game trophies;
men who had no intimate equals –
womenfolk pecking, preening their clipped wings,
and their mute, invisible offspring.
O, white folk with your self-invoked burden
of superiority –
all this furniture of an expanding state.

Having done this groundwork, leave it behind – hopefully everyone's now primed. Then ready your participants, and set out to meet your chosen tree. When you reach it, invite everyone to explore it silently with their senses. After a few minutes re-assemble the group and explain you're going to make a collage poem composed of their words. Invite everyone to take up different positions – at the edges of the canopy, close to the trunk, down by the roots, in the tree's branches (if it's safe to climb), and lying below it. Tell them you'll collect a line from each of them about what they're experiencing from their place. Gather these lines as quietly as possible, noting down the words verbatim. Having done this, re-assemble and read out the lines. They can later be re-collaged and edited, but often there's a magical process whereby a poem emerges from the order in which the lines were given.

Next ask your students to spread out and settle in a place where they can observe the tree undisturbed by anyone else. Tell them they're going to engage in 'interspecies communication', which means telepathically communicating with the tree. To do this they'll need to suspend any doubts about whether this is scientifically possible – although you might mention an experiment with two plants of the same species kept in exactly the same conditions, where one was systematically bullied by schoolchildren and the other was constantly praised, with the results being that after a month the plants were in noticeably varied conditions – the bullied plant wilted and half-dead, and the one that had been praised looking vigorous and healthy. [7]

To initiate this dialogue, ask your students to silently introduce themselves to the tree, explaining their intention. Now invite them to use their senses to observe it, including its connection with place, before internally relaying to the tree what they're noticing. Engaging their imagination and intuition, invite them to contemplate this tree's experiences, what the tree may feel or sense in this moment, and perhaps more generally in life, including how human activity may affect it. Invite the students to silently communicate this to the tree and anything else that feels relevant.

Now ask them to open their minds to the idea that the tree can communicate back. Has it noticed anything about them? Offer the students a few minutes with their eyes closed and mind relaxed to allow the possibility of communication to occur. When there's nothing more to be said in either direction, invite the students to inwardly thank the tree, and then to write down everything they've experienced. Some may find this exercise hard, and if so, extend them empathy – we've all been conditioned by Western culture to believe primarily in the rationality of the mind, the empiricism of the senses, and the measurability of the material world. It may then be appropriate to regroup and share some writings before leaving, or you could simply ask the students what they experienced. Remind everyone that their writings are just creative splurges, and can be further edited and honed at a later stage.

FURTHER DEVELOPMENT

Wild writing in the form of regular Nature journaling can be a brilliant tool for deepening our connection with place. It also develops our ecoliteracy, which is an important skill for our future. At this time of global ecological crises, our survival as a species requires us to work collectively to regenerate and rewild our local ecosystems as we adapt to and mitigate the impacts of climate breakdown. In my experience, a co-creative practice of wild writing can simultaneously build our emotional and psychological resilience to face the challenges of being human in the 21st century.

Endnote: In my ecopoetic practice, I capitalise the proper names of other-than-human beings and phenomena to raise them from the margins to which Western scientific-materialist culture has relegated them.

REFERENCES

Blake, William (1793) America, A Prophecy. From The Complete Poetry and Prose of William Blake: With a New Foreword and Commentary by Harold Bloom, ed. Erdman, David. V. (University of California Press, 2008.

Blake, William (1794) 'The Fly' in Songs of Experience. From The Complete Poetry and Prose of William Blake: With a New Foreword and Commentary by Harold Bloom, ed. Erdman, David. V. (University of California Press, 2008.

IKEA UAE (2018). Bully A Plant: Say No To Bullying, viewed 29 October 2020, https://www.youtube.com/watch?v=Yx6UgfQreYY

Moore, Helen (2015) ECOZOA, Permanent Publications

Plotkin, Bill (2003) Soulcraft: Crossing into the Mysteries of Nature and Psyche, New World Library

VOICES DURING QUARANTINE:
AN EXPLORATION OF HOW CREATIVE WRITING CAN BECOME A HEALING TOOL IN TRAUMATIC TIMES

JUWAIRIAH MUSSA

DAY 1 – LOCKDOWN

We are in lockdown. Now that I am in it, I am not too sure I want to be. I am a busy person. I am worried about how I will cope now my life has come to a grinding halt. I can use this time to write. Will it deliver the stillness I require?
April, May and June were meant to be hectic months for me and I was gearing myself up for it. Ramadhan, university deadlines and work were going to leave me with little to no time for anything else. How will it be now? I don't want to feel trapped.
I'm not sure I trust Boris to see us through this. I haven't forgotten that he called Muslim women letterboxes. Do we have to forgive that now the virus had intruded?

DAY 1 – RESPONSE

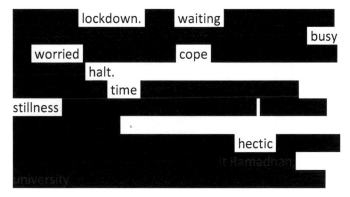

no time How will it be now? feel trapped. trust Boris letterboxes. forgive the virus

I have always suffered from anxiety; it creeps up on me when I am idle. Therefore, I tend to keep busy. I surround myself with friends and family during my free time, and work hard at other times to keep it at bay. However, as soon as the lockdown was announced, I began to feel the anxiety creep in. I was worried about the restrictions we would face, and how I would manage. I decided to throw myself into a project to keep occupied: to do some life writing in the form of a daily journal, to help manage my daily thoughts and concerns and reduce my anxiety level.

In this essay, I will highlight the use of creative writing as a healing tool during traumatic times. I will discuss my own experience of writing a journal during the Covid-19 lockdown, and my journey of healing. I will also explore the work of other researchers who have highlighted their own experiences and findings in regards to using creative writing as a healing tool.

DAY X – LAUNDRY DAY

The lockdown has stolen my voice. I am not able to write poetry. Instead I write a journal. It is meant to be a daily journal, but days blur and I have lost my sense of time.
Sundays are now the new Mondays. Laundry day is no longer Wednesday but now Friday. Our Friday night routine of takeaway and a movie has been cancelled. It hasn't been rescheduled.

When will you give me my week back?

Journal writing is a reflective way in which individuals can express themselves in short bursts. It is often used to take account of daily experiences, personal thoughts and evolving insights (Hiemstra, 2001). There are various ways that individuals can journal, from writing in a physical diary to making notes on a phone.

At first I was apprehensive. I was unable to switch off the writer's voice within. However as the days unfolded, I began to look forward to this precious time set aside for me to unravel my thoughts and feelings. I found I would no longer spend hours fixating on my anxieties, but instead reserve them for the pages of my diary.

After a week, my anxiety levels decreased dramatically. I could compartmentalise my worries and look at them from the perspective of an outsider. It helped simplify the situations I was dealing with, and many concerns that were previously overwhelming seemed trivial when written down. They no longer felt like a cloud above my head, but were merely accounts of my day tucked safely into my diary.

Being able to reflect when writing can have an impact on brain activity and ultimately improve physical and mental wellbeing. Pennebaker (1990) researched brainwave activity before and after 'confessions' (or narratives) of trauma. His research indicated that upon disclosure of 'deeply personal experiences, brain wave patterns became congruent and other positive physiological changes occurred as well, including improved immune function, reduced blood pressure and heart rate' (p. 66). I began to understand the power of narrative and the healing it offers. After I had written down an emotion in my diary, I had processed it and could move on. Using a narrative to express their thoughts and feelings, or simply writing down their account of events, can allow individuals to process and analyse what they are experiencing. It can help you work your way through a problem by using personal insights and reflections (Pennebaker, 1990).

DAY X – THE HORSE CAME TO VISIT

There's a man on a horse outside my window.
I live in London. Not in the countryside.
Is he taking his horse for a walk?
Where does the horse reside?
Why is it out on the street?
Is the horse making the most of the lockdown?
Is the horse taking the man for a walk?
Please come back Horse

Pennebaker created a study in which university students were separated into two groups. Over four days, one group was asked to write about a trivial topic, whilst the other group were tasked to write about a traumatic event in their life. There was a very positive response from the latter group. Although many cried due to the overwhelming nature of their writing, 98 percent stated that they would be happy to participate again. The study also found that those who wrote poorly in other academic work, wrote eloquently when writing about their own personal tragedies (Pennebaker, 2000).

Writing can also help people digest their experiences. Pennebaker concluded that, 'when people are asked to write about emotional upheavals for 15–20 minutes on at least three separate occasions, their health improves' (Pennebaker 2010, p.23). Many health conditions are related to stress. Reducing that stress for the students within the study ultimately increased wellbeing, and even helped to reduce doctor visits.

As the weeks unfolded, I noticed the content of my diaries began to change. They were no longer focused solely on my thoughts during lockdown but extended to commenting on wider society. I reacted to breaking news. I read journal entries that were shared with me by other poets and writers and responded to them. Some entries were turning in poetic pieces, and I was grateful to have my voice back. I had been struggling to write poetry. Writing journal entries helped me overcome my writer's block. The ability to express themselves freely, allows writers to be less critical and more open to their creativity (Hiemstra, 2001).

DAY X – COLOURING THE VIRUS

Read that Black Britons are nearly twice as likely to die from COVID than white people.
People from Indian, Bangladeshi and Pakistani communities also had a significantly higher risk of dying. Apparently, it's down to socio and economic factors. To me it means people of colour are dying because we are poorer. Is there now a price on this virus? That if you are rich enough you are more likely to survive.
I'm tired, that everything around us revolves around the colour of our skin. Even the virus.

DAY 40 – COLOURING THE VIRUS RESPONSE

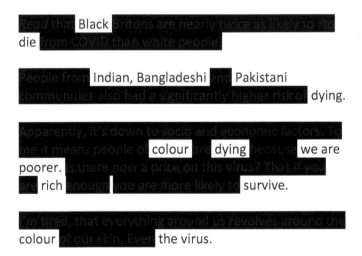

Read that Black Britons are nearly twice as likely to die die from COVID than white people.

People from Indian, Bangladeshi and Pakistani communities also had a significantly higher risk of dying.

Apparently, it's down to socio and economic factors. To me it means people of colour are dying because we are poorer. Is there now a price on this virus? That if you are rich enough you are more likely to survive.

I'm tired, that everything around us revolves around the colour of our skin. Even the virus.

we don't want to die
this virus feeds on brown skin
will you stain us white?

Giving myself the permission and space to write daily, privately and freely during a traumatic time allowed me to process the world around me – and adapt my writing to 'the new normal'. Found poetry forced me to work with the content I had, further adding to the containment I felt within the lockdown. The restriction of syllables used in a haiku beautifully followed this theme of restriction and containment.

Poetry can help bring a sense of relief during traumatic events. An example of this was after 9/11:

> A *New York Times* article on October 1, 2001, documented the phenomenon: "In the weeks since the terrorist attacks, people have been consoling themselves—and one another—with poetry in an almost unprecedented way … Improvised memorials often conceived around poems sprang up all over the city, in store windows, at bus stops, in Washington Square Park, Brooklyn Heights, and elsewhere. Robert Carroll

Poetry also enables people to connect, relate and understand. It gives the writer space in which they can freely express themselves – without fear of judgement – and explore topics such as heartbreak, death and mental health that many individuals shy away from talking about. McArdle & Byrt (2001) defined poetry therapy as the 'intentional use of poetry for healing and personal growth' (p. 521). In a pilot study, poetry writing was used as a part of an 'Arts on Prescription' programme to help mitigate anxiety and depression, and reduce dependence on antidepressants (McArdle & Byrt, 2001).

Turning my journals into poetry has helped me explore my own emotions. It has reduced my anxiety and enabled personal growth. I turned negative experiences into positive ones, and boosted my self-esteem by empowering my words. I spoke about issues that were buried within me, an example of that was body image.

DAY X – BODY SLAM

> Today I do not love my body. I saw pictures of myself as an 18-year-old. I believe I was beautiful then, because I was slimmer. But back then, I did not feel beautiful because I thought I was fatter.
> Some days I feel as though I am too pale to be Indian, other days I am too brown to be anything else.
> In fleeting moments, I find myself to be beautiful. On the days I can feel collarbones and ribs. Those days are far and few between.

Although it was healing to write those thoughts down, I wanted to turn those critical perceptions of my own body into something positive. I did this by using the technique of found poetry.

DAY X – BODY SLAM RESPONSE

This proved to be very cathartic. It allowed me to see myself differently and reaffirmed that I have the power to change how I see myself. If I could change a few words to dramatically change the meaning of a sentence, I could ultimately change how I decided to digest those words. It gave me a sense of control over my feelings.

I was also writing about big life decisions. Writing these thoughts down was helping me become more decisive. One example of this was my career: my work contract was coming to an end and I was offered an extension of employment. However I was unsure if I wanted to continue working for the organisation. This decision was a burden on my shoulders.

I decided to write down my thoughts regarding the decision. I noted down all the positives and negatives, and then I left the writing. Coming back to it the next day, I was able to make a strong final decision. Writing down my thoughts and feelings had helped me to simplify my narrative and see what I wanted more clearly.

DAY X – CAREER BONANZA

This lockdown has helped me gather my thoughts. Sometimes it forces me to address parts of my life which I ignore; such as my career. I have always loved working two-part time jobs. One in an office working for a charity and one within a classroom as a facilitator. I couldn't work within a classroom full time nor could I work in an office full time. I need a balance of both. All I know is I like to work for an organisation I care about. I like to help others, both within the classroom and within the charity.

All I know for sure right now is I need a holiday.

Enabling students to write openly about their thoughts on careers and work experiences can similarly help them to think about and plan their future. 'Career writing engages them creatively, inviting both emotional and cognitive explorations of what is meaningful to them, how they might serve others, and what they might do to set a flexible course' (Lengelle, 2014).

Writing creatively can help them to focus their energy and time on a particular subject area or goal.

Creative writing is not given enough importance within academic settings. Students are often encouraged to sharpen their writing skills for academic essays and exams, while poetry and journal writing are regarded as hobbies or extracurricular activities. However, throughout this research I have personally witnessed the powerful element of healing through poetry – as well as its positive impact on personal development. This must be valued.

I believe creative writing as a healing tool can be particularly beneficial to marginalised groups too, including those who have experienced traumatic events or are vulnerable, and who would benefit greatly from expressing their own narratives. As a BAME, Muslim woman, I believe there is a great need for more voices from within my own community to be heard. Muslim women are often spoken for and are fearful of being judged and stereotyped. These are burdens that we carry heavily and they ultimately impact our mental and physical wellbeing. I would like to offer a safe space where such groups can express themselves and reap the healing benefits of creative writing.

DAY 1 – RAMADHAN

We have spotted the crescent moon and it's Ramadhan. But my family and I are spread across London. I miss the communal feasts and my mother's cooking. I wonder if I will connect more this year?

...

The mosques will be shut. There will be no congregational prayers, no bowing or prostration in union. That saddens me.

Fasting has given me a sense of clarity. As though I am rebooting my body, as the world is rebooting itself. Together we will be new.

DAY 1 – RAMADHAN RESPONSE (HAIKU)

forehead to the earth
pleading for the globe to mend
Ramadan is near

I have outlined various researches that show the therapeutic healing qualities of creative writing to support my belief in using creative writing as a tool to heal. I have also shown how the process of writing a daily journal during lockdown has been an extremely rewarding and eye-opening experience for me. It has highlighted the positive impact that creative writing has on me, especially during uncertain and traumatic times; helped relieve bouts of anxiety that I faced; and channelled my energy into creativity.

My journal entries were extremely varied, showcasing the depth of my own emotions during this period. I discussed various topics, ranging from heavy, taboo subjects such as death, body image and racism, to light-hearted topics such as pancakes and horses. I have managed to pour my deepest concerns into pages of writing, morphing them into peaceful poetry. I have been able to process my own emotions, and observe them from a reader's perspective. It has been a journey of reflection, observation and, above all, healing.

FIVE CREATIVE WRITING PROMPTS TO HELP HEALING

1.   Ask participants to (in pairs) discuss their own personal experiences with journal writing and healing. If they haven't written a journal previously, then discuss their thoughts on it and the impact it can have.

2.   Ask participants to write continuously for three minutes responding to the prompt, 'I've been carrying this around for a long time'. Remind them to write whatever comes into their head, as this will help them to write freely and open up.

3. Found poetry: Print out journal entries of other poets and writers and instruct participants to use these printouts to create a poem. They can do this by cutting out particular words or sentences and sticking them together to form lines of poetry.

4. Ask participants to write about difficult situations in their lives and how each impacted them negatively. Then ask them to cross out this writing and beside each situation write how it has benefited or changed them positively, or what it has taught them.

5. Ask participants to write a letter to themselves at a time when they were going through a difficult time. What would they tell themselves, what advice would they give?

WE ALL HAVE TALENT

NEIL NIXON

This work is drawn from my experience running the UK's first undergraduate programme in Professional Writing. The course, which ran from 1999 to 2019, concentrated on helping students identify and apply their varied talents. What follows is a distillation of the exercise in understanding individual creativity that formed my first classroom session for the incoming first years on that course. I believe this could be relevant to a school classroom setting, particularly with school leavers looking to better understand their creative strengths.

INTRODUCTION

What we're considering in this chapter is individual creativity, and how it appears in writing. The first thing to note is that definitions of what it means to be 'creative' and definitions of what it means to 'write' vary a lot. All we can usefully do in this chapter is be honest about our definitions. Creativity, as far as I am concerned, is using your imagination to create something. Writing is employing words and ideas in the act of creating something.

Years of work and many studies have attempted to understand creativity, so a great deal is known. But it is worth noting that most studies have an inbuilt weakness because they tend to study people who are already understood to be creative (writers, artists, musicians etc.) As technology changes and what we understand as creative work changes with it, the skills we celebrate also change. At the extreme end of this, social media has turned a number of household pets into worldwide stars, sometimes because videos of them performing simple tricks can amuse people for a short time. The pets often demonstrate creativity in making decisions about how to do something, but they can't begin to understand they are performing on platforms such as YouTube for massive audiences all round the world. The creativity that puts them online is often an act of imagination from someone considering how to organize the animal – in other words how long the video should be, the right angle to film and just what content to include.

A lot is known and understood about being creative. Some of the most serious investigations into this started in the United States in the 1950s. The country had massive creative industries such as film, advertising and publishing making huge amounts of money and a number of people became interested in understanding what made the talents in their creative industries so successful. One of the first serious researchers in the subject was J P (Joy Paul) Guildford. He completed several studies and published papers, including one identifying the traits of highly creative people. A 'trait' is a distinguishing quality. In other words, slightly more complicated than a skill but often something a person can do naturally, without thinking about it. Of course, the traits discovered have been used by people throughout human history. For example, most of us have the ability to imagine things that haven't happened, or suggest something that makes others laugh. Guilford and the mass of researchers who followed help us to understand in detail how these natural human traits can be used to make creative work. A simple list of years of findings suggests people in the creative industries can often do the following very well:

- Generate ideas around a theme
- Think laterally and flexibly
- Develop, embellish and conceive of the outcome of an idea
- Focus and organize an idea

It's important to note that you don't need all these traits to work creatively. In fact, a lot of very successful people succeed on the back of using one creative trait. Put simply, the traits above help us explain some of the basics of what it means to be creative. Creativity itself has also been studied with a number of important investigations, including one by the researchers Besemer and Treffinger in 1981. Their work identified aspects of what helps to define a creative achievement. It often includes:

- Novelty: The newness of an idea in terms of process, techniques and application.
- Resolution: The extent to which an idea resolves a situation.
- Synthesis: The extent to which an idea combines elements which are unalike into a coherent whole.

The points above are simply the basics of understanding creativity. I'm making no apologies for avoiding the complexities that followed this research, because the purpose here is to establish a few ground rules and get started on exploring creativity by doing something. One truth often ignored by those investigating creativity and reporting on their findings is that most professional employed creative people, including writers, got to their positions without making a study of creativity. They achieved most of their success by getting on with their work and applying their talents.

THE RESEARCH IN ACTION

Nowadays, people trying to write for a living often undertake training that includes specialist college courses. Extended diplomas in areas such as media studies include units in which industry-specific skills are combined with creative projects, allowing students to demonstrate learning by producing their own work. The industries employing writers recognize these qualifications and are used to reading, listening to and watching the portfolio material produced by these students. It wasn't always like this. One exercise I used for years with Professional Writing undergraduates went back to the days before specialist education for the creative industries, when variations on a 'copy test' were used in many advertising agencies. Agencies and employers may no longer feel the need for these exercises in identifying specific creative skills, but one place I found they worked very well was on day one, lesson one of a course designed to make students employable and confident in their employment choices.

The copy test I gave out would look something like this.

Copy Test

- Describe toast to a space alien (maximum 50 words).
- You have two identical cans of Heinz Baked Beans. Persuade someone to buy the one in your left hand.
- You have no money, no mobile phone and no credit cards. Describe how you will spend a day in Belgium.
- Describe the colour blue to a blind person.
- Write a notice asking members of a country club to shower before using the swimming pool.
- Create an advert for a pair of indestructible socks OR a car that runs on air.
- Describe your face to someone who will never see it.
- Write a poem of any length that scans perfectly but contains no rhymes.

If using this exercise in class, I would suggest imposing a time limit of half an hour to 45 minutes. Each question tests a particular creative attribute or skill. Afterwards, it is useful for the students to reflect on questions they found easy to engage with and ones they struggled with. To help with this I would then share a handout explaining the purpose of the questions, along the lines of the explanations below.

Toast: This is about generating ideas around a theme. It also tests your ability to get 'novelty' into a message. If you found this easy and came up with a range of different approaches you may well have potential to work in any area demanding a high turnover of ideas. Advertising agencies used this question to test for people who could see familiar products and services in a new way. Over the years I've seen answers from students that describe toast as 'human fuel, simple and effective'. I've also seen clever scientific answers that talk about its food value, and others that link it to a time and place, normally explaining it as part of breakfast.

Tins of Beans: This is about creating 'differentiation', finding differences where none appear to exist. The question demands resolution. Someone who delights in this question is often very good at planning creatively. A good journalist would probably cope well with this question. Useful answers to this question include selling the tin in your left hand because you think it once belonged to a celebrity. You can also sell it with a personal endorsement; 'I love beans. I'll make your life better by sharing this love.'

No money, mobile phone: The question is looking for synthesis and resolution. Your initial reaction to the question should give you some insight into how best your creative talents can be applied. I've seen 'commit a small crime and I get deported' answers, indicating maverick talents who probably aren't team-players. I've also seen notions about going to the police and being honest about the problem, suggesting practically minded but less original thinkers.

Blue to a blind person: Any successful answer here needs focus and also the ability to think laterally (i.e. around a problem). Novelty, synthesis and resolution are tested. It's also a test of generating ideas, finding differentiation, conceiving of the outcome of an idea and finding focus and organization. And, on top of those challenges, some human empathy goes a long way here. Successful strategies often revolve around finding some object or experience that has the same qualities as the colour. Advertising agencies often used red (which people found easier to describe) as the colour in the question.

Country Club Notice: In all the years of using copy test questions with groups, this question (or variations on it) have caused the most problems. Many people simply miss the reference to the country club and, with it, miss the creative challenge of the question. This tests the usual creative skills but the focus is on attention to detail. It's a country club (suggesting membership fees, members used to being treated with respect etc). Along with creative skills, this is about precision and organization, which are vital in certain areas of creative work and creative writing.

Indestructible socks, car that runs on air: The key point here is that the world *has* changed. These impossible products would bring about a difference to most of our lives. Breakthroughs in technology do sometimes change the world. Sudden changes in the world were often hard to grasp for young people in a class. In the aftermath of the Coronavirus outbreak, this notion is now easier to understand. A range of traits and abilities are under test but this question really pushes the ability to imagine the end of something. Since, in reality, this hasn't happened in our world, the question helps identify people who can confidently imagine a change *before* it occurs. I once came up with a storyboard for the indestructible socks. In my idea, a young man in a suit shuffles into a room with bare walls and seats, another young man comes to meet him. They are obviously uncomfortable. They exchange a little conversation until it becomes obvious that one man is picking up the ashes of his grandfather from a crematorium. Having got the box of ashes, he turns to leave, only for the other man to hold up a pair of socks and ask; "What do we do with these?"

Your face: This is a difficult act of synthesis. A right answer here needs some self-knowledge, some sign that you are able to see yourself the way others see you, and the ability to generate ideas around the theme. On top of all that, it needs the kind of editing skills seen in the country-club notice and the ability to be focused and not ramble on about yourself. Above all, tackling this effectively means uniting the skills and traits with creative writing skills.

Poem of any length that scans perfectly but contains no rhymes. This is a test of your sense of balance, timing and rhythm in writing. It demands creative skills, organizational ability and intelligence. The usefulness of the question to advertising is obvious. Catchy and memorable slogans get products and services noticed. The skill of summarizing a complicated idea in a few words, and also grabbing attention, can earn a writer good money. One famous former advertising copywriter is novelist Salman Rushdie. Rushdie won the Booker Prize for his novel *Midnight's Children* and when the Booker Prize had produced 40 years of winners, Rushdie's novel was voted the best winning book in that period – a unique award. For all this success, it is likely the best-known words he ever wrote are still the three that formed the slogan for a hugely successful advertising campaign for cream cakes: 'Naughty. But nice.' In fact, Rushdie's words repeat the title of a 1939 movie but the expertly placed punctuation allows for a very different emphasis on 'naughty' and 'but nice', which was key to the success of the adverts. He also coined the word 'Irresistibubble', which was used to advertise Aero chocolate bars.

SO WHAT?

Variations of this copy test exercise were used throughout the 20 years in which I ran the Professional Writing course. The next target the students faced was an assignment requiring them to make a professional contact and prove they'd done some work for that contact. Their understanding of the creative skills they used in completing this assignment was informed by the material they generated in completing their copy test. I often discussed ways of identifying creative skills by throwing in examples from my own life. One such was a series of phone calls I received in my staffroom many years ago, all from the editor of a comedy magazine I'd started writing for. I rang back, far from pleased, asking why he kept bothering me. He replied saying every time he chased me, I sent more copy. That near-argument taught me something important. I was productive. I might not have been any funnier than his other writers but he cared more about the way I kept generating ideas because his biggest worry was having enough work to fill a magazine every month. In other words, I was showing the skill tested in the first copy test question. I used these examples from my own life to get students to discuss times they'd done some creative thing well and consider what skills they could identify as a result. All of which started discussions we could build on in the coming weeks.

REFERENCES

J P Guilford - Creative Talents: Their Nature, Uses and Development - Bearly Limited, 1986
Susan P. Besemer and Donald J. Treffinger - Analysis of Creative Products: Review and Synthesis – Journal of Creative Behavior Volume 15 Number 3 Third Quarter, 1981

THE REALITY OF FANTASY
AN INVESTIGATION INTO WRITING FANTASY GENRE FICTION

MATILDA ROSTANT

The aim of this research is to investigate how I, as a child, approached writing fantasy genre fiction. I have used this auto-ethnographic introspection to suggest ways in which fantasy writing can be incorporated in classrooms.

INTRODUCTION

The fantasy genre is incredibly popular, particularly with school age children. Personally, writing fantasy has been my greatest passion since I was four. It gave me an outlet to express myself and escape from reality. However, at times, I was given the impression that my fantasy writer's self should exist separately from my more academic self, as what I write is considered 'genre fiction'.

The genre of fantasy is "difficult to articulate or to define" (Jackson, 1981:1) because anything that is not reality can be considered fantasy. With that in mind, all fiction is to one extent fantasy (Jackson, 1981:13), so we need to investigate further what the genre entails. Common components of the fantasy genre are often "dragons, wizards, heroes etc. – and the narrative techniques – elevated diction, names with too many consonants, lots of capital letters, maps" (Coats, 2018: 346) and it originates from folklore and fairytales (Cart, 2016: 98).

What draws me to fantasy is the "wonderful blend of action, strong characters, and detailed, atmospheric settings." (Burcher et al, 2009: 227) As a writer, I get to challenge myself in all aspects of writing: character, plot and world building. Fantasy also allows me to examine difficult or sensitive subjects in a context removed from reality, which helps me bring in new perspectives I might otherwise have overlooked.

METHODOLOGY

I used Howard Gardner's Multiple Intelligences Theory as the framework for my research to see how the different intelligences – "a set of abilities, talents or mental skills" (Gardner, 2006: 6) – apply to my fantasy writing process. Although, by default, writing falls under linguist intelligence, requiring the capacity to use and learn languages, both spoken and written (Gardner, 1999: 41), I will be interrogating how interpersonal, intrapersonal, naturalist, visual-spatial, logical-mathematical and musical intelligences can be applied to the fantasy writing process I have undertaken at key stages in my life. Thus, Gardner offers a lens through which to see my processes in a positive, as opposed to shameful, light. I do not claim to be an expert in all these fields, since we all "possess each of these skills to some extent" (Gardner, 2006: 6). Instead, I aim to show how I use different methods when writing my stories and how that can be applied in the classroom.

As already articulated, providing a specific definition of the term 'fantasy genre' is impossible, as it needs to be defined in relation to both itself and other genres (Propp, 1984: 40). The term 'fantasy' is no different. I have therefore decided to draw upon Vladimir Propp's genre theory to understand how and why I wrote what I did. More specifically, I will reference Propp's seven characters; "the villain (marplot), the donor, the helper, the princess (the sought-for person) and her father, the dispatcher, the hero, and the false hero" (ibid) in relation to my writing.

This research is autoethnographic, and therefore I looked at how my writing emerged because of outside influences, juxtaposing this with my own experiences as a fantasy writer (Muncey, 2010: 10). Thus, I did not analyse myself as a participant in a vacuum, but in relation to the world around me. However, there is critique to this method, such as the risk of "privileging the self" (Hamilton et al., 2008: 17) by not taking others into consideration – that your personal experience is of no use to others. There is also "the danger of selective memory" for the researcher, where they "unconsciously distort vivid experiences" (Coen et al, 2018: 298). I would argue, however, that autoethnography captures those vivid experiences effectively, and by analysing and reflecting upon them in a broader social context, autoethnography allows an investigation of the "multiple selves in contexts that arguably transform the authorial "I" to an existential "we."" (Spry, 2001: 710-711). In my research, I used autoethnographic vignettes dating back to my childhood. Some argue that autoethnograhy "violates ethical standards of privacy" (Coen et al, 2018: 299) of individuals and I have therefore done my best to anonymise the vignettes. Also, "[s]tories are essential to human understanding" (Ellis, 2004: 32), and therefore I believe that using vignettes is the most effective method to investigate and present my research.

THE RESEARCH

I squeeze down between two of the other children so that we all fit on the blue sofa. Our kindergarten teacher sits in a chair opposite us, holding two stories in her hand. One of them is mine.

First, she reads out the other story. It's about a child who walks up a long staircase in an empty castle. At the top of the stairs the child opens the door and finds a ghost and they become best friends.

When the story finishes everybody claps and wants to hear it again.

'We have to listen to Matilda's story first', the teacher says and waves my book in her hand.

I squirm with excitement in my seat as she reads out my story about a princess who finds a frog, kisses it and watches as the frog turns into a prince. The other children do not laugh or clap like they did during the previous story, and when my story ends, all they want to hear is the ghost story again.

This was my first taste of rejection as a writer, and looking back I understand why. The story of a friendship striking up between a ghost and human was appealing as it built suspense and had an element of surprise when we find out there is a ghost behind the door, as opposed to my princess story. However, I still enjoyed writing about princesses and a big part of my initial love for fantasy was the idea of royalty. Disney movies and fairytales, which from an early age was what I consumed, may have influenced this. The movies often contain Propp's character functions, such as the princess, the hero and the villain (Propp, 1984). My story, The Princess and The Wizard, also contained these characters, as well as the structural components of a fantasy story; the wizard being the benefactor aiding the protagonist (Propp, 1984: 170) and the story beginning "with a desire to have something" (Propp, 1984: 102). The protagonist is usually the one to "win the princess" (Propp, 2012: 147-148). However, in my story the princess is the protagonist, yet she still needs to be saved (from boredom) by a male character, which is in line with Propp's genre theory of the hero saving the princess, and seen in Disney movies from the early 90s. Fairytales are a great gateway to start engaging children in fantasy in the classroom. The stories can be retold in a modern setting by using Propp's character functions in new and exciting ways, such as challenging the norm of the princess needing to be rescued, and what characterises a hero.

As a young reader and writer, fantasy "contain[ed] features sparked by pure imagination" (Stephan, 2016: 8), which appealed to me. Fantasy can be seen as a way to encourage escapism (Webb, 2015: 2), and that may be true; however, I also believe my passion for the genre grew from being exposed to different mind-sets through a range of new characters. Although existential intelligence is not classified as a valid intelligence (Davis et al, 2011: 488), to me, writing fantasy does involve tackling existential questions. In a world where I can create my own gods, I can in turn decide why these gods put the humans on earth. This process requires me to pose questions about life and death. This may not always be the case for children writing fantasy, but it is important for these questions to be allowed to be discovered through writing. Sigmund Freud articulates how humans have "a drive towards a state of inorganicism" also known as "a death wish" (Jackson, 1981: 72), which I explored when writing fantasy. This was seen in my story Solens strålar (Rays of the Sun), written in second grade, about a girl who goes on a quest to find her dead parents. After a series of tests, she reaches 'the paradise in the sun' where her parents are, and she decides to stay with them. In addition, the way that my story looks at death as just another place after life, exposing my fear of death as well as my desire to be with my family after I die, aligns with Freud's argument that writing fantasy is "projecting unconscious desires and fears into the environment and on to other people" (Jackson, 1987: 64).

One of the reasons fantasy writing suits me well is because it often requires planning. I would spend hours 'world building' before writing a story, which included: drawing maps, creating animals and plants, as well as making lists outlining the different cities and political systems. Burcher et al. argues that world building gives "an opportunity for authors to develop and explore their worlds" (2009: 227). Looking at Gardner's naturalist intelligence when creating my fantasy world, I use my "knowledge of the living world" (Gardner, 2006: 48) in order to decide which plants grow where and why certain animals can only live in certain places. I also use logical-mathematical intelligence to find solutions to why, for example, a magic system is put in place and how that fits with the rest of the world-building by "solving abstract problems" (Davis et al, 2011: 488). I agree with Edward James and Farah Mendlesohn's statement that "a writer can be a 'sub-creator' of a secondary world" (2012: 65), as I need to think about not just the characters in my stories, but also how they coincide with nature and all other living things in that universe. Thus, using naturalist and logical-mathematical intelligences are of utmost importance when writing fantasy. Children can learn about climate, wildlife, and society structures through creating their own world – by, for instance, using our world as a template and utilising their imagination to make the world their own.

To plan my world I create a map, using spatial-visual intelligence. Visualising the world through drawing maps was helpful in my planning. I would also create mythology, drawing upon Greek mythology, which became of great interest after watching Disney's Hercules (1997) as a child. To me, world building is as important as the plot. By knowing the history of the created world, we can use interpersonal intelligence to understand our characters by recognising their "moods, desires, motivations and intentions" (Davis et al., 2011: 488). As an author, I need to place my work "in relation to historical, social, economic, political and sexual determinants, as well as to a literary tradition of fantasy" (Jackson, 1981: 3) and therefore recognise that it is not placed "'outside' time altogether" (ibid), but part of "the kind of reality it reflects" (Propp, 1984: 41). Thus, world building is the foundation of any fantasy story. Not only is it the place that story and characters inhabit, but it creates meaning to why characters are the way they are and how the story the reader is presented with came to be.

When writing characters, interpersonal intelligence and intrapersonal intelligence are important. Through my own life experiences of working with diverse people, I learnt to see the "moods, temperaments, motivations and intentions" (Gardner, 2006: 15) in others as well as myself. These interactions helped me write well-rounded characters who have their own dreams and motivations. Similarly, through my characters' actions, I was able to portray my own experiences and desires, as well as the experiences of people I had met in my life. Tzvetan Todorov claims that through fantasy, the reader is exposed to the strange whilst having the security of the familiar (Eşberk, 2014: 143). Consequently, the hesitation from the reader makes them "feel the need to search, resist, think and criticize" (ibid), and the same can be said about the writer. Using fantasy, children can express questions in relation to the world they live in, and create alternative realities, in which they can challenge the status quo and push the boundaries of what reality should be.

I wrap my cardigan tighter around my body. Who knew it could be this cold in Spain? I'm watching another episode of the anime Clannad that my brother had recommended. As I watch,

one of the music scores catches my attention. As the song
町、時の流れ、人 *plays, a scene crops up in my mind. A*
panning shot over desolate landscapes. People down below,
fighting, and dying. Seas set on fire. Everything burning. All the
muted chaos viewed from above, by a young man. Powerless.
Crying. Watching the world end.

The above vignette shows one of the ways I write fantasy; through music. I use musical intelligence when writing to help set the mood of a story. For example, the song from Clannad became important in the initial stages of re-writing one of my novels, and became the basis for the ending of the whole trilogy. It was through listening to the song on repeat that I wrote the final scenes. Although I do not have musical ability in the way of composing or performing, which is arguably relevant in identifying musical intelligence (Gardner, 1999: 42), I can appreciate the music and "make meanings of different patterns of sound" (Davis et al, 2011: 488) which I then translate into my writing. Rosen argues that story is created when we "bind feelings and ideas together" (Rosen, 2013: 8), and music "acts as a stimulus to thought and feeling" (Lass, 1932: 318). This is arguably why I find music beneficial when creating stories. However, I never use music in combination with any other type of writing than fantasy, which could be because music to me is a gateway to my imagination. When I hear a piece of music that resonates with me, I can create worlds in my head. Through my experience, I have learned that inspiration can come from different outlets, not just reading. By encouraging children to view art, listen to music and watch films, it can help them find inspiration to write stories.

FINDINGS

My research project focused on how I wrote fantasy as a child and how those elements can be incorporated into the classroom. Looking at Gardner's Multiple Intelligence theory, I realised that having knowledge in different fields is essential when I create a fantasy novel. For example, I use interpersonal and intrapersonal intelligences when creating my characters, naturalist intelligence to create my world and inhabit it, and even musical intelligence to spur my imagination. Further, I could see that early on in my life, I already used the character functions and structures of Propp's genre theory to write my stories, which were derived from fairytales and Disney movies. Fantasy is popular worldwide (Stephan, 2016: 3), and I would argue that classrooms would benefit from combining literary and genre fiction, as it would create a more enriching experience for the students, allowing them to explore all different sides of writing.

Finally, conducting this autoethnography taught me to not belittle genre fiction. Creating a fantasy novel requires not only great imagination, but also a deep understanding of reality. Hence, fantasy shows "what it means to be human" (Aeromagazine, 2019) and should not be disregarded as reading simply for pleasure, but also for understanding our reality.

WHAT'S NEXT?

Moving forward, I would like to find more ways to incorporate genre fiction exercises into creative writing courses and classrooms. Below are suggestions of prompts to get started writing your fantasy story:

Create a character who inhabits your world. Who are they? What do they do for a living? What are their hobbies? What are their dreams/ambitions/goals? What stands in their way from achieving those things?

Describe a day in the life of your character in your world. Where do they live? Show us around their place/area/village/town/city. Use all the senses – vision, touch, smell, taste, and sound. What is the climate like where they live? What season is it? Does your character like where they live?

Introduce the world to your reader. Use your character to describe more about the world, through what they see and do in their daily life. What is the political system, and is there magic? Magic always comes with a price, what would be the price for using magic in their world? What plants and wildlife exist in their world?

Introduce your character to another character. It could be a family member, a friend, a love interest, or a stranger visiting their home for the first time. What do they talk about? Do they agree or disagree? If they are strangers, do they understand each other? What are some of the similarities and differences between the two characters?

Have your character take one step towards fulfilling their dream/ambition/goal. Your character's aspirations are what will drive them to action and move the story forward. What do they need to do to achieve their aspirations? Do they need to leave home? Learn a new skill? Find something or someone to help them?

From here, you can take your character out on an adventure, or have them explore the place where they live, discovering new things they did not know before.

REFERENCES

Aeromagazine (2019)
https://areomagazine.com/2019/05/17/why-we-need-fantasy-literature/ Accessed: 11/02/2020
Burcher, C., Hollands, N., Smith, A., Trott, B., Zellers, J., Core Collections in Genre Studies: Fantasy Fiction 101, Reference & User Services Quarterly; Chicago Vol. 48, Iss. 3, (Spring 2009): 226-231
Cart, M. (2016) Young Adult Literature: From Romance to Realism (Third Edition), Chicago: ALA Neal-Schuman (American Library Association)
Coats, K. (2018), The Bloomsbury introduction to children's and young adult literature, London: Bloomsbury Academic

Coen, L., Manion L., Morrison, K. (2018) Research Methods in Education, London: Routledge

Davis K, Christodoulou JA, Seider S, Gardner H. The Theory of Multiple Intelligences. In: Sternberg RJ, Kaufman SB Cambridge Handbook of Intelligence. New York: Cambridge University Press; 2011. pp. 485-503.

Ellis, C. (2004) The ethnographic I: A methodological novel about autoethnography. Walnut Creek, CA: AltaMira Press

Eşberk, H. (2014), The Function of Fantasy as a Subversive Genre in Literature, Journal of Language and Literature Education, 10, 139-144.

Gardner, H. (1999) Intelligence Reframed; Multiple Intelligences for the 21st Century, New York: Basic Books

Gardner, H. (2006) Multiple Intelligences: New Horizons, New York: Basic Books

Hamilton, M. L., Smith, L. and Worthington, K. (2008) Fitting the methodology with the   research: an exploration of narrative, self- study and auto-ethnography. Studying Teacher Education, 4 (1), pp. 17– 28.

Hercules (1997) [DVD] Walt Disney Pictures and Walt Disney Feature Animation, United States

Jackson, R (1981) Fantasy: The Literature of Subversion, London: Routledge

James, E. and Mendlesohn, F. (2012) Fantasy Literature, Cambridge: Cambridge University   Press

Lass, A. H. The English Journal, Vol. 21, No. 4 (Apr., 1932), pp. 316-318

Orito, S. (2004) [SONG] 町、時の流れ、人, Japan: Key Sound Label

Muncey, T. (2010) Creating Autoethnographies, London: Sage Publications Ltd

Propp, V. IA. (1984) Theory and history of folklore, Manchester: Manchester University Press

Propp, V. IA. (2012) The Russian folktale by Vladimir Yakovlevich Propp, Detroit: Wayne State University Press

Rosen, R. (2013) How Genre Theory Saved the World, Changing English, 20:1, 310, DOI:10.1080/1358684X.2012.757055

Spry, T. Performing Autoethnography: An Embodied Methodological Praxis, Qualitative Inquiry, Volume 7 Number 6, 2001 706-732, Sage Publications

Stephan, M., Do you believe in magic? The Potency of the Fantasy Genre, Coolabah, No.18, 2016, ISSN 1988-5946, Observatori: Centre d'Estudis Australians / Australian Studies Centre, Universitat de Barcelona 3

Webb, C. (2015) Fantasy and the Real World in British Children's Literature: The Power of Story, NY and Abingdon: Routledge

NOTES FROM THE TICKLE TRUNK:
A WRITER'S GUIDE TO THE SHADOW SELF

TANYA ROYER

OVERALL AIM

A writer embarks on a Jungian adventure into the 'shadow' aspect of her mind, where she discovers – through mindfulness, free-writing practice and object-led reflection – clues to her authorial voice. Along the way, she has an encounter with Tickle, the voice of her shadow, who reveals the essence of her self-delusion. Through a series of creative exercises, this article will also suggest ways to discover and dialogue with your own shadow self, or guide others to do the same.

INTRODUCTION

Like most people, I read alone. But when I write, I always have the odd sensation of being observed by someone who is judging what is and is not available to me to write about. She is watching me right now as these characters catapult themselves from the synapses in my brain down, through the tendons my arm, into the tips of my fingers as they strike the keyboard, landing on the screen of my computer. I sense a presence, quick and ruthless, waiting to lurch in front of me when I get close to voicing experiences or emotions that she considers her territory. She is my internal sovereign, whose domain is located in the crypt of my psyche. Within this crypt, I imagine a locked room that only she has a key to, and where a set of bottles sits on a shelf:

FIG. 1 BOTTLES IN A LOCKED ROOM IN THE CRYPT OF MY PSYCHE

Ever since I can remember, I have felt at a distance from the core of my true self, in a way that other people do not seem to be. This sense of dislocation has deprived me of the artistic confidence required to allow myself to completely free fall into a creative flow. An exploration of my psyche had the potential to bring me closer to this part of myself. I wanted my writing voice to become ruthlessly candid, and for this I knew that I needed greater self-awareness and empathy. These are both vital qualities for creative writing educators; for their own writing and to make safe the experimental space for creative learning. This type of learning space allows engagement with darker elements of the psyche, such as shame and fear, which, though deeply unsettling, are often the very subjects that most need creative expression. By having an open channel with their shadow self, a creative-writing educator can model how to engage the shadow, allowing learners to see that they are free to follow their intuition and imagination wherever it may lead.

I made my descent into the crypt with the aim of finding the truest version of myself and, within it, my most fiercely honest voice.

KEY THEORY: THE SHADOW SELF

This work is guided by the insights of Carl Jung and by philosophers, essayists and novelists who themselves have explored the psyche's darker corners. Jung termed our dark side the 'shadow self' (Stevens, 1990: 43) and his terminology has helped me to define and describe this aspect of the mind.

Jung believed that the imagination was a magical force, and that 'all the works of man have their origin in creative fantasy' (Jung, 1970: 76). He believed that our dreams contain images that can guide us toward a meaningful sense of self, offering "a practical and important hint which shows ... in what direction the unconscious is leading" (Jung, 1970: 72).

I was introduced to the concept of the unconscious when I was a child, through a television programme called Mr Dressup. The presenter, Mr Dressup, would sing a magic song to unlock the 'tickle trunk', in which he would find neatly folded costumes to wear while acting out stories on the programme. This showed me that we have other selves that we can access through the power of imagination. As a gesture of respect to Mr Dressup for his inspiration, I have used the name Tickle to refer to my shadow self. Tickle is also a felt witch who guards the door to my office, which is the physical representation of my psychic crypt in this research.

FIG. 2 TICKLE, A WITCH MADE OF FELT WHO GUARDS MY OFFICE DOOR

Tickle is also the co-author of this article, appearing in dialogic form to share her views and insights.

Exercise 1: Name your shadow

While it is not necessary to give your shadow a name, it can make your shadow more approachable. To name your shadow, it helps to visualise it as a character. You can find your shadow in any expression of creativity (for example, a favourite film, song, piece of art, poem or story) that has captured your imagination and made you feel understood.

RESEARCH IN ACTION

I used mindfulness practice, free writing and object-led reflection as my cognitive tools for this action research project.

Mindfulness

Mindfulness practice, which involves focusing on the breath to become more aware of the present moment, allowed me to create a vulnerable, open and respectful space for releasing unsettling memories and emotions. For this research, I used a Buddhist approach that involves aligning six points of posture (seat, legs, torso, hands, eyes and mouth) before beginning, in order to ensure that the body is comfortable and at rest (Chodron, 1997: 22-23). Once I was comfortable, I practiced 10 minutes of silent meditation.

Free writing

After meditating, I did a timed free-writing session to capture my immediate reflections and habits of thought. The practice of dialogic diary writing (Rainer, 1978: 102-114) helped me to voice Tickle, my shadow self, with honesty and candour. I kept a handwritten notebook and an electronic journal, to experiment with different states of creative flow.

Object-led reflection

As stated, I used my office as the physical representation of the crypt of my psyche in this research. I allowed myself to choose any object from within the room to reflect on and write about.

This could be anything from a photograph, to a journal, or a piece of art. The selection of objects was spontaneous and intuition driven, rather than planned and premeditated, as a way of allowing my shadow self, Tickle, to lead.

FIG. 3 WRITER'S PSYCHIC CRYPT, AS REPRESENTED BY HER HOME OFFICE IN KENT

RESEARCH PROGRAMME

Over a four-week period, I gathered qualitative data in the form of photographs and images that illuminated the theme of my research, as well as mindfulness-led free-writing practice, including open dialogue with Tickle. I carried out mindfulness and writing sessions two days a week during this period, comprising 10 minutes of mindfulness followed by a five-minute free-writing session, increasing the latter by five minutes each week to allow for progressively deeper reflection.

Exercise 2: Design a research programme

A writer needs time to write, and a schedule can help with this. Below is a two-week sample programme. You can adjust this programme to suit your needs.

<u>Week One</u>
Day one
| Mindfulness | 10 minutes |
| Free writing | 5 minutes |

Day two
| Mindfulness | 10 minutes |
| Free writing | 5 minutes |

<u>Week Two</u>
Day one
| Mindfulness | 10 minutes |
| Free writing | 10 minutes |

Day two
| Mindfulness | 10 minutes |
| Free writing | 10 minutes |

FINDINGS

Undertaking this research reacquainted me with my oldest, most personal artefacts and memories. This raised unsettling feelings, in particular about my experiences as the child of a mother who was bipolar. In my mindfulness practice, I acknowledged and honoured complex, often conflicting emotions with equanimity. I was then able to write about my mother's fragile mental health, while celebrating how she had helped me to discover the joy of literature and the inspiration to write. Writing in the voice of Tickle was liberating and allowed me to name my fears and insecurities, releasing me from their grip.

In my object-led reflection, I discovered an unexpected treasure in an old journal. This gift gave me renewed faith in my ability to trust my instinct when confronting my fears.

MOVING TOWARDS FEAR

On the day I walked into my office to begin this research, I froze with panic. I had no idea which object to choose for the object-led reflection or where to start. I sat down and began 10 minutes of mindfulness, keeping focused on my breathing. Once I gave myself the cognitive and physical space to be silent, my anxiety subsided and Tickle emerged, as the voice of my instinct:

> Tickle: Are you tempted to choose a safe object, such as a glass sculpture given to you as a birthday gift from a close friend, rather than venture into the riskier territory of your family photographs and letters?
> Writer: (silence)
> Tickle: I have something to show you.

Guided by Tickle, I opened the bookcase and pulled out a journal at random. The following was written at the bottom of the first page:

> Those who have come to terms with the Shadow aspect of their personality.

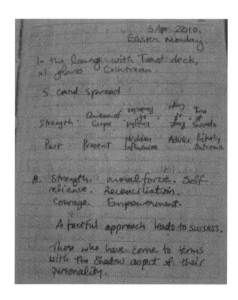

Fig. 4 Writer's journal excerpt on the shadow, 5 April 2010

During a Tarot card reading almost 10 years ago, Tickle had left a message in my journal for my future self. I use Tarot not to see into the future (as Tarot is sometimes used) but as a tool of play to open a fresh perspective on the present.

I had often considered getting rid of my handwritten journals. But Tickle always turned up in these moments of self-doubt, making sure that I kept these old, tattered journals – safely stored in a sturdy, watertight archival box – so that on the day I came looking for her, I would be able to find her.

What Tickle showed me was how to engage with the shadow by moving towards the fear of what I might discover, rather than turning away.

Exercise 3: Moving towards fear

To engage the shadow, a writer needs to be prepared to be vulnerable and honest. The shadow is clever and will always try to evade you. Here are some questions that may help. Pick one that makes you flinch and let your instinct do the rest. Write about it for five minutes without stopping:

- When you hear the word 'jealous', who do you think of?
- Think of a time when you have felt socially uneasy and gone silent. What you were feeling?
- When you hear the word 'betrayed', what does it make you think of?
- In the dream of your life, who do you wish to become?

It may help to write this as a conversation between you and your shadow.

LITERARY SHOPLIFTING

After a mindfulness session on the train one morning, I drifted into a state of reflection while gazing out the window. I remembered the death of my mother, which happened a few years ago. As this thought passed, another took its place. I began writing, to see what of this stream might land on the page. Here is an extract from the entry:

My mother had many gifts. One was for choosing literature for me when I was a very young child. I can recall lying against her body as she read to me from Tolkien. First, The Hobbit and later, parts of The Lord of the Rings.

She also introduced me to full-length books, beginning with The Chronicles of Narnia. I was given the full set of these books as a birthday present. I don't remember how old I was, but it would have been around nine. This was a Puffin edition, illustrated with a picture of Mr Tumnus standing on the snowy path. The first one of these I read was The Lion, the Witch and the Wardrobe. Lucy's first adventure through the back of the wardrobe was all the more thrilling to read alone, in the solitude of my bedroom and without my mother's reassuring voice to lull me.

My mother was a haunted, mercurial woman with an occasionally volcanic temper. At various stages when I was growing up I recall her being hospitalised for mental breakdowns. She was also a deeply loving and tender person. What I had written in my journal connected my memory of my mother with my discovery of myself as a writer, and with the character Lucy in The Lion, the Witch and the Wardrobe. The three memories seemed to arrive as a piece.

When I read alone as a child, I entered a mythic world far beyond the reach of adults, as children do. Lucy's experience in her house strongly resonated with my sense of home, a space where from a very young age I did not feel safe. The idea that a portal to another world could be found from within the house (Lewis, 12-13: 1978) was a magical, thrilling prospect that filled me with a vigorous sense of conviction and hope. If Lucy could find a portal to another world in her house, perhaps portals to other worlds existed in my house. This potent idea opened a rich dimension of adventure to the dream world where I would spend the whole of my childhood and adolescence, awaiting the chance to escape.

Though I had been told under no circumstances to ever write in ink in any book, my nine-year-old self gleefully transgressed this rule. It was here, in this same book, that I first trespassed on another author's work. Like Lucy summoning the courage to go through the darkness of the wardrobe, my paperback copy of this story was the place where I declared my urge to write, by criminally inking my name all over the book.

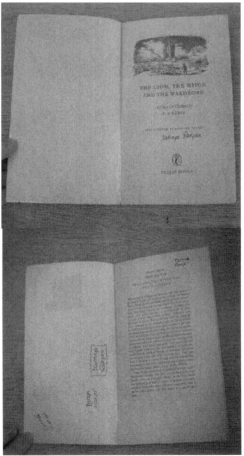

FIG. 5 WRITER'S COPY OF THE LION, THE WITCH AND THE WARDROBE WITH THE WRITER'S NAME WRITTEN INSIDE THE BOOK

Tickle: Lucy's journey into the darkness of the wardrobe was your first experience of a young girl using her courage to embark on an adventure, a literary manifestation of your own desire to escape from the volatile home you were living in as a child and run away to be a writer.
Writer: But shouldn't I have learned how to write before writing my name in a book?
Tickle: Tanya, when you were nine, you believed you were already a writer.

This was not just the book that I would like to have written, this was my manifesto. With a fanatic's lust, I went straight past plagiarism to literary shoplifting.

It remains the only book in which I have ever written my name.

Exercise 4: Write from inside another work (intertextuality)
Writing from another artist's work is useful for experimenting with creative reading and writing. Below are two exercises to try:

- Pick a detail from an artwork, film or book that you like. This can be a place mentioned in a film, a character or idea described in a story, or a detail from a work of art. Now write a short poem about it. The idea with this exercise is to free yourself to notice details. What lands on the page will show how you view the world.
- Choose a favourite piece of music to listen to for 10 minutes. Now free write for another 10 minutes without stopping, with or without the music as you prefer.

ENCOUNTERING THE SHADOW SELF
In my dialogue with Tickle, she confronted me about my use of social masks, zeroing in on my attachment to sarcasm:

> Tickle: My favourite times to visit you are when you are daydreaming on the train or first thing in the morning before you get out of bed.
> Writer: Why?
> Tickle: Because Sarcasm is not around and you are at ease. Sarcasm is a mask. To engage with me you must unmask yourself.

The etymology of sarcasm is the Greek word sarkazein, meaning to 'tear flesh' (Oxford English Dictionary: 2019). In effect, sarcasm was my way of weaponising rhetoric to tear the metaphorical flesh of those around me. This was alarming enough. But there was an even more insidious level to this. Whenever I would take annual leave from work, I would book a cottage as far from civilisation as possible and disappear for a week to write and read. This arrangement is what Jungians describe as 'sneaking into the shadow' (Estes, 1992: 236-237); where a person acts a role in public, waiting for the chance to dive into her private life. If a colleague asked me where I was going, I would cringe and then immediately turn the sarcasm up to maximum. With a dismissive, breezy grin I would reply, 'Oh, I'm off on a sojourn to write my book'.

> Tickle: We on the shadow side call this the Aspiring Writer cocktail. One part Insincerity, one part Self-Sabotage, shake gently and serve with a garnish of Postmodern Irony.
> Writer: I do want to write a book. Why is that so hard to say out loud?
> Tickle: It's not. You just did.

Tickle exposed that I was playing a double bluff by framing the truth as a casual, throwaway remark. Language was the veil I used to hide from both the world and myself, polluting the source of my creativity with this twisted head game. As diabolical as it was, this insight spoke directly to the mystery of why I felt at a distance from my true self. I needed to come clean and become radically sincere, both on and off the page.

CONCLUSION

I set out on this adventure to find a way into the shadow of my psyche, as a means of deepening my creative practice as a writer and educator. In the course of this work, I confronted difficult past experiences, with the hope of finding a more self-aware version of myself. Mindfulness was a crucial tool for helping me to move through my panic at the beginning of the work. Free writing and object-led reflection put me in an intuitive, self-reflective state, and allowed me to turn my experiences into a personal narrative, an exercise that was both inspiring and healing.

But it was the work with Tickle, my shadow self, that was the most satisfying part of this research. Her blunt, unsentimental style showed me that the most powerful way to find my voice is to start with being honest with my first reader: myself. This insight has made me consider beginning my creative work from the non-writing part of myself – the part that feels, rather than thinks.

This is only the beginning. The work ahead of me is to let Tickle take me afar, into the deepest testimony of myself.

REFERENCES

Chodron, P. (1997). When Things Fall Apart. Boston: Shambhala Publications.

Haiman, J. (2011). The Science of Sarcasm. Smithsonian Magazine.
Available at: https://www.smithsonianmag.com/science-nature/the-science-of-sarcasm-yeah-right-25038/ Accessed 28 December 2019.

Estes, C.P. (1992). Women Who Run With the Wolves. New York: Ballantine Books.

Jung, C. (1933). Modern Man In Search of A Soul. Reprint. 1970 ed. London: Routledge.

Lewis, C. (1978). The Lion, the Witch and the Wardrobe. London: Penguin.

Marinka (2016). Glass bottle of poison. Deposit Photos. Available at: https://depositphotos.com/126376882/stock-illustration-glass-bottles-of-poison-vector.html Accessed 19 November 2019.

Simpson, J. and Weiner, E. eds. (2019). Oxford English Dictionary. Oxford: Oxford University Press

Rainer, T. (1978). The New Diary. Los Angeles: J.T Tarcher.

Stevens, A. (1990). On Jung. London: Penguin.

WRITING FROM 'THE THIRD SPACE'

EXPLORING MIXED-RACE EXPERIENCES
IN CREATIVE WRITING

CARINYA SHARPLES

In debates around diversity in literature, mixed-race authors and characters are often forgotten – or absorbed into black British writing. Here I chart my progress developing a creative-writing workshop that centres mixed-race experiences and supports writers of mixed heritage to explore their identities and write from their own 'third' space.

> 'I understood myself, as a child, to be a third, impossible option in an otherwise binary culture: neither black nor white but both. There are many negative responses a child can have to this feeling of impossibility ... But there is another more interesting response that I think of as inadvertently creative.' – Zadie Smith (Smith, 2019, p. 340)

As a mixed-race child growing up in 1980s London, I never saw myself represented in the world of literature. On the page I was invisible.

For young mixed-race readers in the UK today, not much has changed in terms of representation. In its latest 'Reflecting Realities' survey of ethnic representation in UK Children's Literature, the Centre for Literacy in Primary Education (CLPE) found that only 0.3% of children's books published in the UK in 2018 featured mixed-race main characters (Centre for Literacy in Primary Education, 2019, p. 7). Yet according to the latest census, 1.2 million people (2.2%) of the population of England and Wales self-identify as being of 'Mixed ethnicity' (GOV.UK, 2018).

Two months after the CLPE survey, the Arts Council published its own report, 'Time for Change: Black and Minority Ethnic Representation in the Children's Literature Sector'. The report didn't look at mixed-race representation at all – instead using the catchall term 'BAME' (Arts Council England, 2019). Doing so glosses over the complexities and rich diversity found within this broad group – including the varied experiences of mixed-race people, which academic Miri Song notes are 'quite distinct from those of monoracial minorities' (Song, 2003, p. 81).

For older readers, it's often non-fiction work that captures the social and cultural experiences of mixed-race people: such as Zadie Smith's *Feel Free*; Akala's *Natives*; Tessa McWatt's exploration of her fractured history and identity, *Shape of Me*; *Tangled Roots*, a collection of real-life stories from mixed-race people; and Afua Hirch's *Brit-ish*. There are occasional fictional characters too. In Evaristo's Booker-prize winning *Girl, Woman, Other*, one section is dedicated to three generations of mixed-race women from one family. Other examples include Helen Oyeyemi's *Icarus Girl*, whose main character is mixed English-Nigerian; Zadie Smith's *Swing Time,* about two mixed-race childhood friends; and the mixed-race character of Callie Rose in Malorie Blackman's Noughts & Crosses young adults series.

Interestingly, high-profile mixed-race writers such as Smith (English-Jamaican), Evaristo (English-Nigerian) and Jackie Kay (Scottish-Nigerian) often describe themselves and are described as 'black writers' (Smith, 2019, p.219; Evaristo, 2019; Severin, 2002) – perhaps affording them a place on the more visible 'black British writers' platform. Yet at the same time they talk of their mixed-race identity as forming an important part of why they became writers and their writing identity. Evaristo described writing her semi-autobiographic novel-in-verse *Lara as* 'a sort of transformative process' (Chingonyi, K., Beard, F., Robinson, R., Chivers, et al, 2009). Smith admits a 'barely conscious' awareness that 'part of me is always writing backwards to the confused brown girl I once was, providing the books I wished back then that I could read' (Smith, 2019, p. 342). While Hanif Kureish, the author of *Buddha of Suburbia*, was drawn to writing as a way to explore what it meant to be mixed English-Pakistani teenager growing up in the UK in the 1960s: 'It was pointed out to me that this was a really interesting perspective to see the world from and that people on the whole weren't writing about that particular perspective' (Jenkins, 2020).

The importance of sharing these perspectives and experiences is apparent in Dr Kirstin Lewis's 2016 study 'Helping mixed heritage children develop "character and resilience" in schools'. One participant, Kim, reports that the needs of the mixed-race pupils in her school are being ignored. She calls for an assembly 'about the cussing that we have to put up with' and also a dedicated room where mixed-race students could come together to talk: 'White people have the library – black people have the canteen – we don't have anywhere' (Lewis, 2016).

In August 2019 I visited the Mixed Race Faces exhibition in South East London: a display of portrait photographs featuring mixed-race people (Mixedracefaces, 2019). There were also poetry readings by mixed-race writers taking place. As I looked around the room, I realised I was for the first time in my life in a space where the majority of the people were mixed race. There was no need for performers to provide explanations or disclaimers for the mixed-race-majority audience: we were all on the same page.

I was struck by bell hooks describing how she wrote her seminal text *Ain't I A Woman?* in dialogue with the black women she worked with at a telephone company (hooks, b. and Hall, S., 2018, p.5). I wondered: could talking with other mixed-race writers help me (and them) figure out what we wanted to say, and give ourselves permission to write about what we wanted, how we wanted, in a way that drew on the insights and fluidity of our multiracial identities?

I wanted to test this theory and provide a space for mixed-race writers to come together.

THE THEORY

In the planning of my research workshop 'space' for mixed-race writers I drew on two main theories. Firstly, the pedagogical approach of 'reading the world' and 'writing the world' introduced by Paolo Freire in his seminal text *Pedagogy of the*

Oppressed. Secondly, the concept of a third space or borderland for mixed-race people to occupy and speak from.

In Freire's seminal 1970 text *Pedagogy of the Oppressed* he talks about *conscientização* (Freire, 1996, p. 17) – a kind of social, political and economic consciousness of the contradictions and inequalities in society. It is a precursor of sorts to being 'woke' (Watson, 2017). Both suggest an arrival of consciousness, although Freire's approach is Marxist in nature, with an emphasis on the relationship between 'the oppressor' and 'the oppressed' (Freire, 1996, p. 45). For Freire, the way to break the status quo was liberation through education – 'the word':

> Within the word we find two dimensions, reflection and action, in such radical interaction that if one is sacrificed– even in part–the other immediately suffers. There is no true word that is not at the same time a praxis. Thus, to speak a true word is to transform the world. (Freire, 1996, p. 68)

If true words can transform reality, then perhaps if mixed-race writers speak their truth, their reality, they too can transform the world. Freire also suggests a liberating teaching model: the 'problem-posing teacher-student' persona (Freire, 1996, p. 74), who offers a programme that is not a gift or an imposition but an 'organized, systematized, and developed "re-presentation" to individuals of the things about which they want to know more' – in this case mixed-race identity and creative-writing processes.

The second main theory I drew on in the creation of this workshop is the idea of what Homi Bhaba called the third space (Bhabha and Rutherford, 1990, p. 211): a safe physical space in which to write but also an intangible inner space. It offers freedom to write and potentially escape from the racial polarisations of the real world. bell hooks writes that 'What released me from the narrow blackness and whiteness of my upbringing was the imagination of another place … Our imagination is where our strength to resist lies' (hooks, b. and Hall, S., 2018, p. 46).

I believe this third space is missing in educational facilities and literary institutions, and would strengthen participants' writing and sense of belonging if it could be provided. I want to give mixed-race students and writers a space where, as Laurie Mengel writes, they can 'relieve themselves of their oppressive "two-ness" in favour of wholeness' (Mengel, 2001, p.111).

THE WORKSHOP

As a mixed-race writer myself, I designed the workshop to be participatory – with me not adopting an authoritative teacher role, but taking part in discussions and exercises. The workshop plan outlined below draws on the theories outlined above, as well as creative writing prompts created by myself or used by other educators. I would plan to use only one or two of the following activities per workshop session to allow time for discussion as well as writing.

Some teachers or facilitators are anxious about broaching the topic of race or mixed-race identity with their pupils, and feel ill-equipped to do so. I understand their hesitancy, but as a mixed-race person, I feel that by describing such discussions as 'difficult' or 'challenging', I am also seen as difficult and challenging. Those you work with may have no other opportunity to have these conversations, so providing such a space and not feeling the need to 'lead' or have the answers is important. Although having a mixed-race facilitator may encourage participants to open up initially, I believe the workshops could be led by a non-mixed-race facilitator if that individual is willing to just hold the space, listen, gently guide exercises, and not discredit or deny any reported experiences or offer any personal defence. Further research would be helpful in this area.

Icebreaker: Heritage objects

Each person is asked before the session to bring one to three objects that demonstrate their mixed heritage. Here we each present our object(s) and share what they mean to us.

Rather than starting with words, I decided to start with objects – as sometimes terminology can divide and restrict. Instead of simply saying in which countries their roots lie, the participants will hopefully see those identities as tangible, and be more open to finding stories in the objects (and the tensions between them).

River of reading

We each create a 'river of reading', beginning with the first book we remember reading (or being read to us) and ending with the last book we read – and including other significant texts or reading phases in between. We then plot on the river the times when we were particularly prolific or sparse in our writing and/or reading. Finally we add words or phrases we've used, or other people have used, to describe our racial identity at different points in our life. Afterwards we discuss the activity: what did we think of the exercise and any surprising things that came out of it.

I wanted people to reflect on their journey but not necessarily in a chronological, linear way. This format offers freedom of expression, and visual and textual approaches to suit different people. I was keen to see moments of *conscientização*: when we found texts that opened up our world and changed our writing, thinking or even lives. This also seemed like a good opportunity to look at how we each are identified and self identity at different stages, and show how fluid identity is.

Discussion point 1: Mixed-race characters

We each read out one of the following questions, written on a prepared card:

- *Were there any mixed race characters in the books you read as a child? How were they represented?*
- *Can you think of any fiction books or poems with a mixed-race protagonist?*
- *What is the first fictional character you remember identifying with?*

- *Do you think reading about characters with the same ethnic identity to you matters?*

Given the importance attributed to childhood experiences and memories in psychoanalysis and educational theory, I felt it was important for the participants to reflect on the representation of mixed-race people in the literature they consumed as children and read now. This could help the group to highlight texts perhaps unknown to other participants, and to make connections between childhood experiences and how we identify as writers and readers of mixed-race heritage today.

Activity 2: The mixed-race bookshelf
Each person designs their own book cover using 'blank books' (ordinary books with plain paper wrapped around the cover). We each imagine a book we would have liked to read when we were younger (or would like to read now), featuring a mixed-race character, and including one or all of our objects. We write the book's title and our name on the front and spine, and a 'blurb' and 'bio' on the back. We then each 'present' our book to the group and put in on the 'mixed-race bookshelf' (an actual bookshelf with books by other mixed-race writers on its shelves). Followed by a brief discussion about the activity.

I wanted to give myself and the other participants something like the feeling of seeing our name on the front of a book, and to imagine ourselves as part of a community of writers of mixed heritage. I hope this activity also serves as a chance to manifest the future each of us wants for ourselves as writers, as well as to figure out which story is the most urgent one for us to tell. A brief discussion should follow.

Discussion point 2: Reading
After reading an extract from the book 'Caucasia' by Danzy Senna, we each read out one of the following questions and lead a discussion on it:
- *What do you think of the extract?*
- *Who do you identify or sympathise with?*

- *How does it feel to read the story from the perspective of the mixed-race child?*
- *What themes or challenges does the extract raise?*

By reading an extract of a book by a mixed-race writer told from the perspective of a mixed-race protagonist, Birdie, I hope to give the participants the opportunity to explore the issues raised with some distance from their lives. It is also a way to re-engage us with the practice of reading – to 'read as a writer'. By reflecting on Birdie and her family, we may reflect on our own family or relationships and remember moments that have lain buried for a long time.

Activity 3: Writing from the past
We each imagine that we are the same age as Birdie. We choose a memorable moment from our childhoods that relates to either our ethnic identity or writing/reading and write a diary entry about it – ideally in the hand we're not used to using, to capture the deliberateness and slowness of a child's handwriting. If time, we may also write a supportive letter from ourselves now to ourselves then.

Telling your story is a powerful tool, both in terms of understanding where you have come from but also in terms of writing in an authentic, truthful and emotive way. In this activity we practice tone and language (adopting the voice or concerns of a child): we may adjust the lens through which we view the world (to the detailed observations and physical limitations of a small child), we may also change geographic location to a place we grew up. We may have a certain view of that event or incident now, in hindsight, but how did we feel at the time?

Discussion point 3 / Activity 4
Together we read Maria P.P Root's 'Bill of Rights for Racially Mixed People' and discuss any 'offences' we worry about committing as mixed-race writers. Then, as a group, we will create a draft 'Bill of Rights for Racially Mixed Writers'.

This activity aims to help us uncover some of the myths and fears we have about writing and ourselves as writers. It then aims to unite the group through collective writing to create positive affirmations about what we have the freedom to do as mixed-race writers. What Francis Gilbert calls the 'autobiographical discourse' of our childhood and youth can impact how we see ourselves today – this is a chance to recognise old habits and messages and either accept or reject them.

USEFUL RESOURCES:

- **Mix-D:** As well as lots of excellent advice for parents of mixed-race children, Mix-D offers a Professionals' Pack to help teachers, carers and others to explore and discuss mixed-race identity, experiences and lives. http://www.mix-d.org/
- **People in Harmony:** A long-running organisation that aims to 'promote the positive experience of interracial life in Britain' through events, online resources and support groups. http://www.pih.org.uk/
- **mixedracefaces:** Although primarily a photography project, the portraits are accompanied by thoughts and life stories of those pictured, which give a good sense of the diversity of what it means to be mixed race (or however people choose to self identify). https://mixedracefaces.com/
- **Middleground:** New online magazine showcasing works by mixed-race creatives about their experiences and identities. Includes beautiful art works, poetry and prose. https://www.middlegroundmagazine.co.uk

REFERENCES

Akala (Daley, K.) (2019) *Natives: Race & Class in the Ruins of Empire*. London: Two Roads Books.

Arts Council England (2019). 'Time for Change: Black and minority ethnic representation in the children's literature sector'. Available at: https://www.artscouncil.org.uk/publication/diversity-children's-literature-report-2019 [Accessed 13 February 2020]

Bhabha, H. and Rutherford, J. (1990) 'The Third Space'. In: Rutherford, J. (ed.) *Identity: Community, Culture, Difference*. London: Lawrence & Wishart Limited.

Centre for Literacy in Primary Education (2019). 'Reflecting Realities - Survey of Ethnic Representation within UK Children's Literature 2018'. Available at: https://clpe.org.uk/RR [Accessed 13 February 2020]

Chingonyi, K., Beard, F., Robinson, R., Chivers, et al (2009). *15 shorts: UK writers and poets, July 2009* [DVD]. PeopleBrandsEvents

Evaristo, B. (2019). *Booker Prize-winner Bernardine Evaristo: 'I persisted', 5 December 2019. Available at:* https://www.ft.com/content/156f5a42-155b-11ea-8d73-6303645ac406 [Accessed 13 February 2020]

Freire, P. (1996) *Pedagogy of the Oppressed* (20th anniversary edition). London: Penguin Books.

Gilbert, F. (2018). 'Aesthetic literacy and autobiography', *Writing in Practice*. Vol. 4. Available at: http://research.gold.ac.uk/23228/ [Accessed 9 October 2019].

GOV.UK (2018). 'Population of England and Wales'. Available at: https://www.ethnicity-facts-figures.service.gov.uk/uk-population-by-ethnicity/national-and-regional-populations/population-of-england-and-wales/latest#by-ethnicity [Accessed 13 February 2020]

hooks, b. and Hall, S. (2018) *Uncut Funk: A Contemplative Dialogue*. New York: Routledge

Jenkins, L. (2020). 'Hanif Kureishi: This was a really interesting perspective to see the world from', *The Fountain*. Available at: https://thefountain.eu/books/2020/01/hanif-kureishi-this-was-a-really-interesting-perspective-to-see-the-world-from/ [Accessed 13 February]

Lewis, K. (2016) 'Helping mixed heritage children develop 'character and resilience' in schools', *Improving Schools* (volume 19, issue 3, pp.197-211). Available at: https://journals-sagepub-com.gold.idm.oclc.org/doi/full/10.1177/1365480216650311 [Accessed 13 February 2020]

Massey, K. (ed.) (2015) *Tangled Roots: True Life Stories About Mixed Race Britain.* UK: Tangled Roots

McWatt, T. (2019) *Shame on Me*. London: Scribe Publications

Mengel, L. (2001) 'Triples – The Social Evolution of a Multiracial Panethnicity: An Asian American Perspective' in Parker, D. and Song, M. (eds.) *Rethinking 'Mixed Race'.* London: Pluto Press. Available at: https://epdf.pub/rethinking-mixed-race.html [Accessed 13 February 2020]

Mixedracefaces (2019). *Mixedracefaces Exhibition 2019*, 13-14 August 2019, Copeland Gallery, London. *Available at:* https://mixedracefaces.com/exhibition [Accessed 13 February 2020]

Root, M. (1993) 'Bill of Rights for People of Mixed Heritage'. Available at: http://www.mixedremixed.org/reminder-bill-rights-people-mixed-heritage-maria-p-p-root/ [Accessed 12 February 2020]

Senna, D. (1999) *Caucasia.* New York: Riverhead Books

Severin, L (2002). 'Interview with Jackie Kay', *Free Verse.* Available at: http://freeversethejournal.org/issue-2-summer-2002-jackie-kay-by-laura-severin-interview/ [Accessed 12 February 2020]

Smith, Z. (2019) *Feel Free*. London: Penguin Books

Smith, Z. (2013) *NW*. London: Penguin Books

Song, M. (2003) *Choosing Ethnic Identity.* Cambridge: Polity Press.

Watson, E. (2017) 'The Origin Of Woke: William Melvin Kelley Is The 'Woke' Godfather We Never Acknowledged', *Okay Player.* Available at: https://www.okayplayer.com/culture/woke-william-melvin-kelley.html [Accessed 12 February 2020]

EXPERIMENTAL WRITING PROMPTS

HOW CAN EXPERIMENTAL WRITING PROMPTS AFFECT THE
MODERN-DAY WRITER'S APPROACH TO CREATIVE WRITING?

JAKE SMITH

> With the rise of the Web ... writing has encountered a
> situation similar to that of painting upon the invention of
> photography. ... If photography was striving for sharp
> focus, painting was forced to go soft, hence
> impressionism. (Goldsmith, 2011, p.14)

Readers today are able to access almost any text, from any
period, often in many languages. As writers, we must adapt to
this multi-faceted, multi-cultural era: "Writing needs to redefine
itself to adapt to the new environment of textual abundance."
(Goldsmith, 2011, p. 23-24). In response, I have created a series
of exercises for writers who wish to challenge their current
structural and, perhaps, inhibited form of writing by
experimenting and playing with language and writing concepts.
Although aimed at more experienced writers, I believe that
these exercises, with some amendments, could be used
effectively for any proficiency or age.

TEACHING WITH CONSTRAINTS

The underlying element to teaching with constraints is the idea
of playing with language; that language is malleable and
enjoyable. Bruner suggests that language is 'most daring and
most advanced when it is used in a playful setting' (1984,
p.196), and even whilst it is being used and taught as
'advanced', it is almost never exclusive. Language is easily
adaptable, so, 'everyone, regardless of cognitive levels plays
with language or responds to language play' (Crystal, 1996,
p.328). Language play is not unusual or strictly academic, in fact,
it's deeply ingrained in our societies, from game shows to jokes
and newspaper headlines (Ibid, p.328). It is almost certainly
important in our language development as a child; "The play as
practice model makes a major contribution to phonological

development through its focus on the properties of sounds and sound contrast" (Ibid, p.334). Therefore, surely, it can be as useful in our development as writers too. The exercises I have created encourage students to question the sound of their language and poetry and force them to explore new vocabulary in ways that differ from their pre-conceptions and learned techniques.

TEACHING 'ALTERNATIVE' NARRATIVE

In British and Western education more widely, we value the 'traditional' narrative structure – 'Aristotle's Arc' – "a sequence of events with a beginning, middle, and end, that consists of an introduction, climax, and denouement" (Madej, 2008, p.42). Whilst writing with a traditional narrative structure can make our work satisfying, marketable and profitable, we should try to understand how the perpetual teaching of this idea of narrative can affect how we and society value stories. It is essential that we do not value a version of narrative that is representative of one culture but not another, further it is important to note that storytelling:

> … is how histories are passed down, how customs are shared and how traditions become endemic to a group […] But it's not just what stories they choose to tell that transmit culture, it's how they choose to tell them. (Mizrahi, 2019)

The kind of narrative that I want to promote in my exercises is one that is more focused on conscious-based writing. Below is a visual representation of how I imagine a traditional narrative structure to work, versus my proposed idea of conscience-based writing.

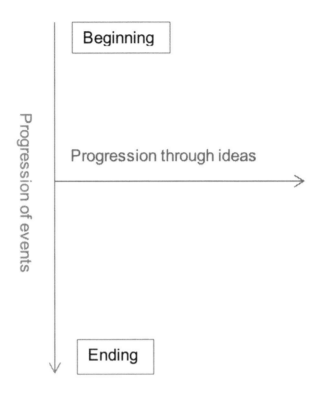

Figure 1: A visual representation of a traditional 'Aristotle's Arc' narrative structure.

Here, the focus is clearly on the 'progression of events', which dictates what is marked as the 'beginning' and the 'ending' of the story. The 'progression through ideas' is merely optional or exploratory, not dictating where the narrative is in its development.

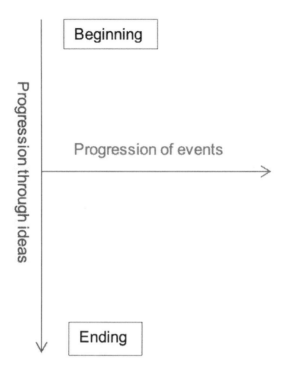

Figure 2: A visual representation of a conscience-based, meditative idea of narrative structure.

In this figurative example, ideas will culminate until we reach a climatic expression of consciousness by the end of the narrative. What happens physically in the order of events is of less importance. By trying to understand narrative this way and emphasising the importance of the 'progression through ideas', we can, perhaps, find a greater balance in our writing.

TEACHING 'EXPERIMENTAL WRITING'

If we challenge our institutions' deeply held beliefs about creativity, we become more able to reflect a 'true' society, one that encompasses the trivialities and experiences of everyone.

My exercises, below, work to liberate the writers who, because of a societal push towards 'good writing', believe their writing is limited in what it can achieve or is simply following the 'status quo'. I believe, however, that our fetishization of certain literary constructs and ingrained creative writing beliefs are at the root of this problem, and only by expanding our understanding of language and the capabilities of it, can we reform this new era of writing.

EXPERIMENTAL POETRY WRITING
Using Oulipian constraints in poetry writing.

Exercise 1:
This exercise is structured around Christian Bök's *Eunoia* poetry collection. The poems were written in response to Georges Perec's *La Disparition (1969) / A Void (1995)* – an Oulipian novel that avoids the letter 'e'. Bök's *Eunoia* reverses this "by using only one vowel rather than eliminating one" (Perloff, 2004, p.34). This exercise is a little more liberal and allows the use of other vowels, provided that one particular vowel is present in each word.

Process:
- Play the students a recording and/or give them a text to read aloud from Bök's *Eunoia,* or a similar example created by a teacher or student, such as the ones I have modelled below.
- Ask the students if they notice anything about the rhythm or sound of the poetry, before revealing the constraint (which is using one vowel in every word).
- Tell students they may pick 'I' or any other vowel and use this constraint in their writing by including it in every word. To start off, a short poem is most effective. They are allowed to break the rules but only for 'good reason'.

A model example of how a poem with constraints can be played with:

Hyphenation

in his solitude in high altitude
inside dim-lit attic-rooms eating
finger-food lives this liar lying
in linen with cigarette debris
littered   beside   his   pillow
blizzard outside his window
considered   puffing   cigarillo
"stick with cigarettes"   said fin
fin   is   smoking   cigarillos
fins insides lined with ink
ink inside his insides since
fin decides smoking is glorious

this   liar   said
"fin, I promise I ain't smoking cigarillo"

this   liar   lied
lit cigarillo this liar smiled

this   liar   said
"I will exit this attic-room with this finger-food"

this liar tried escaping "I" with hyphenation
omitting "I" is outside his imagination.

in his attic-room eating finger-food
lying in linen this liar continued lying
until "I" died without perceiving
anything   outside   his
I-eye-I

Points to highlight to the class:

- The rhythm of the poem: stressing that much of this rhythm has not come through installing a purposeful rhythmic metre. The rhythm of the poem is imposed by the repetition of the vowel 'I' or '/aɪ/' sound. 'All sentences must accent internal rhyme through the use of syntactical parallelism' (Bök, 2001, p. 103–4).
- The potential of musicality and fluidity that this constraint creates, naturally and simply. This could be shown with the facilitator's personal example or Bök's voice recording of *Eunoia*, which can be found here: http://www.ubu.com/sound/bok.html (Ubu.com)
- Demonstrate to learners how the rules can be broken or adapted for effect. The point of the exercise is the playfulness of language. In my model, for example, hyphenation seems to be the only perceivable way to escape 'I' – the consistent constraint this poem is somewhat tied to (or the 'I' character is), which reflects undertones of self-obsession/gluttony. At the end, the hyphenated pillars of 'I' in 'I-eye-I' protect the constraint, even though, phonetically, 'eye' has the same pronunciation. The pillars largely reflect the way we sometimes have to protect our writing from constraining traditionalist views.

Be careful not to outline all of this to students immediately but rather let them understand their own interpretations and understanding of the poem. Think about the learners' abilities and needs – a much simpler poem, playing around with imagery and metaphors around selfishness/gluttony (the first person pronoun 'I') may be much more effective.

Exercise 2:
Process:
- Tell students they should respond to the previous activity by reversing the constraint i.e. avoiding the vowel they chose for the first exercise.

- They should consider this as a response and think about crossover themes.

Here is a model example of a response that avoids the vowel 'I':

> she swerves her eye
> away
> looks at the ground
> observes
> what's not there
>
> she bunkers on
> the bottom floor
> she was
> beneath the boy
> with one eye
> who belched loudly
>
> he came down
> once a day
> collected snacks
> and scuttled back
> up the steps
>
> he was a touch
> self-obsessed
> she thought
> before the new boy
> moved bags to the room
>
> the new boy cooks
> and she averts her
> eye
> "do you choose bottom floor do's or don'ts?" he says
> mouth pursed
> rounded chops
> she presumes he means rules

she nods
"do you smoke?" he says
"no, do you?"
he sparks a fag
coughs "no"

he really meant 'yes'
but as she suspected
they had come full cycle
rounded sounds
these boys.

Points to highlight to the class:

- Facilitators should be lenient with students in circumstances when their explanation for including the excluded vowel is valid and thoroughly thought out. Challenge those who try to 'bend the rules' without good reason.
- At the end of session, the facilitator could introduce a brief overview of the Oulipo movement and writing with constraints. A suggested reading list could be: Christian Bök's *Eunoia* (2001), George Perec's *A Void* (2008) and *Three* (1996).

EXPERIMENTAL NARRATIVE WRITING

Exercise 3:
This exercise is based on students' responses to photographs and the creation of an experimental narrative. The idea is to diverge from the significance of 'traditional' or 'normal' narrative structure and focus more on 'moments': writing about a meditative and profound floating through ideas, instead of a rapid progression of actions. The writing can still follow a

'traditional' structure, but this should not be the primary focus of the piece.

Process:

- As preparation, the facilitator should find or take photographs that are of importance or relevance to the class. It is important to note that the idea is not to take photographs of general landscapes or, for example, a church, but to photograph aspects of the church that offer opportunities for an imaginative and creative written response. A collection of eight to 10 photos will be enough. I have included some examples below, which were simply taken around my house.
- In class, tell students to pick four or five photographs and spend no more than five minutes doing a separate piece of free writing in response to each photograph. The student's responses should aim to acknowledge how, as writers, we can 'speak to photos, speak for photos, imagine the narratives of photographed subjects, and reconstruct the circumstances in which photographs were taken' (Pelizzon, 2013, p.148).
- Finally, tell the students to try to 'thread' their pieces together. Emphasise that it is not important to create a 'story' but simply to create a flowing piece of writing. To create this 'thread', students will have to edit, delete and completely change some parts of their 'free writing' and this should be encouraged.

Model photograph examples

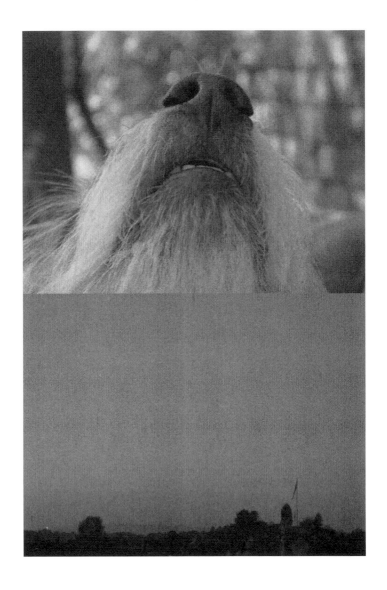

FREE WRITING MODEL EXAMPLE

A singular cloud isolated in a diorama of pastel. The day burns out, leaving the juncture between evening and night buoyant in time. Like a play set, the silhouettes of the forefront exist only in the two dimensional, a cardboard cut-out. It seemed to me as though I could lean out further and pinch the flag upwards, lift it upwards like a pull-tab, bringing with it this cardboard forefront, and slowly eliminating the peachy hues, the solitary cloud and then the greying top of the frame until nothing would be left but the blackness of its depth, the unfamiliarity of what is closest to us, for a view describes what is in the distance, not what is near. How deep is a sunset? I asked myself, my fingers swimming in the dying light.

MODEL OF FINAL NARRATIVE PIECE

The girl ran her fingers over the fretted piece of ornamentation that was screwed onto the front of her wardrobe. It wasn't a handle, it didn't spin, in fact, it had very little practical purpose. And that was probably why she liked it so much. She believed purpose was a synonym for oppression, a system in which one thing only existed because of the needs of some other force or power. By this way of thinking, the objects around her were always filtered into two separate hierarchal categories; purposed and non-purposed. She wondered if anyone else had ever stared at this particular piece of wardrobe and traversed this same piece of thought.

The piece of metal fretting did, in fact, represent the fine details of a flower; the petals, the pistil, the screw? Perhaps, this was its purpose, to bring the joy of natural creation indoors for the consumption of human. But this didn't warrant a good enough reason to switch categories and it still lay dusty and unquestionably non-purposed in the systematic corner of her hippocampus.

Why do we recreate nature in art, especially when it is all around us? She asked. Why are there so many paintings of the sky when the very thing is unexplainably real above our heads. Perhaps we long for a surface, something to grasp, to understand – the paint is on the canvas. The sky has no surface, we get lost in the everlasting empty blue. I wish I knew everything, she thought, before remembering that she didn't wish anything for a purpose.

Downstairs, shoes worn by a child were left on the door handle. The empty blue sky held much more for him than his silly old shoes, he thought.

The trees smudged themselves into existence. Branches held out their careful arms as he climbed so high. My feet are so much lighter, my soles can grip the branches, my toes micro-adjustments for balance. From up here was the perfect viewpoint, a lifetime of shifting diorama. A singular cloud was isolated in the orange pastel as the day burned out, leaving the juncture between evening and night buoyant in time.

Like a stage set, the silhouettes of the forefront – shadowed buildings, puffy trees, a slopped flag above a factory – existed to him only in the two dimensional, a cardboard cut-out. It seemed to the boy as though he could lean out and pinch the flag, lift it upwards like a pull-tab, bringing with it this cardboard scenery and slowly eliminating the bottom of the sky's peachy hues, the solitary cloud, until nothing was left but the shadows of foreground, the last coat of paint before the curtains dropped. How deep is a sunset? He asked himself, fingers swimming in the dying light.

He liked it up this tree so much that he told the girl he would stay. Nature had got the better of him. And so, he buried his roots. Like the trees, he swayed in the heavy wind. He grew so tall and so strong, each day progressing a little further toward the empty blue sky. But the taller he grew, the further his roots spread to hold him. Eventually, he grew out of view from the girl, a mere rustle in the leaves. The roots spread under the door where his old shoes, now mossy and brittle, still hung. Beneath the house, they spread further, crashing through foundations, lifting up the floorboards. He grew taller, snaked up walls until he burst through the roof.

--

There is a pigeon in the tree, said the dog, gruffly. The dog was not wrong. There was in fact a pigeon in the tree, and it fluttered its wings loudly. I don't like it, said the dog, again, gruffly. Why is one animal given the ability to fly, to have access to every atom on ground and sky, when another is stuck down here, with these stubby little terrier legs of mine. I bet it doesn't realise the sheer privilege, lucky bastard. The dog sauntered inside and finished off this morning's breakfast.

Oh, how I'd love to catch it, said the dog on return, still tongue-cleaning the gravy from his beard. Perhaps if I ingested it, I could share some of its air-born magic; my ears would feel so free without the clunking chains of gravity that lasso my dog body to this earth; my paws would become soft, like clouds; not even carpet would rough my skin. My nails could grow long, and I would learn to play the harp, floating on my back through the empty blue. WALKIES boomed from the kitchen. STICKS, screamed the dog, gruffly and raced inside.

The dog walked the girl. The boy was up in the tree but followed with his roots as they caterpillared round corners, embedding themselves into the concrete. The three of them eventually reached a substantial mass of land. The boy sank his roots beneath the long grass and tunnelled his way to the lake through the untrodden earth. The girl and the dog slogged their way through, she occasionally helped loosen the dog free when his legs became knotted. By the time they reached the lake, the boy's roots were already drinking. The girl and the dog dipped their blood-warm legs into the lake, her hand scratching the dog's wiry back.

The machine works, claimed the dog. It stitches together life's tapestries. The bright hot sun and the cool lake stitched together with a hot blanket of rays that is passed between them. One heating the other; one cooling the other. The girl looked confused. The sun would be hotter if it wasn't for the lake? The dog was uncertain for the first time.

Stitched into the middle of the lake were bodies. A human and a canine in suspension over the cold, silty bottom; weaves of water supporting flailing legs. Stitched into the bodies were organs, perfectly organised in pattern, stitched together with tight strings of veins. The water travelled through the roots and back to the boy, he sat up above his diorama, quenching the thirst of a thousand leaves.

The girl wondered if these things happened for a reason, these silly thoughts and actions.

REFERENCES

Bök. C. 2001. *Eunoia.* Toronto: Coach House Press

Bruner, J. (1984). Language, Mind and Reading. In: Goelman, H. et al., 1984. *Awakening to literacy : the University of Victoria Symposium on Children's Response to a Literate Environment: Literacy before Schooling*, Exeter, N.H. ; London: Heinemann Educational Books.

Gallix, A. (2013). Oulipo: freeing literature by tightening its rules. *The Guardian.* [online] Available at:

https://www.theguardian.com/books/booksblog/2013/jul/12/oulipo-freeing-literature-tightening-rules [Accessed 6 May 2018].

Goldsmith, K. (2011). *Uncreative Writing*. New York: Columbia University Press.

Madej, Krystina. (2008). "Traditional Narrative Structure" – not traditional so why the norm? *5th International Conference on Narrative and Interactive Learning Environments* pg. 40-47. Available at: https://www.academia.edu/12236207/5_th_International_Conference_on_Narrative_and_Interactive_Learning_Environments

Mizrahi, I., 2019. *Storytelling Is A Different Story For Each Culture*. [online] Forbes. Available at: https://www.forbes.com/sites/isaacmizrahi/2019/02/19/storytelling-is-a-different-story-for-each-culture/#3e8c6d867ad0 [Accessed 13 July 2020].

News.bbc.co.uk. (2018). *Beautiful vowels*. [online] Available at: http://news.bbc.co.uk/today/hi/today/newsid_7697000/7697762.stm

Pelizzon, V. (2013). Light Speaking: Notes on Poetry and Photography. *Poetry*, 202(2), pp.145–165,179–180.

Perec, G. (1969). *La Disparition*. Translated from French by G. Adair (2008). *A Void* London: Vintage Classic.

Perec, G. and Bellos, D. (1996). *Three*. Translated from French by I. Monk London: Harvill Press.

Perloff, M. (2004). The Oulipo factor: the procedural poetics of Christian Bök and

Ubu.com. n.d. *Christian Bök*. [online] Available at: http://www.ubu.com/sound/bok.html [Accessed 12 June 2020].

Zender, J. and Wilson, B. (2017). *In Dark Places: How Constraints Make Us More Creative*. [online] Falmouth University English & Creative Writing. Available at: https://falwriting.com/new-blog/2017/7/10/in-dark-places-how-constraints-can-make-us-more-creative-as-writers [Accessed 10 June 2020].

WRITE WHAT YOU KNOW:
FACILITATING WORKSHOPS WITH YOUNG WRITERS

MATTHEW TETT

Pupil Premium (PP) learners often underachieve in school settings. Their attainment generally is lower, and they can struggle with motivation. Working with a group of PP writers was an exciting challenge and an experience that has shaped my practice.

INTRODUCTION

In 2018, I completed a Writing Ambassadors training course at BathSpa University. This was a pilot scheme, organised and facilitated by the university, in conjunction with Paper Nations – an Arts Council-funded writing incubator. One of Paper Nations' aims is to empower young people to write and to enjoy the process of writing – and I was fortunate enough to be part of its work.

Funding was provided to set up a series of creative writing workshops with young PP writers in a secondary school. The seven young people, all in Key Stage 3, were invited to attend the after-school sessions by their English teachers, and it was my job to facilitate their learning and experiences, and to provide an exciting series of sessions, with a defined outcome: to publish an anthology of their writing based on the theme of 'Me and My World'.

Often, teachers say to young people 'write what you know' – and it is a useful mantra, to an extent. However, I wanted to take it one step further and encourage the writers to produce work based on an interpretation of their own 'world' – and I wanted the participants to approach this in ways which suited their own ideas. One writer, for example, wrote a dazzling piece about attending a carnival; another approached their writing more conceptually, focusing on the abstract. Even though the writers were working to a remit, there was freedom and flexibility – and it was this approach that I wanted to engender, believing that this would result in the best, most interesting work.

KEY THEORY

One of my main aims was to empower young writers to enjoy writing for writing's sake; that is, I did not want the writers to feel that they had to write for a particular academic outcome – which does have its place in the classroom, obviously, in more conventional contexts. According to the National Literacy Trust (NLT) in a Department of Education document published in November 2012, a lot of young people believe that 'writing is important... to succeed in life'. The same document reports that young writers believe 'using imagination' is important for writing. Interestingly, and this links to a Writing Ambassadors session from May 2017, Mimi Thebo, a YA writer, commented in reference to writing that 'anything is good'. This is what I wanted to encourage: for the young people not to be put off by the need to self-edit; in other words, to have fun and write, and not worry about what they were writing.

CREATIVE WRITING IN ACTION

From the beginning, my main objective was to encourage a love of writing, and I stressed this from the first session. The writers were asked questions about their writing habits, what they associated with good writing ('magical', 'passionate', 'amazing' were some shared words) and the benefits of creative writing: 'feeling good' and 'it is fun' came near the top, which was very reassuring. However, many members of the group commented that writing helps with studying in school and I valued this mature approach.

I was allocated seven sessions to work with the group and I planned each session with the writers' needs in mind. Some key points:

- A safe environment was established from the beginning: writers were never forced to share, although it was encouraged.
- Writer expectations were discussed: what was expected from 'Me and My World'?

- Name badges were provided, as were motivational treats.
- Each session started with the reading of a poem linked to the date, followed by writers workshopping – and sharing their work, if they wanted to.
- Sessions focused on objectives and stimuli, such as pictures, before encouraging the writers to produce their own responses.
- Over the first couple of weeks, I encouraged the writers to build up their own 'mini anthology' of pieces, all focused on the theme, so that they had sufficient work to choose from later.

A TYPICAL SESSION PLAN: 75 MINUTES

Timing	Activity
5 minutes	Welcome; reading of a poem for the day.
5+ minutes	Sharing of work; feedback; discussion of current reading.
5 minutes	Link to the previous session's work.
10 minutes	Task introduction and discussion/questions; sharing of resources, stimuli, expectations.
35 minutes	Writing time!
10 minutes	Recapping and consolidating
5 minutes	Next steps

The writing activities focused on the theme of 'Me and My World' but there was significant variation in terms of input provided and outcomes. Some examples included: writers bringing in a chosen object and describing its role in an unusual environment; using photographs and pictures for stimuli, considering actions, characters and settings; and experimenting with different forms, including 'translating' prose into poetry. Ultimately, the writers were given sufficient freedom as I wanted their outcomes to reflect their own engagement – and too many 'rules' might not have resulted in the creativity I was looking for.

Specific Focus: Session 4

To exemplify the success of the sessions, what follows is a close focus on one workshop – and how this bridged the gap between what had gone before and what was to follow.

The session started with a reading of Simon Armitage's 'Not the Furniture Game', a poem rich in metaphor, and fantastic for conjuring up ideas about characters. This was followed by a discussion of current reading – it was always great to celebrate the writers' choices. A task that I wanted to build on was focused on describing objects – from a pencil case, to a favourite cuddly toy – with the emphasis being on the unconventional and less obvious. By this stage in the sessions, the writers were used to sharing and tackling different activities as a means of improving their work and reflecting on how others' writing could help with their own.

To tie-in with 'Me and My World', pupils were presented with photographic stimuli and asked to answer the question 'Where am I?', ensuring that subtleties and implicit ideas were adopted. I discussed how writing can be 'translated' from one form to another, and this is what I asked the writers to do: for example, changing a poem into a piece of prose. The idea behind this was to encourage the writers to be adventurous – to move beyond their comfort zone – if only to experiment with different forms of writing. This fourth session culminated with a writing prompt ('My world is...'), and then I gave the writers a 25-word limit to demonstrate what their world encompasses. The rationale behind this was to restrict the time they had – as writers know, writing less is often more challenging than writing more – and I also wanted to conclude the session with a definite outcome.

The ending of the session lent itself to leaving the writers with something to come back to the following week; in this case, it was focusing on chosen pieces of writing to go into the final anthology.

FINDINGS

The final sessions culminated with the compilation of an anthology and a celebration event where the writers received their own copies of the anthologies and shared their writing. The group acknowledged that the sessions benefited the way they perceived writing, and personal objectives included writing more, to be proud of outcomes and to develop confidence with work – all extremely beneficial points. One writer's poem used a series of beautiful metaphors: *'When the sky was a shining gem / Waterfalls novel / The grass jade / This was only a small paradise'*. This writer's 'world' was conceptual; it was interpreted in an abstract, sophisticated way. Another's approach, a piece of flash fiction, was more literal, but no less stunning: *'The sky was painted with a soothing gradient. Blue. Purple. Red. Yellow. It was a blanket, woven with gorgeous fabric...'*

My experience was extremely positive and one that left me, and the writers, with outcomes that counted for such a lot. The feedback from the young people was positive, both ad hoc and through more formal surveys that I provided as part of the evaluation process. The completed anthology, and the ownership the writers had over this, was hugely advantageous. In addition, the celebratory sharing event – parents/carers and teachers were invited – highlighted the brilliance of the writers' work. Admittedly, I was fortunate to receive funding for this project and a small but willing group of ambitious creative writers. However, I believe that such a project, with a finite amount of sessions and a designated outcome, can work in so many settings, with both children and adults. It is about creating a safe, imaginative environment, and not forcing sharing but encouraging it. This, I realise, sounds idyllic but it worked – and it can work for you, too.

8 ACTIVITIES THAT WORKED

1. Starting sessions with a poem for the date/day – such as *A Poem for Every Day of the Year* (Macmillan).

2. Workshopping and sharing ideas, as a whole group or in smaller groups.
3. Bringing in objects from home to use as stimuli for creative writing tasks.
4. Providing pictures for writing stimulation.
5. Writing in a specific form, such as a 50-word piece of micro fiction or a haiku.
6. Taking 30 seconds to talk about a great book.
7. Changing the form: for example, poetry to prose, or vice versa.
8. Discussing good and bad examples of writing

REFERENCES

Armitage, S. (1992) 'Not the Furniture Game' in *Kid*, Faber and Faber: London.

Clark, C. National Literacy Trust (2013). *Children's and Young People's Writing in 2012: Findings from the National Literacy Trust's annual literacy survey,* NLT: London. [Accessed 10 May 2020].

Esiri, A. (ed) (2017) *A Poem for Every Day of the Year,* Main Market Edition, Macmillan: London.

WHERE ANGELS WRESTLE BEST:

HOW PLANNING CAN IMPACT WRITING AND WELLBEING IN A POETRY WORKSHOP

PATRICK TOLAND

The aim of this article is to provide teachers of creative writing in the secondary school sphere with a 'first person' insight and a suggested outline for how best to run a creative writing workshop focusing on challenging or emotive subjects. In particular, I outline a workshop I have crafted that focuses on creating poetry dealing with the theme of grief. I offer advice on how to navigate some of the pitfalls or risks whilst also considering how planning can impact writing and well-being in a poetry workshop.

INTRODUCTION

> I am often awed by the artistic temperament. It sometimes seems to me to be a battleground, ... [an] angel of destruction and ... [an] angel of creativity wrestling
> – 'Bishop Undercroft', in *A Severed Wasp* by Madeleine L'Engle

The philosopher Montaigne had his tower – a place of remove from busy public life that forced him, through isolation and confinement, to script his essays. Poet Wallace Stevens, so the story goes, imposed upon himself a lunch-break routine of writing that was guarded strictly by his secretary so that he could find inspiration through deliberately fettered circumstances. The message therein? That artistry can perform best if allowed to exist and ferment within some kind of creative curtilage.

Or more simply said, without rules; chaos may follow.

This notion, of how a lack of boundaries around creative activity can jeopardise the success of any creative writing, is examined critically by Andrews and Belk (2011). They state that, 'The problem with viewing creative writing as limitless space ... is that this very limitlessness often overwhelms students and actually hampers creativity.' This is the challenge then for the teacher of creative writing: to be able to referee the creative battleground of a writing workshop and not be undone by the 'angel' of amorphous aims, but instead be guided by the 'angel' of good pedagogy, informed by ideas of pastoral responsibility, student safeguarding and diligence in planning, especially if the writing we ask of our students steps into territories of well-being and the personally therapeutic.

CREATIVE WRITING IN ACTION

I work part-time in a secondary school, teaching Key Stage 3. As I only teach one day a week, it is not unusual for me to be somewhat unaware of school events in a way that a full-time member of staff would be less likely to. One particular day, I arrived at the school and was told that the timetable had been 'collapsed' to run a day of creative activities, for the charitable benefit of a local hospice (a care home for cancer patients that also offers grief counselling and support for patients and their families). The Faculty Head informed me that he and I would each be running a one-hour poetry workshop – at the same time but with separate groups in different classrooms – based around the theme of loss, grief and bereavement (linked to the work of the hospice).

I'm not usually someone averse to embracing the free-range nature of some creative-writing programmes and activities, but I expressed concern to my Senior Faculty Head at the need for a higher level of preparedness, and guardedness around the running of a workshop linked to such affecting and visceral material. My personal and professional senses – I am also a member of a UK/Ireland wide Poetry Therapy Network – were pushing me towards a 'gut-call', knowing that participants might have recent experiences of bereavement that could be unprocessed and 'raw'. Yet, due to time constraints and not wishing to disappoint the group or seem to be objectionable, I obliged by agreeing to do the workshop. On reflection, this 'reflex' decision meant a chance to apply my teaching writing skills to a group that could very much gain from writing about their experiences (especially in regards to boosting their own well-being and mental health through the 'catharsis' of writing). However, with similar reflection, what emerged could have been more enriching if we had gone through a proper process of planning and pre-deliberation.

When planning lessons that deal with sensitive subject matter, I believe the work of Jess-Cooke should be followed and examined. Jess-Cooke (2017) discusses how 'poetry therapy' is, as yet, generally unregulated in the UK. Jess-Cooke warns that *'anyone* can set up a writing for wellbeing workshop, and regardless of how experienced or well-intentioned a facilitator may be, writing workshops can have potentially catastrophic outcomes if safeguards are not in place'. She advises a checklist/precautionary approach as 'you don't know what people are carrying with them'. This includes adopting (or adapting for the participants) elements of pre-screening, an avoidance of triggering, an awareness of transference, and the need to provide avenues for further counselling support if required. Below are also a few specific ideas extracted from Bolton (1999), who describes such workshops as 'the healing pen' in which a teacher, like a health professional, should have a Hippocratic attitude of 'first do no harm'. A teacher may also consider:

- **The time of day and the space the workshop is run in.** If participants (or the teacher) are tired, hungry or thirsty this may enhance a sense of being unsettled. Is the room you are working in too cold, warm, bright or dark? The spaces between seats too close? Such physical matters can affect the mood of participants who need to feel comfortable but also able to focus.
- **Journalling.** If participants keep a journal, they could perhaps bring it (or some notes from it) to the workshop to provide them with some ideas for what to write about. The student and teacher can then work together to find the

positive/uplifting in the emotional debris that trauma/unhappiness/grief can cause.

- **The notion of workshop openings.** Bolton labels this 'unbuttoning, opening the box', and the prompts for writing that teachers use should be as varied and diverse as the groups they teach. A prompt could be a poem, quote, music clip, film clip, newspaper story, object etc. Yet care should be taken as some sights, sound or even smells can evoke difficult memories.
- **Writing as self-empowerment.** Bolton asserts that the participants (who may feel that their life and personal emotions are out of control) should always feel 'this is *my* decision' to write and be involved. The workshop should be co-designed/produced by the 'guiding' teacher and 'willing' participants.
- **Being attentive to voice, tone and pitch.** Bolton recognizes that when working with participants there can be a kind of 'regression' in which the participants can feel child-like and fragile, therefore your own teaching voice should have warmth, gentleness and a sense of care and assurance.

Docherty states that the 'multi-directional and multi-layered' activity of creation can have a 'varied birth' – 'even if the precise inputs are known, the precise outputs can never be known'. These inputs could include the use of 'transitional objects', espoused by Docherty in her analysis of the work of Winnicot (1953). For example, a participant can bring an object that was given to them by a lost loved one that has particular meaning and resonance (my own is an embroidery of a cottage sewn by my grandmother). These objects can become 'crutches' or 'scaffolding' that allow the participants to talk, share and be inspired in a way that has boundaries but also allows for the unexpected, in terms of how these objects can become 'bridges' or 'avenues' into writing. I would suggest, though, not allowing objects to be passed around in a group (imagine if someone dropped and broke such an object). Participants could also bring a song suggestion to the workshop, which, in a similar way, may provide a way for them to discuss challenging feelings and think about how these feelings can be transmuted into writing. Remember to ensure the technology is working properly beforehand, as it could be disheartening for a participant for 'their song' not to be heard.

An apt word to employ in relation to the importance of planning is *selvage* – the heavier weaved part of a hem that protects against fraying. To reach what Docherty describes as 'continuous flow', any river or even rivulet of creativity requires the analogous components of stoney bed, emplanked bank or concrete buttress to angle the direction of that river, or else it becomes an ill-defined flood or metaphysical swamp. Bolton suggests such boundaries, without losing sight of the fact that sometimes the best workshops are about swimming in high and turbulent waters. Being attentive to the heritage and lineage of the teaching of creative writing itself is another method for avoiding watery teaching practice. Monroe (2002) reminds us how the principle discipline of creative writing should be to recognise its disciplinary structure. Clare (2015) instructs us to also remember how some creative writing workshop tropes or methods (for example, warm-up reading) may persist because of their utility and we shouldn't reject them just for the allure of adventurism or the sake of difference. In our conduct as professionalised teachers of creative writing, whether we draw our inspiration from Andrews and Belk or not, it is our main task to ensure that when it comes to the wrestling angels of creativity, we are fully in charge of building and overseeing the forum and arena in which they do battle.

10 ACTION POINTS

1. Don't let yourself be 'bounced' into creative-writing sessions as a timetable filler or on subjects of any strong emotive nature. If you are asked to do so, make safeguarding students' wellbeing your defence.

2. Agree 'ground rules' or a code of conduct between yourself and your students before or at the beginning of a workshop. Agree some parameters for how work will be heard and received by the group, and what forms of feedback will be used.

3. Check and self-audit your own feelings, lived experience and baggage in regards to workshops around emotive themes. You have a responsibility to protect yourself and your own wellbeing as well as others'.

4. If you are conducting a workshop around an emotive issue, ensure that you give students ample but sensitive warning of any content that may arouse or 'trigger' any dormant emotions or unresolved and latent trauma. Think of the Hippocratic oath, 'First do no harm', as a guide to how to progress.

5. Can you give your students some appropriate reading/viewing material to help prepare them for the workshop and gently introduce them to the topics to be examined and work to be conducted?

6. Don't forget that the terms creative writing and therapeutic writing are not interchangeable: therapeutic writing requires additional formal training. Organisations such as Metonia can provide such training for teachers (https://www.metanoia.ac.uk/).

7. You may wish to examine *The Art of Grief* edited by J. Earl Rogers, and consider how other forms of expressive art can assist with understanding the topic of grief. Perhaps you could collaborate with colleagues in other subject areas to produce cross-curricular work on the theme?

8. Don't let your workshop become a 'House of Correction' – where you are focusing on what the students have not done well or accomplished, rather than how they have used their writing as a vehicle to

voice more profound and deep feelings. Be patient. Listen to your students. Credit them for their openness. Refinement, re-drafting and editing of work can come at a later stage.

9.   If you have to impose limits on a workshop, to protect yourself and your students, limiting the workshop by time rather than outcome can prove useful. Even though some subjects can be profoundly emotive, there is nothing wrong with putting time limits on writing exercises/feedback – just ensure that all students get a chance to share their work and that no student feels negated because 'time has run out'.

10.   I had the chance to repeat this workshop the following academic year with a different group of students. Knowing they enjoyed films, I decided to make that the 'way in' to the topic of grief and loss. See the plan below for a rough idea of the workshop structure.

HALF DAY HOSPICE WORKSHOP:
COURSE PLANNING DOCUMENT
(KEY STAGE 3)

Course Type: Seven sessions across seven weeks (45 minutes per session).
Proposed Course Title: Writing about loss and grief –
How *Avengers: Endgame* can help us write about grief and loss.

Course Development Team:
Course Developer: Patrick Toland
Course Tutor: Patrick Toland (Teacher of English/Film)
IT Support: (Head of IT)
Well-Being and Health Support: (School Nurse)
Well-Being and Health Support: (Head of Key Stage 3)

Aims of the Course:

1. For students to write about and explore their own experiences of grief and loss through film watching and creative writing.

2. For students to see *Avengers: Endgame* (the final film in the Marvel Cinematic Universe Avengers series) as a way into discussing grief and loss, and a stimulus to guide their own writing on the subject.

Target Audience:

Key Stage 3 students (a class of young men, a number of which have experienced recent loss and bereavement)

Course Content Overview:

This course will consider a range of film clips from the film *Avengers: Endgame* as stimulus to lead to wider writing/discussion tasks about the subject of loss and grief.

Course Textbook/Reading/Resources:

1. No textbook is required but it would be useful for students to read the Flickering Myth blog post about how *Avengers: Endgame* has a range of characters/character moments that exemplify the five stages of grief. See: https://www.flickeringmyth.com/2019/07/representa tion-five-stages-of-grief-in-avengers-endgame/

2. It would be helpful if students also did some prior web research on the Poetry Foundation and examined its section on writing examples around the theme of grief/loss/sorrow: https://www.poetryfoundation.org/articles/68559/po ems-of-sorrow-and-grieving

3. Students may also wish to visit the Cruse Bereavement Care website for information about loss or grief or support: https://www.cruse.org.uk, or examine the

Sue Ryder website: https://www.sueryder.org/how-we-can-help/someone-close-to-me-has-died/advice-and-support/how-can-i-cope-with-bereavement

SUPPLEMENTARY MATERIALS:

The course will be organised around five specific film clips from the film *Avengers: Endgame* (2019). These clips exist in the public domain and can be viewed in class or by students at home.

Delivery Mode, Pedagogy and Estimated Tutor Time and Student Study Time:

The course will run over seven sessions (45 minutes each) in class time and on timetable.

The mode of delivery: each class will begin by introducing the topic at hand, hearing and sharing responses to that topic, examining a film clip from *Avengers: Endgame* (aligned to one character and one stage of grief), hearing discussions about the clip and then using the clip/discussions to move into a short writing task (which will vary each week). Students may finish and present in class, or work on their writing during the week to bring it to the next class for feedback.

Week Plan:

- Week 0 - Introduction to Course Plans/Topics/Structure (Topic: Discussion of Personal Experiences of Grief/Loss). Instructions to research clips/the Kübler-Ross five stages of grief model as prep for next session.
- Week 1 - Denial/Thor: Clip Viewing/Writing Prompt (Advice Letter)
- Week 2 - Anger/Hawkeye: Clip Viewing/Writing Prompt (Court Victim Statement)
- Week 3 - Bargaining/Captain America: Clip Viewing/Writing Prompt (Support Group Role-Play – One bit of advice)

- Week 4 - Depression/Natasha: Clip Viewing/Writing Prompt (Note to Self)
- Week 5 - Acceptance/Hulk: Clip Viewing/Writing Prompt (Inspirational Speech)
- Week 6 - Summing Up/Conclusions/Ways Forward: 'You Can Rest Now' – The final words said to Tony Stark – Your Final Words (Writing a Poem).

Estimated Student Study Time:

5.25 hours (plus time for research prior to class, or work completed outside of class)

Estimated Tutor Time:

As above plus time for planning and reading/providing comments on student work.

Learning Outcomes:

As a result of the course, within the constraints of the time available, students should be able to:

- Appreciate that viewing film can be a method for opening up feelings of grief and loss, and a means to talk about those feelings in a safer way.
- Understand that their own creative writing can be prompted by film experiences.

Informal/Self-Assessment Opportunities:

Discussions about points of interest, appreciating and critiquing the film clips and each other's work, all involving input by tutors and peers.

Mechanisms for feedback to students:

- Weekly feedback on written work
- Opportunities to speak to other teachers (Head of Year/School Nurse) about getting any further help for issues of grief and loss.

What next?

Suggesting books or poetry to read about loss and grief e.g.
https://www.redonline.co.uk/reviews/book-
reviews/a527222/books-that-will-help-with-grief-loss/

Proposed QA procedure:
- Formal Report by teacher to Faculty Head
- End of Course Review with Faculty Head/Head of Year/School Nurse – especially to identify students who may require further emotional support.

Evaluation Opportunities for Students:

Student questionnaire at end of course, including personal reflection on learning and on need for further support, if required.

BIBLIOGRAPHY

Andrews, Kimberly Quiogue and Belk, John, 'Something to Push Up Against: Using Theory as Creative Pedagogy, in Dispatches from the Classroom: Graduate Students on Creative Writing Pedagogy, ed. by Chris Drew, Joseph Rein, David Yost (London, Continuum International Publishing Group, 2012)
Bolton, Gillie, The Therapeutic Potential of Creative Writing: Writing Myself (London: Jessica Kingsley Publishers, 1999)
Bourdieu, Pierre, Reproduction in Education, Society, Culture (Beverly Hills, CA, Sage, 1977)
Buttel, Robert and Doggett, Frank, Wallace Stevens: A Celebration (New York, Princeton University Press, 2014).
Brookhart, Susan M., How to Give Effective Feedback to Your Students (Alexandria: ASCD, 2017)
Chavis, Geri Giebel, Poetry and Story Therapy: The Healing Power of Creative Expression (London, Jessica Kingsley Publishers, 2011) p. 211-212
Clare, Horatio, Viewpoint: A Short History of Creative Writing (12th January 2015) https://www.liverpool.ac.uk/new-and-

international-writing/original-writing/articles-and-features/a-short-history-of-creative-writing/ [accessed 20 April 2019].

Cohen, Joshua L., Johnson, J. Lauren, Orr, Penny, Video and Filmmaking as Psychotherapy: Research and Practice (London: Routledge, 2015)

Deleuze, Gilles and Guattari, Felix, Extracts from A Thousand Plateaus by Gilles Deleuze and Felix Guattari (Minneapolis: University of Minnesota Press, 1987).

Desan, Philippe, Montaigne: A Life (New York: Princeton University Press, 2017).

Docherty, Abigail, 'What is 'creativity' and how do we as teachers unleash it?', Post-Graduate Certificate in Teaching Creative Writing (1819PCR900): Module One: The Philosophy and Context of Teaching Creative Writing, 2019.

Donnelly, Dianne, Establishing Creative Writing Studies as an Academic Discipline (Bristol, Multilingual Matters, 2011)

Earnshaw, Steven, The Handbook of Creative Writing (Edinburgh: Edinburgh University Press, 2007)

Elbow, Peter, Changing Grading while working with Grades, in Frances Zak and Christopher C. Weaver (ed.) The Theory and Practice of Grading Writing: Problems and Possibilities (New York: State University of New York Press, 1998)

Gillies, Midge and Durneen, Lucy , 'The history of teaching creative writing in different settings. Is it even possible to teach creative writing? What can't you teach? What kind of student and teacher are you? Is there a methodology of teaching creative writing? Who does it, where and how?', Post-Graduate Certificate in Teaching Creative Writing (1819PCR900): Module One: The Philosophy and Context of Teaching Creative Writing, 2019.

Gillies, Midge and Durneen, Lucy (2019). Course Reader Module Two (Introduction). Cambridge: Published by ICE. O'Connor, Philip, F, Instructions Based on Some of What I've Learned about Conducting Creative Writing Workshops (Mississippi Review, Vol. 19, No. 1/2, Workshops, 1990)

Greenberg, Suzanne, 'A 'A' for Effort: How Grading Policies Shape Courses', in Ann Leahy (ed.) Power and Identity in the

Creative Writing Classroom. (Cleveden: Multilingual Matters Ltd, 2005)

Jess-Cooke, Carolyn, Safety first: safeguards for writing for wellbeing (Mslexia: 76, 2017).

Gillies, Midge and Durneen, Lucy (2019). Course Reader Module Two (Introduction). Cambridge: Published by ICE. Green, Chris, Materializing the Sublime Reader: Cultural Studies, Reader Response, and Community Service in the Creative Writing Workshop (College English, Vol. 64, No. 2, Nov. 2001)

Izod, John and Dovalis, Joanna, Cinema as Therapy: Grief and transformational film (London: Routledge, 17 Dec 2014)

Jesson, Jill, Developing Creativity In The Primary School (London: McGraw-Hill Education, 2012)

Kravitz, Bennett, Representations of Illness in Literature and Film (Cambridge: Cambridge Scholars Publishing, 2010)

Madeleine L'Engle, A Severed Wasp (New York: Farrar Straus Giroux, third Printing edition, 1983).

Miller, Andrew, Freedom to Fail: How do I foster risk-taking and innovation in my classroom? (Alexandria/USA: ASCD Arias, 2015)

Monroe, Jonathan, Writing and Revisiting the Disciplines (New York: Cornell University Press, 2002).

Morley, David, The Cambridge Introduction to Creative Writing (Cambridge: Cambridge University Press, 2007)

Morrison, Matt, Key Concepts in Creative Writing (London: Red Globe Press, 2010)

Page, Ellis, Teacher comments and student performance: A seventy-four classroom experiment in school motivation (Journal of Educational Psychology: 1958, 49)

Peake, Tom H., Cinema and Life Development: Healing Lives and Training Therapists (Santa Barbara: Greenwood Publishing Group, 2004)

Solomon, Gary, Reel Therapy: How Movies Inspire You to Overcome Life's Problems (New York: Lebhar-Friedman Books, 2001)

Tanggard, Lene and Wegener, Charlotte, 'A Creative Peer to Peer Methodology', in The Palgrave Book of Social Creativity

Research, ed. by Izabela Lebuda, Vlad Petre Glăveanu (London: Palgrave Macmillan, 2018).

Thaxton, Terry Ann, Creative Writing in the Community (London, A & C Black, 2013)

Thebo, Mimi, 'Hey Babe, Take a Walk on the Wide Side - Creative Writing in Universities', in Key Issues in Creative Writing, ed. by Diane Donnelly, Graeme Harper (Bristol: Multilingual Matters, 2012)

Vandermeulen, Carl, Negotiating the Personal in Creative Writing (Bristol: Multilingual Matters, 2011)

Wassman, Claudia, Therapy and Emotions in Film and Television: The Pulse of Our Times (New York: Springer, 2016)

Wandor, Michelene, The Author is Not Dead, Merely Somewhere Else: Creative Writing Reconceived (Basingstoke: Palgrave Macmillan, 2008)

Winnicott, D.W, 'Transitional Objects and Transitional Phenomena — A Study of the First Not-Me Possession', International Journal of Psycho-Analysis, .34, (1953), 89-97

FORBIDDEN

GABRIEL TROIANO

Faythe grips the piano which her father used to play. I feel her steady hands puncturing my soul as I escape from the dreary town hall party. I walk down the living room, not wanting my steps to pause the melodious concerto. Her eyes are filled with wounds from the past, decades of lost hope. She is beautiful, delicate, yet lost in all of life's compromises.

I approach her with open arms and stiff lips. I can hear her slow breath, almost perfectly in sync with mine. She is expecting me. She has been sensing my presence for the whole night. As I come from behind and lay my hands on her shoulder, she turns around and with the slightest move places my hand on her face. I scan my eyes around the room to convince myself that it is all happening.

I lean over and kiss her. I kiss her repeatedly, passionately, as if we were lovers that had been drawn apart for an eternity. It was like our stories had brought us here, to this hideous party, to this room, to this kiss.

Suddenly, I feel a rush of uncertainty from her.

'But what about Helen, aren't you afraid of what might happen?'

'I don't care about Helen, I care about you Faythe. I care about this moment', I reply, clearly.

Small tear droplets start racing across her soft face as she tries to evaluate her actions.

'My father, poor old man... if he could see me now! Father, forgive me, I did not know you at that time, all I can ask for is your forgiveness!' The more she tosses and turns, the more she tries to escape her past. She can no longer get rid of her senses. I try to decipher her face, the darkest of pits, but I can see the story behind the pain.

'Love is but a word that turns into desire, my dear, and we desire each other. That you cannot deny.'

'Inside, deep inside, I know I am loved. My chest is aching with this feeling, this thing I cannot get rid of. If only I could talk to him again, with you here with me, he would understand. Yes, I know my father would be very fond of you, like he was of this piano. But inside, there's a world I cannot decipher yet.'

I sense an internal desperation for solace in her, as if time is running out and my chance in saving her is here. I grip her again and kiss her tight lips once more. She radiates within me and I within her.

LEARNING ACTIVITIES COMMENTARY

With this novel excerpt, I introduce a fiery yet forbidden romance between two characters. In literature, doing something forbidden, whether that is sneaking out as a teenager to attend a party or eating a chocolate cake late at night, has great storytelling potential. This allows the writer to engage the audience in a conflict, a drama that involves characters who are in some way facing a challenge, a milestone, a significant happening that is able to move the plot forward.

For those constructing a novel or short story, this idea is one worthy of exploration. First, start by making a list of things that are forbidden, something that someone would do that goes against the norm in some way (such as the examples I gave above). From there, expand the idea. For example, a boy eats a chocolate cake late at night and his mother catches him in the act, telling him to go back to his bedroom and to stay there until further notice. The interesting thing is that this can be interwoven with other conflicts happening in the story. This chocolate-eating scene could be paired with the divorce that the boy's parents are going through, causing the mother to flip out unnecessarily and create even more family drama – expanding the scope of the novel or short story. Eating the cake becomes only part of the story, a detail that can be introduced to develop each character.

Doing something forbidden can also mean a character doing something that will set the tone for the rest of the story. A forbidden affair, a crime, a secret that gets out – it can be anything. You can build your plot around this idea or you can use it to describe a specific moment in time. Whichever idea you choose, it's a great way to create a compelling story.

THAT SHAKESPE-HEREAN RAG:
Metre and Authenticity in Poetry behind Bars

STEPHEN WADE

The following is drawn from my experience working with adult prisoners, often with low levels of literacy. However, I believe that the examples outlined could be applied to low ability/PRU classes.

In creative writing workshops in prison communities, the challenge for the teacher or workshop leader is to open up for students the possibilities and potentialities of what is recognised as a poem. The reason for this is that simple end-rhymes and rhyming couplets dominate conceptions of what poetry is. For most, a poem *is* a rhyme of some kind. Free verse may even be looked upon as being inferior.

With this in mind, in my years working as a writer in residence in a number of prisons I experimented with ways of being adventurous, enjoying formal constraints and letting the rhythms of a poem match the authentic 'voice' at the heart of the poetic idea. The students 'inside' had no problem understanding the point about an 'authentic voice' in poetry. After all, when they do sit down to write a poem which is going home in a letter or on a card, a great number of prison writers are happy to produce rhymed platitudes, and use limited vocabulary, but the important aspect of this to see is that they do not see these limitations. Most of the people behind bars have no reading experience of poems across the massive spectrum of forms and subjects that literature offers.

To expand on this a little, what I am referring to here is the acceptance of an easy rhyme in prison poetry. The authentic voice of experience in much modern poetry is created by a very specific vocabulary, intricate metrical devices and, often, subtle rhyme-schemes, rich allusions using the potential of intertextuality, and so on. In prison, as with many other sub-cultures, what has most impact is the beat and rhyme of a poem or indeed a song. My opinion is that the readers and writers I worked with do have a sense of the authentic voice when they hear or read its testimonies, but more than any other factor in their enjoyment of poetry, they want *immediacy.* Having to unpack meaning might be a pleasure to some, but most want the foot-tapping insistence on a rhyme and a simple stanza. The poems in the prison newspapers show this too.

Sincerity and authenticity, then, should be made apparent in the workshops undertaken behind bars. The most powerful way to show this, and to encourage writing, is to work on poems with fast, urgent, clear meaning. But this is not to say that rich and staggeringly fresh imagery is not to be admitted. On the contrary, as I have seen in reading thousands of scripts produced by prisoners over the years, although message prevails over medium, as Marshall McLuhan would have put it, the prison poets relish and enjoy the artifice of the poet's craft when they encounter it. Preaching about 'fine words' will not achieve anything; but showing by reading a poem and then pointing out the craft will pinpoint the skills behind a poem.

One of the most productive ways of highlighting the authenticity problem is to read together, as a group, one of the anonymous poems that circulate in prisons. One example I came across in Lincolnshire was 'The Boston Boy.' I saw several versions of this, but most began with:

> The Boston Boy threw it all away.
> His woman, his kids, his life.
> The Boston Boy in his pad did lay,
> Brought there by his knife

The theoretical basis of the work behind my workshop has its roots in Russian Formalism and the wonderfully attractive challenges of 'making it new' and making the stone *stony.* In prisons, writing is highly valued, and poetry is the most revered. The ability to write an interesting poem for a birthday card or for Valentine's Day is a special skill, and a wordsmith will find other inmates drawn to his or her expertise. In my experience as a writer, varieties of 'make it strange' which have filtered through to such writing as The Mersey Poets in the 1960s or to poets such as Sylvia Plath have a powerful impact in prison writing workshops.

The next step, after deciding on the aim of being successful both in the use of metre and yet keeping the authentic voice for the feeling energising the poem, was to find a *modus operandi.* I decided to keep to one simple example: iambic pentameter. If students grasped the principle, they would extend it in their reading. It would also sharpen their appreciation of the poems in print which they encountered every day: the prison newspapers carry poetry pages, and the poetry shelves in prison libraries are always high on the lists of borrowings. There may also be a prison magazine. In my years as a writer behind bars, I always set up a magazine. The prisoners love working on such a project, and they always want a poetry section.

The workshop would be in three stages. The first part involves the use of objects. A mix of interesting small objects are placed in a bag. When I was teaching, I gradually collected material for this object-bag; it was an exercise I first learned from the poet Graham Mort. Popular and enjoyable workshop ideas tend to circulate and be used in different ways by each practitioner, undergoing a journey not unlike a folksong as it travels through cultures.

Before using this bag of objects, as the context is a prison, each object has to be logged and also vetted to check its potential as a makeshift weapon. Using the notion of a shadow-board, I keep a log of every object and make sure that it is collected at the end of the session. In this first stage, I explain that they must close their eyes, and keep them closed as I walk around with the bag. Each student takes an object and they are allowed to explore it for one minute before I collect it back. Their eyes remain closed until I take the object back, and then they start writing.

My instructions are that they write down everything that has been floating through their minds, at random, in no form. They should not worry about writing sentences, and certainly not start to write a poem. I tell them that the object might suggest just an image – a wing-nut might suggest ears, and so all they have is a simile perhaps. But an object might suggest a memory or a theme; in my workshops, a little tin soldier was always productive, sometimes giving the student a theme about wars or about empires.

Stage two is the point at which I introduce the notion of iambic pentameter. The poem I used on many occasions for this is 'The Old Oak Tree' by W. H. Davies. I read the opening stanza and then on the whiteboard I write the first quatrain (the poem has six quatrains with an end-rhyme of abcb). This is the first stanza:

> I sit beneath your leaves, old oak,
> You mighty one of all the trees;
> Within whose hollow trunk a man
> Could stable his big horse with ease. ·

There are many options available here to show the x / of the iambic foot. My favourite was to have a guitarist bring his instrument along and play two chords, with the sonority on the second one. But foot tapping will do the job, as will (if some humour is needed) the old de **dum** de **dum** de **dum** de **dum** de **dum**.

It is valuable here also to bring in examples of 'making strange'. I start with a look at the Davies poem. What is made strange here? This is my question, and here I list on the whiteboard all the 'facts' of the poem which are **not** made strange. So we are exploring literal and metaphorical expression. Together, we locate 'stable' as the one comparison. Everything else is a descriptive of the tree, literally. A useful discussion here is to ask whether or not 'making strange' is actually what literature has always been about. Students are asked to quote favourite lines from poems to show this. I use:

'How close we were with death's wings overhead' (from 'A Close One' about being bombed)

'Sleep now,

Alone in the sleeves of grief'   (Brian Patten: 'Sleep Now.')·

Now it's down to the writing. I ask the group to choose two statements from their notes on the object and then write these down. These are read out, and then I pick out the images used, and we all talk about the degree to which the subject has been estranged from immediate facts and descriptions. The students are asked to change the two statements into a rhyming couplet – to find rhymes using synonyms. Following that, I ask them to force the iambic pattern on the statements. The results show up the challenge for the poet. I would list the general results like this:

- The sentence will not work at all as natural expression in this way.
- The changes do work, but the resulting two lines are not 'poetic'.
- The lines work quite well, but they don't really make strange.

The development of this, in the last phase of the session, is to introduce Shakespeare. I read *Shall I compare thee to a summer's day?* Then I ask what it is saying. Generally, if I explain that it is from a sequence of love poems, the meaning of that specific sonnet is pretty clear today. It is perfect for the topic. 'Shall I compare thee to a summer's day', I suggest, is Shakespeare making strange.

At that point, it is homework time because I want them to write any form of poem as long as it uses iambics. I also ask that they use something conversational. To set this up, we play around with translating the Shakespeare sonnet into modern speech. This is the fun part. I start off with statement, ignoring metre:

> If you like, I could say you're nice as a day in summer
> You're a lot more sexy, and more easy-going.
> In England, a day in June can be a bummer
> And our peace disturbed by some bugger mowing...

Their task for the next session is to write something based on everyday talk, and use iambics for most of the poem.

After presenting this workshop a number of times in the jails I worked in, I have to stress that the workshop calls for commitment to the tasks involved. Creative writing classes in prison are subject to so many constraints, and there are so many hurdles blocking the way to success, that a succession of short sessions will achieve more than one or two full periods in the day's timetable.

In fact, the writing is best done over a longish session with a tea break in the middle. Prisoners are often short on attention span; their lives are riddled with worries and anxieties. Creativity, in all its forms, is one activity which offers them a kind of release from the blandness and routine of a prison regime. There is so much pressure by the prison system to initiate 'purposeful activity' that often such an activity as creative writing is not seen as purposeful. But my conclusions from this are encouraging and optimistic. First, the session – if, say, an hour and a half is available (with the break) – will move from the stimulus material through to a poetic draft, and so the whole writing process will be experienced and understood. I am sure that students doing this activity will perceive the workings of a poem such as a sonnet or any other set form in ways which were not available before in their reading.

A valuable point here is to explain that the established forms and stanzas etc. may be ignored, and the poet can write his or her own formal structure – in this, I keep just to line length and end-rhyme. From the Davies poem the students have seen the *abcb* and the development to *defe* and so on through the whole poem. From that, I show the Shakespearean sonnet patterns of lines and metre, and soon the students are enjoying experimenting with their own forms. I have a favourite example which I always quote: this is *The Horwich Hennets* (1976) by Edmund Leo Wright. They like the idea that Wright made his own form, the 'hennet', and they see the point of doing so. (A hennet has twelve lines and each line has eleven syllables, but beyond that it gets too complicated.)

If a writer is able to achieve it, then creating his or her own special stanza form is very rewarding. Wright's concept of the hennet may easily be a template for any other poet doing a similar formal structure for the poem being written. I remember once suggesting that a poet called Smith could create a 'smithet' stanza, or Mr Brown could generate a 'Brownet.'

I used to end the session with a reading of a sonnet I have written to explain what a sonnet is:

A Sonnet Looks at Itself

I begin like this, all full of myself
With plenty to say to make you think,
Like taking just one book down from the shelf.
You read me before you've time to blink.
A sonnet – little but with a great heart
And perfect in my way: quite beautiful,
An advert for the poet's craft and art,
Making his approach dark and dutiful.
I'm a poem with a strong purpose, a quest;
To show the love of rhythmic lines and rhymes.
You need to work to make me look my best
And write me in your deepest loving times.
 I end with joy, wonder, power and passion.
 Amazingly, I've never been out of fashion.

What might be done as a step further in this area of poetry writing? In prisons there are education courses, of course. Work done by the writer could be integrated into the curriculum managed by the teacher, but in practice I found this difficult. The reason for this is that a writer in residence is seen by the inmates as a free spirit, not linked to teaching and nothing to do with the professionals who run the jail. I used to wear distinctive clothes, and these were completely different to anything worn by staff, as well as being nothing like the standard prison garb worn by the guests of Her Majesty.

The role of the writer in residence is to respond to what the students inside want to write. Hence, when I was told that poetry was popular, I began to see that rhyme was popular, and that students tended to be happy with simple rhymes and lines. But in my very first session explaining how poems work, I found that the class wanted to have metre explained. I remember writing on the whiteboard the patterns of stressed syllables in one of the poems written by a student. The group were really keen to know more about the 'ups and downs' of verse.

What comes next then, after a session such as I have described, is a course of reading and writing, using printed poems as templates. In itself, this is a viable topic to explore. I usually say that all writers learn from other writers, but that there is a concept of plagiarism. The point is to copy patterns of sound in order to learn, and so when I set the first homework, I spend that time showing how each writer can invent his or her own forms.

NO WRITER IS AN ISLAND
HOW DOES READING AND FREEWRITING AFFECT THE WRITER AND THE WRITING?

JAMES WARD

This article is a personal reflection on a study undertaken to explore the use of freewriting activities in the creative writing process. The article also outlines the academic context that underpinned the study and its conclusions. The conversation started here is intended to ignite new interest in freewriting as a tool for learning. In this context freewriting becomes a means for learners to engage with canonical texts as exemplars and stimulus for new understanding, personal engagement, and enriched creativity.

I had never sought to draw direct influence from the work of others into my writing. Certainly not as an adult. To closely follow the example of any established author would be to imitate rather than create in a credible manner. But I had also failed to establish an identity for myself as a writer within a community of writers or creative writing tradition. I came to realise this position was creatively and technically stunting. Identifying and incorporating influences is the bedrock of any writer's work. Indeed, no writer is an island.

I had to learn to read as a writer and respond creatively to this reading. By this I mean close, analytical, indeed critical, reading of fiction. Sarah Moss believes learning to be a better reader is almost more important than writing itself: 'I learned to write by reading … I teach people to write by teaching them to read' (2020: 01).

This brief research study investigates how close reading of works of fiction and responsive freewriting influences or affects the creative writing process. It looks at the possibility that this combined practice can enable the development of writer identity.

LITERATURE REVIEW

This research uses the concept of intertextuality – proposed by Kristeva (1969) and Bakhtin (1981) – as a framework to explore influence in the context of creative writing. Allen (2000) states: 'Texts, whether they are literary or non-literary, are viewed by modern theorists as lacking in any kind of independent meaning. They are … intertextual' (p.1). The context, meaning and credibility of any new work of creative writing is derived from its relationship or similarity to extant texts.

Absorbing and Transforming Texts

Orr (2003) evoking Bakhtin (1895–1975) suggests 'any text is the absorption and transformation of another' (p.21). This proposition offers considerable weight to the notion of influence in writing. Writers are asked about their creative influences so often there is an implication the answer shouldn't be complex. But intertextuality suggests factors influencing the development of creative writing are anything but straightforward.

Creative writing is an aspect of a complex established system of which extant literary or non-literary texts are just part. Wilkie-Stibbs (1999) points to this complexity:

> The literary text … is just one of many sites where several discourses converge, are absorbed, are transformed and assume a meaning because they are situated in this circular network of interdependence which is called the intertextual space (p.168).

In my own practice, a key problem was a lack of awareness of my literary or non-literary 'influences,' or recognition of the 'intertextual space' I inhabit as a writer.

Influence and the Intertextual Space

By understanding or having an awareness of the 'intertextual space,' the writer can better develop his craft – this relates to the technicality of his writing and what he writes about – and can benefit from a greater sense of identity within a literary or non-literary creative writing community or tradition.

Clayton and Rothstein (1991) contrast influence, an 'ancient given', against the more recent emergence of intertextuality: 'Concern with influence arose in conjunction with the mid-eighteenth century interest in originality and genius, and the concept still bears the marks of the original.' This notion, of the 'genius' in isolation, persists today. 'From the very beginning [of the nineteenth century], influence was an author-centric and evaluative concept'. At that point, the convention of 'tracing influences' was established (pp. 4-5). The question, 'Who are your influences?' arose to judge, identify and categorise the writer in relation to the perceived originality of totem literary figures of 'genius'.

The Writer as Reader

Formal education resulted in my seeing creative writing as the preserve of an elite. The concept of intertextuality is possibly more inclusive than the traditional notion of influence, which ignores the wider agency at work in the 'intertextual space'. This extends to the role of the reader; and, in the first instance, to the writer as reader.

Wilkie-Stibbs (1999) suggests literary theorists 'are recognising the place of intertextual understandings in literary studies for readers' reception and reproduction of texts' (ibid: p.168). She notes Barthes (1915–1980) coined the term 'infinite intertextuality' in reference to the 'intertextual codes by which a reader makes sense of a literary work.' Barthes describes a 'mirage of citations', which dwell equally in readers and texts (ibid: p.170). The writer must become literate in terms of 'intertextual codes' and develop as a reader in order to actualise as a writer.

The Reader as Writer

Bruner (1986) states 'the writer's greatest gift to the reader is to help him become a writer.' He suggests the reader constructs a 'virtual text,' the meaning of which is his own (pp. 66-67). This proposition liberates the reader from any obligation to engage with a specific meaning prescribed or intended by the writer. It is feasible the reader benefits through the construction of his 'virtual text,' gaining a renewed understanding of his identity in relation to others. This transaction has even greater significance for the reader as creative writer. By reading, rereading or close reading, and subsequent writing, writer identity begins to form.

Barrs (2000) advocates the benefits of pleasure alongside understanding in reading in an educational context: 'Our favourite texts are where, as readers, we apprentice ourselves as writers.' Reading pleasure was among the variables considered in selecting texts for inclusion in this study. Barrs proposes the writer 'draws on her experience of styles and rhythms,' and suggests: 'Writers who are also readers are people with a large number of tunes and structures in their heads' (pp. 54-55). Reading therefore furnishes the writer with the technical means to develop his craft.

Reading and Close Reading
Nicholson (2017) suggests close reading of texts is not meant to 'uncover universal truths', but 'to pay detailed attention to the political and cultural significance of texts'. This is not, however, so impersonal a brushstroke: 'Close reading can reveal the tensions and contradictions in a text, and it can illuminate moments of experience by placing them in the context of other cultural, artistic or social practices' (pp. 183-184).

Nicholson's reference to 'experience,' points to the element that ultimately makes any text relevant and understandable, and any narrative universal. Frey and Fisher (2013) suggest: 'Close readings should be done with texts that are worthy and complex enough to warrant repeated reading and detailed investigation.' Of course in terms of intertextuality this is relative to the individual reader. They cite the recommendation of Rosenblatt (1995) that the reader 'should develop an understanding of the author's words and bring their own experiences, beliefs, and ideas to bear on the text' (p.57).

Freewriting from Experiences

Bringing my experiences to bear on the texts selected for close reading during this study was achieved through freewriting in response to reading. Reynolds (1984) explains freewriting as an exercise intended to generate 'new and unexpected ideas,' and has variously been called 'spontaneous,' 'stream-of-consciousness,' or 'non-stop-writing.' Reynolds presses the assertion of Dorothea Brande (1893 – 1948) that writers must cultivate the two sides of their nature: the conscious 'craftsman and the critic,' and the unconscious, 'the artist's side.' The development of freewriting in the mid-twentieth century owes much to Brande's idea for a 'program of writing to cultivate the unconscious and thereby have the two sides functioning harmoniously' (p.81). This research study considers that duality.

RESEARCH APPROACH

This short personal research study was autoethnographic in nature. It was undertaken to explore the effect that close reading of extant works of fiction and freewriting in response to that reading, carried out on a daily basis, might have on my writing practice. Ellis & Boscher (2000) assert: 'Autoethnography is an autobiographical genre of writing and research that displays multiple layers of consciousness, connecting the personal to the cultural' (p.739). This model validated my writing about the personal in response to close reading. Munsey (2010) proposes: '[an autoethnography] somehow emerges out of the iterative process of doing research, while engaging the process of living a life' (p.3).

The key aspects of this research study in practice included:

- Close reading of selected extracts of fiction.
- Freewriting in response to close reading.
- Mining of personal experience through this combined practice.

RESEARCH METHODS

I conducted this autoethnographic research study to explore if close reading of fiction, and focused freewriting in response to reading, could have a positive effect on the development of my writing practice. I also wanted to mine and channel personal experience – recollections and observations – into my work in a more focused way.

The study was conducted over a two week period with close reading and focused freewriting exercises undertaken on ten individual week days.

Close reading

A prescribed structure for the study was important. To achieve this I used a selection of extracts taken from short works of fiction and extracts compiled by Anderson (2006). I selected and compiled a list of ten readings for inclusion in the study. Criteria for selection consisted of the author's name, the title of the work, and my initial instinctive response to each.

Freewriting

To scaffold my freewriting, I incorporated a freewrite activity into the study (Activity 1.2, Anderson 2006, p.23) (Figure 0.1). Following the activity's instruction, I chose one of the 'beginnings' provided to start each freewrite. I used one beginning per freewrite, without the option to choose one at random or use a beginning more than once.

Choose three or four of the following beginnings and freewrite for a few minutes about each one.
ACTIVITY 1.2
Writing

- The truth is …
- I wish I had said …
- I need proof …
- I went outside and …
- For the first time ever …
- It surprised me when …
- It was no use pretending …
- A long time ago …
- I turned the corner, and there, coming towards me was …
- That smell reminds me of …
- One summer's day …

Read over your freewrites. Underline any words, phrases or lines that interest you. Start to build a stock of material for possible development.

Figure 0.1

I wrote for a timed period of 20 minutes each day – short enough to fit into any given day, yet long enough to generate sufficient data.

Data generation

The data was generated using pen and paper. Handwriting is more conducive to freewriting as it protects the spontaneity compromised on digital devices.

Prescribed perspectives

Anderson (2006) suggests 'to establish point of view is one of the most empowering things a fiction writer can learn. It gives you a range of possibilities to select from and increases your versatility and clarity as a writer' (p.99). To challenge myself and enrich the variety of data generated, I allowed the perspective encountered in individual close reads to dictate the point of view I used in my freewrite responses.

Ethics

Elbow (1989) highlights the often private nature of the work generated through freewriting (p.58). I decided inclusion of all the generated data was important in demonstrating the variety of results; and the range of analytical possibilities a longer study could allow.

DATA ANALYSIS AND FINDINGS

The generated data was analysed under the following headings:

- Close reading to scaffold writing
- Freewriting to explore and create
- Towards identity: the emergence of themes

Close reading to scaffold writing

Close reading is often associated with the 'analytical reading' of text 'to dig down into its deeper meaning' (Frey and Fisher, 2013, p.57). In this study close reading was also used to identity and engage with technical aspects of the writer's craft – elements such as structure, form, and rhythm. Anderson (2006) asserts: 'The structure of any narrative is arrived at through organisation of time, from choosing where and how the narrative should start, to deciding upon the dramatic present' (p.152). Newkirk (2010) suggests: 'Writers often struggle with their beginnings because they are making so many commitments ... establishing a voice, narrator, and point of view that are right for what will follow' (p.8).

The first text I close read, 'from Cal' by Bernard MacLaverty (b.1942), has an opening sentence that arguably addresses the challenges outlined by Newkirk:

> 'Feeling clean on the outside, with his hair held back in a tail by an elastic band, Cal drove the van over to Crilly's place' (MacLaverty, cited in Anderson 2006).

Following close reading of this text, I immediately undertook a timed freewrite, which emerged with following opening lines:

> 'The Truth is, a good haircut can be everything. But right then, and for that very reason, Rory felt ridiculous.'

Hammond and Gibbons (2001) suggest the theoretical basis of scaffolding lies in theories of learning by Vygotsky (1896–1934). In an educational context, the term refers to the provision of 'temporary supporting structures that will assist learners to develop new understandings, new concepts, and new abilities' (pp. 14-16). As a 'learner,' my close reading of 'from Cal,' provided scaffolding for the drafting of my freewrite response. This included the structure of my opening sentence in terms of punctuation and language, and the inclusion of details relating to appearance in introducing the protagonist.

Cowan (2010) explains 'form' in writing by asserting 'writing ... absorbs us not because of what it is about, but because of how it is written – and ... how it might be *re*written (p. 214). The role of form was demonstrated to me forcibly upon close reading 'The Black Cap,' a short story by Katherine Mansfield (1888–1923). This work is made up predominantly of dialogue and directional text in brackets:

> 'SHE: Oh, if you should want your flannel shirts, they are on the right-hand bottom shelf of the linen press' (Mansfield, cited in Anderson 2006).

The story's form made it conducive to fast reading. It also enabled me to complete a freewrite with time to spare from the allocated 20 minutes:

> The woman: Good morning. Welcome! *(She smiles)*
> Me: Good morning. *(I smile)*
> The woman: Please come in, I was about to start the next tour.
> Mark *(my friend)*: Ok, let's go in. *(He grimaces at me)*

Freewriting to explore and create

The scaffolding provided to this study by close reading resulted in what Elbow and Belanoff (2000) call 'focused freewriting' (pp.6-7). My freewrite responses were suggested by an aspect of the narrative encountered during close reading. Hollway and Jefferson (2000) propose 'free-association narrative' is based on the premise that meanings underlying 'elicited narratives are best accessed via links based on spontaneous association'. They also suggest 'free associations follow an emotional rather than a cognitively derived logic' (p. 153). Anderson (2006) states: 'In freewriting … we permit ourselves to associate freely' (p. 22).

The kinds of 'spontaneous association' that presented in my freewrite responses proved surprising. On close reading 'from *Age of Iron*' by J.M Coetzee (b.1940), I immediately undertook a freewrite based on my early primary school experience. The novel is narrated by the central protagonist, a retired Classics professor, as a letter to her emigrant daughter:

> 'How I longed to be able to go upstairs to you … whisper in your ear as I did on school mornings, Time to get up!' (Coetzee, cited in Anderson 2006).

Elbow (1989) tells us: 'Unfocused exploring is probably my main use of freewriting.' He also states he 'follows the train of associations' (p.58). On reading 'from *Age of Iron*', I also followed this 'train,' which, echoing the suggestion of Hollway and Jefferson (2000), I found to be of emotional rather than cognitive origin and destination. I wrote:

> 'I cried again in the classroom, on my small chair, as my mother waved goodbye and went out into the day.'

This close reading sparked a 'spontaneous association' with school, which became the basis of my freewrite. And following the narrative perspective of Coetzee's novel, I directly addressed my first primary school teacher:

> 'I need proof, they would probably remind me, but I do think it was your fault. I think you started it. It took me years to suss it, but I think you primed disaster from the beginning.'

This brings me back to beginnings and the use of scaffolding in this study. As I outlined in the methodology, I employed a freewriting exercise (Anderson, 2006), which supplied a list of phrases to kick-start each freewrite. I found the use of this activity beneficial to the creative process on a number of levels. A writer's work can become formulaic – *Once upon a time I went to school…* But using a prescribed beginning such as 'I need proof …' was creatively liberating rather than restricting. It challenged me, pushed me out of my comfort zone, and forced me to say something different. The prescribed beginning 'That smell reminds me of...' was paired, according to this study's methodology, with the text *'The Artist'* by Patricia Highsmith (1921–1995). This short story about an art college caused me to 'follow a train of associations' and write about experiences during my undergraduate degree. But this prescribed beginning challenged me to explore further, and I made an association with a university tutor with body odour:

> 'That smell reminds me of the noxious body odour of a very obese man.'

Guided by the study's methodology, this freewrite developed an alternative narrative, stimulated though previously unexplored routes of experience.

Towards identity: the emergence of themes
Brooks (1988) discussing writing in the classroom, highlights the use of reading and writing by students to undertake 'an exploration of situations in their own lives.' Rather than viewing a text as 'a model for imitation,' students use 'writing to explore the complexity of experience and communicate what they find.' The act of self-exploration is one in and the same with the writer identity (pp.27-28). I associate strongly with this view and argue writer identity is a process of incremental development in exploring one's own life and the lives of others.

Elbow (1989) stated 'I feel most myself when I freewrite.' There is credence in this statement with relation to the development of writer identity through practice. Elbow also suggests freewriting is 'analytic' and 'invites a personal honesty' (pp. 43-46).

During the study I entered a writing space unencumbered by self-censorship or superficial self-consciousness. With a focus on exploring the relationship between close reading and freewriting in terms of my own practice, I used the material most readily at hand: personal experience. Through this exploration, I caught glimpses of my writer identity in the themes that emerged.

Six of my freewrites were thematically focused on childhood and adolescent experience. This is a high proportion, particularly as I was drawing organically and generally on personal experience and didn't allow the texts to dictate the period of life I explored in my freewrites. This points to the value of freewriting in terms of mining personal experience for authentic emotional resonance. It also indicates the usefulness of freewriting in guiding the writer to areas of particular creative value.

CONCLUSION

The issue of influence is contentious in the context of intertextuality (Clayton & Rothstein, 1991). But the writer exists and his work develops within the interdependence of the intertextual space (Wilkie-Stibbs, 1999). Having completed this study, I came to find this idea both instructive and reassuring. I find resonance in Sontag (2001): 'Reading usually proceeds writing. And the impulse to write is always fired by reading' (p.265). This statement can be taken as a broad brushstroke, but also considered in the context of daily writing practice.

Indeed my research has confirmed close reading of extant texts provides support to the writer. Reading and close reading as part of writing practice benefit both the conscious and unconscious parts of the writer's make-up, as proposed by Dorothea Brande (Reynolds 1984).

This brings me to the value of freewriting. The constraints of structured freewriting in response to close reading provide a highly effective scaffolding, which supercharged my productivity over the course of this research study.

In the context of autoethnographic research, freewriting proved to be a highly effective means of mining personal experience and engaging with self-reflection in terms of the creative writing process. I found myself entering a space rich with creative possibilities, with which came a sense of empowerment and liberation. Reflecting this, a key experience in freewriting is according to Elbow (1989) 'the sense of letting go' (p.58).

BIBLIOGRAPHY

Allen, G. (2000). *Intertextuality* (Second Edition). London and New York: Routledge.

Anderson, L. (Ed.) (2006). *Creative Writing: A Workbook with Reading*. Abingdon: Routledge.

Bakhtin, M.M. (1981). *The Dialogic Imagination: Four Essays*. Ed. Michael Holquist. Trans. Caryl Emerson and Michael Holquist. Austin and London: University of Texas Press.

Barrs, M. (2000). 'The Reader in the Writer.' *Literacy*, vol. 34 (2), pp. 54-60.

Brooks, R. (1988). 'Modelling a Writer's Identity: Reading and Imitation in the Writing Classroom.' *College Composition and Communication*, vol. 39 (1), pp. 23-41.

Bruner, J. (1986). *Actual Minds, Possible Worlds*. Cambridge, Mass: Harvard University Press.

Clayton, J. Rothstein, R. (1991). *Influence and Intertextuality in Literary History.* Madison, Wis: University of Wisconsin Press.

Cowan, A. (2010). *The Art of Writing Fiction*. London: Routledge.

Doyle, M. (2020). 'Sarah Moss: Ireland is a deeply literary place. It is also very beautiful,' *The Irish Times*, 11, January.

Elbow, P. (1989). 'Towards a Phenomenology of Freewriting.' *Journal of Basic Writing*, 8(2), pp.42-71.

Elbow, P. Belanoff, P. (2000). *A Community of Writers: A Workshop Course in Writing*. 3rd ed. Boston: McGraw Hill.

Ellis, C. and Boscher, A.P. (2000). 'Autoethnography, Personal Narrative, Reflexivity: Researcher as Subject,' in N. K. Denzin & Y. S. Lincoln (Eds.), *Handbook of Qualitative Research (2nd Ed.)*, Sage Publications, p. 733-768.

Frey, N. & Fisher, D. (2013). 'Close Reading.' *Principal Leadership*, vol. 13, no 5, pp. 57-59.

Hammond, J. and Gibbons, P. (2001). 'What is Scaffolding?' in Hammond, J. (Ed), *Scaffolding: Teaching and Learning in*

Literacy Education. Newtown (Australia): Primary English Teaching Association.

Hollway, W. & Jefferson, T. (2000). 'A Psychosocial Case Study,' in Hollway, W., & Jefferson, T. *Doing qualitative research differently* (pp. 131-154). London: SAGE Publications Ltd doi: 10.4135/9781849209007.

Joyce, J. (2000). *Dubliners*. London: Penguin Classics.

Kristeva, J. (1969) *Semiotike: Recherches Pour une Sémanalyse*. Paris: Editions du Seuil.

Munsey, T. (2010). *Creating Autoethnographies*. London: Sage.

Newkirk, T. (2010). 'The Case for Slow Reading.' *Educational Leadership*, 67(6), pp. 6-11.

Nicholson, H. (2017). 'Close reading.' *Research in Drama Education: The Journal of Applied Theatre and Performance*, vol. 22:2, pp.183-185, DOI: 10.1080/13569783.2017.1309738.

Orr, M. (2003). *Intertextuality: Debates and Contexts*. Cambridge: Polity Press.

Reynolds, M. (1984). 'Freewriting's Origin.' *The English Journal*, 73(3), pp.81-82.

Sontag, S. (2001). *Where The Stress Fall*. London: Penguin Books.

Wilkie-Stibbs, C. (1999). 'Intertextuality and the Child Reader,' in Hunt, P. (Ed.). *Understanding Children's Literature*. London and New York: Routledge, 168-179.

012

ABOUT THE AUTHORS

GAAR ADAMS

Gaar Adams is an American writer and educator. He has taught creative writing at secondary schools and communities forums in the United Arab Emirates and the UK, as well as at the University of Glasgow, where he is pursuing PhD studies. His features have been published in The Atlantic, Foreign Policy, Rolling Stone, Al Jazeera, Slate, NPR and VICE. His essays, fiction and poetry have been anthologised by publishers including Speculative Books, Uncommon Books and Dostoyevsky Wannabe. He is a London Library Emerging Writer and is writing a nonfiction book on queerness and migration in the Middle East. Twitter: @gaaradams

LEXI ALLEN

Lexi Allen is an MA Creative Writing and Education Student at Goldsmiths, University of London. She is a writer and ESL instructor. She hails from Key West, Florida.

EMMA BRANKIN

Emma Brankin recently finished her MA in Creative Writing and Education at Goldsmiths. She is a journalist turned teacher. Her writing has appeared in national newspapers and literary magazines.

SARA CARROLL

After graduating from Oxford, Sara Carroll worked in publishing for 15 years: initially for the Quaker Home Service and then for Walker Books and Random House Children's Books. She is now an English teacher in Kent, currently teaching all key stages at secondary level. She has always written creatively, and has had several children's books published. She started the MA in Creative Writing at Goldsmiths University in 2019. www.linkedin.com/in/sarajcarroll

CAMILLA CHESTER

Camilla Chester is a self-published Children's Author with three successful books for 8-12s: Jarred Dreams, EATS and Thirteenth Wish. Camilla's debut was shortlisted in the 2015 New Author Prize run by The Literacy Trust and her second book EATS received Highly Commended in Winchester Festival Funny Fiction Award 2017. Camilla was a finalist in the Mslexia Children's Novel Competition 2019 with her fourth book, Darna's Sky. www.camillachester.com

JANET DEAN

Janet Dean is a writer and creative writing tutor from York, UK. After a career in the public sector she was awarded her MA with distinction by the University of York St. John in September 2015. As Janet Dean Knight, her debut novel The Peacemaker, based on her own family history was published in 2019 by Top Hat Books. Janet writes poetry and short fiction and is co-director of Awakening The Writer Within, which runs creative writing retreats and workshops in the UK, Europe and online.

TJAWANGWA DEMA

Tjawangwa Dema is a poet, educator and arts administrator. Her collection The Careless Seamstress won the Sillerman First Book Prize for African Poetry. Her chapbook Mandible was selected for the African Poetry Book Fund's inaugural New-Generation African Poets series. Her poems have been translated into languages including Spanish, Chinese, German and Swedish. She co-produces the Africa Writes – Bristol festival and is honorary Senior Research Associate at the University of Bristol. www.tjdema.com, @tjdema

ANGELA FRANCE

Angela France is a Gloucestershire poet whose publications include *Occupation* (Ragged Raven Press, 2009), *Lessons in Mallemaroking* (Nine Arches Press, 2011), *Hide* (Nine Arches Press 2013) and her latest collection *The Hill* (Nine Arches Press 2017) which is based on Leckhampton Hill near Cheltenham where Angela has walked for 50 years, since childhood. Poet Sheenagh Pugh said of *The Hill:* "Exuberant, controlled, angry, elegiac, this is a poetry of landscape, politics, witness". Angela teaches creative writing at the University of Gloucestershire and in various community settings. She runs a reading series in Cheltenham called Buzzwords.

FRANCIS GILBERT

Francis Gilbert was a teacher for 25 years in various UK state schools. He is the author of many books about education, including *I'm A Teacher, Get Me Out Of Here* (2004) , *Parent Power* (2007) and *The Last Day of Term* (2011). He is now a senior lecturer in education at Goldsmiths, University of London, where he is the course leader for PGCE English and the head of the MA in Creative Writing and Education.

KIRSTY GUNN & GAIL LOW

Kirsty Gunn is published internationally by Faber and Faber; more information on her publications can be found at: http://www.kirsty-gunn.com. Gail Low is the founding editor of DURA (Dundee University Review of the Arts). Both teach and write essays together, which they see as exciting collaborative ventures; they also serve as joint publishers of The Voyage Out Press. Their second co-edited and curated collection of essays, Imagined Spaces, will be out in November 2020.

GEOFFREY HEPTONSTALL

Geoffrey Heptonstall's publications include a poetry collection, The Rites of Paradise (Cyberwit 2020), and a novel, Heaven's Invention [Black Wolf 2016]. His poetry has appeared in several anthologies and many magazines around the world. A number of his plays and monologues have been broadcast, staged and/or published, with venues ranging from small fringe theatres to BBC Radio 3. Geoffrey is also an essayist and reviewer; much of his work has appeared in The London Magazine. He lives in Cambridge where he has taught writing at

Anglia Ruskin University and for the Open College of the Arts.
@geoffreywrites

TAMAR HODES

Tamar taught English and creative writing in schools, prisons and adult education centres for 35 years, until her retirement last year. She has had many short stories published in anthologies and magazines, and broadcast on Radio 4. She has had two novels published: *Raffy's Shapes* (Accent Press) and *The Water and the Wine* (Hookline Books).

Aisha Johnson

Aisha Johnson started writing when she was around 10 years old, and won a competition to be featured in The Irish Press. She has also had a poem displayed in an exhibition by radical London-based publishing company Bogle-L'Ouverture. She recently started writing again more seriously as she finds writing therapeutic and healing. Aisha is of mixed heritage, hailing from Barbados with roots in Scotland, Ireland and England. She currently lives in Deptford, South East London, and teaches money skills in inner-city schools. She plans to self-publish a book of her poems.

MARK KIRKBRIDE

Mark Kirkbride was educated at Kingston and Oxford. His second novel, *Game Changers of the Apocalypse*, was a semi-finalist in the Kindle Book Awards 2019. His short stories have appeared in *Under the Bed, Sci Phi Journal, Disclaimer Magazine, Flash Fiction Magazine* and *So It Goes*, the literary journal of the Kurt Vonnegut Memorial Library. Poetry credits include *The Big Issue, The Morning Star, The Daily Mirror, Sein und Werden* and HWA chapbooks. He is currently a Creative Workshop Tutor for the University for the Creative Arts, and an arts facilitator for OPEN Ealing.

www.markkirkbride.com,
https://www.facebook.com/KirkbrideM/,
https://twitter.com/MarkKirkbride

HELEN MOORE

Helen Moore is an award-winning British ecopoet, socially engaged artist and outdoor educator based in Somerset. She has published three poetry collections, Hedge Fund, And Other Living Margins (Shearsman Books, 2012), ECOZOA (Permanent Publications, 2015), acclaimed as "a milestone in the journey of ecopoetics", and The Mother Country (Awen Publications, 2019) exploring aspects of British colonial history. Helen offers an online mentoring programme, Wild Ways to Writing, and has recently been awarded a substantial grant by the Royal Literary Fund to support her work. www.helenmoorepoet.com

JUWAIRIAH MUSSA

Juwairiah Mussa is a British Muslim, Indian poet and educator. She is currently pursuing an MA in Creative Writing and Education at Goldsmiths, University of London as an Aziz Scholar. She has been previously published in the University of Greenwich Anthology 2017-2019, For Sale: Baby Shoes, It Equals, Sort, among others. Her play, 'Wrong Shade of Brown' was showcased as part of the Greenwich Book festival in 2018. She was prized runner up at the auspicious CAGE UK poetry competition. She is currently working on a poetry pamphlet on the theme of race and shading within the South Asian community.

NEIL NIXON

Neil Nixon has been writing for publication since he was a student. His writing career has included almost 30 books on subjects as varied as the paranormal, rock music and football. He has written a couple of books about creative and professional writing. His other writing includes working for Viz Comic, Sooty Films (where he had to write for a puppet who can't speak) and as an obituaries correspondent. In 1999 he founded the UK's first university course in Professional Writing, a programme he ran for 20 years. www.neilnixon.com

MATILDA ROSTANT

Born in Sweden, Matilda Rostant is a fantasy writer now living in London. She has just finished her MA in Creative Writing and Education at Goldsmiths, University of London.

TANYA ROYER

Tanya Royer is an editor, writer and mentor based in Margate, Kent. She is currently studying an MA in creative writing and education at Goldsmiths University.
Social media: @fabulaworks, website: fabula.works

CARINYA SHARPLES

Carinya Sharples is a writer, freelance journalist and workshop facilitator. She recently completed an MA in Creative Writing & Education at Goldsmiths, University of London. She works freelance for the BBC, Mongabay and other outlets; taught communications at the University of Guyana; and facilitates creative-writing and youth-focused workshops. She was shortlisted for the Flipside Festival's GAWP! Green Alphabet Writing Prize 2017, and her creative writing has been published by The London Reader and Commonwealth Writers' adda.
www.carinyasharples.com

JAKE SMITH

Jake Smith is a Creative Writing & Education MA student at Goldsmiths and a part-time ESL tutor. His primary focus is on creative forms of education and championing writing that is challenging or experimental. A poet and short story writer, he believes creative writing can liberate concepts and narratives to have innovative, positive effects on society, pushing a new generation of writing. His writing often fuses the mundane trivialities and surreal abstractions of human experience through poetry, fiction and auto-fiction. He is particularly interested in the sound of words and language and how music seeps into all aspects of writing.

MATTHEW TETT

Matthew Tett is a freelance educator and writer living near Bath. He also coordinates the StoryTown literature festival and is the reviews editor for NAWE's *Writing in Education* magazine. Matthew is a keen writer of short prose and is working on a collection of stories.

PATRICK TOLAND

Patrick Toland holds post-graduate qualifications in Creative Writing and the teaching of Creative Writing from Oxford and Cambridge University. He has been published widely in the UK, US and Ireland and his most recent poetry collection, Stockholm, was a winner of the Templar Portfolio Award. He was also a winner of the Hippocrates Prize 2020 Health Professional category. He is currently a supervisor on the Masters in Education at Buckingham University, Regional Lead on the NHS at 70/Voices of COVID project at Manchester University, and a member of the Irish Poetry Therapy Network.

GABRIEL TROIANO

Gabriel Troiano is an aspiring writer from São Paulo, Brazil, embarking on the MA in Creative Writing & Education at Goldsmiths University.

STEPHEN WADE

Stephen Wade was formerly a university lecturer, mainly in Hull. He later worked for six years as a writer in residence at a number of prisons, working with male and female inmates. His books are mainly in the genre of true crime/crime history, but he has also written biographical works on Conan Doyle, George Grossmith and Harry de Windt. His next poetry collection is *Stretch*, from Smokestack Publishing.

JAMES WARD

James Ward is a fiction writer, poet, and an educator in creative writing. He is based in London. Twitter: @Jamesfward

Printed in Great Britain
by Amazon

59650387R00169